THROUGH BLOOD
AND BROTHERHOOD

THROUGH BLOOD AND BROTHERHOOD

Comrades and Enemies in WWII Yugoslavia

BRIAN R. JOHNSON

CASEMATE

Pennsylvania & Yorkshire

Published in the United States of America and Great Britain in 2024 by
CASEMATE PUBLISHERS
1950 Lawrence Road, Havertown, PA 19083
and
47 Church Street, Barnsley, S70 2AS, UK

Hardback Edition: ISBN 978-1-63624-405-1
Digital Edition: ISBN 978-1-63624-406-8

A CIP record for this book is available from the British Library

Printed and bound in the United Kingdom by CPI Group (UK) Ltd, Croydon, CR0 4YY
Typeset in India by Lapiz Digital Services

For a complete list of Casemate titles, please contact:

CASEMATE PUBLISHERS (US)
Telephone (610) 853-9131
Fax (610) 853-9146
Email: casemate@casematepublishers.com
www.casematepublishers.com

CASEMATE PUBLISHERS (UK)
Telephone (0)1226 734350
Email: casemate@casemateuk.com
www.casemateuk.com

Disclaimer

The views and opinions expressed in this book do not reflect or represent the opinions of Grand Valley State University. Neither the author nor any associated parties shall be held responsible for any consequences arising from the opinions or interpretations expressed within this book.

Dedicated to my family

Contents

Acknowledgements

While my name is on the cover of this book, there are several people who contributed to it. First, I would like to recognize my wife Shari for supporting me in the research and writing of the book and going on my trips with me throughout the US to interview veterans. I would also like to thank Bernie Siehling and his wife Brigetta for their countless hours spent translating the diaries, and Bernie's one question that fueled this book: "Do you think he is still alive?" Then, there is the University of North Alabama that funded my trip over to Europe to re-trace Gottfried's path. A big thanks also goes out to my former colleague at UNA, Phil Bridgmon, Ph.D. for his support and ideas for the book. Dave Kalinich, my professor and mentor in graduate school, and later a co-worker, has always been there encouraging me on and making me laugh. Dave also connected me with his uncle, Dan Cupković, who was a Chetnik fighter in World War II. Everyone should have a friend like Dave. I also had many fact-checkers and readers. They include Martin Super who, in my opinion, is an expert on Croatia in World War II. Martin was also my translator on the trip to Europe. Some of my reviewers included Christopher Kierkus, Ph.D., Brian F. Kingshott, Ph.D., FRSA, and my mother who attributes her excellent grammar and writing to her paralegal career and her parochial school education. Steven and Michelle Dyke, Dick Grossenbacher, and my dean at GVSU, Paul Stansbie, Ph.D., also spent many hours reviewing drafts of the book and providing constructive feedback on how to improve it. The photos used in this book were also edited using advanced software, thanks to Sara Alsum-Wassenaar at the GVSU School of Communications who gave me access to their studio and was always there when I had questions. Vico Marelic, on the island of Korčula was also very helpful in narrowing down where Gottfried took some of his photos and answering many other questions I had about the city and island. Thank you so much for your time. There are also the veterans and their families who took time out of their lives to share their stories with me. This book could not have been completed without their help. Finally, a big thanks to Ruth Sheppard and the staff at Casemate for seeing the book's potential and bringing it to life.

Introduction

This is a story about a set of old World War II diaries and the journey they took me on. The story has a simple beginning in 2007. But it soon became complex. One day while surfing the internet, I came across a set of World War II German diaries for sale. Having always been attracted to military history, particularly World War II, I thought they looked interesting. It seemed like a fun thing to do: translate and read some old diaries to learn more about the life of a German soldier in World War II. I took German in college, so it would also be a good way to brush up on my German-language skills. Being a military history buff, I had already done a similar thing with some American diaries from World War I where the writer's unpublished thoughts took me back to a time, perhaps a more simplistic one, in American history and culture. These diaries revealed a time in America where writing was basically the only way of communication and an art, where wordsmithing and penmanship was paramount, compared to the 21st century where video blogs and e-mails are the preferred way of recording one's thoughts. These diaries were also time capsules where forgotten words like lads, chaps, and fellas were common vernacular, while "having a gay time" simply meant having fun. These young men, some the first time away from home, recorded their days in boot camp and comradeship, writing about the excitement of journeying across the United States by train, proudly wearing their new uniforms, and marching through impromptu parades at whistle stops as citizens cheered them on. Some included entries about their journeys on the troop ships that would take them to faraway England and eventually to France where they would write about the boredom, excitement, and horrors of war. These stories also provided a glimpse into the innocence of these long-dead youth who now only exist as a photograph tucked away in an old box where future descendants wonder who that person in the photo is—and was.

I hoped that these diaries would provide me more insight into the glimpse of a day in the life of a German soldier—not what is found in the objective history books, but a personal narrative of the life of a soldier, expressed by the soldier himself from a simple, individualistic, and human perspective that is often overshadowed by other World War II history books. These books tend to report the facts of historical battles and tactics. But they fail to capture the details and the point that human beings, young men full of life and dreams regardless of which side they were on, were propelled into a maelstrom of violence that was out of their control.

The diaries did not look like much when they came in the mail. Just a few old tattered pocket-sized journals and 77 photographs of a German soldier. Perhaps other individuals thought the same. I was the only bidder on the item. What was immediately apparent was that the writer had good penmanship. He was also very detailed in his writing. In most cases, there were daily entries in the diaries, making me wonder when a soldier had time to write, especially in 1945 when the German army was basically on its heels and in a constant state of retreat. The writer also included sketches and maps of where he was, a direct violation of *Wehrmacht* (armed forces) orders that prohibited the writing of diaries out of concern that if the soldier was captured or found dead, the information found in the diary would assist the enemy. I soon found, through the maps and a quick skim of some words, that the original owner of the diaries was Gottfried Weber, who served in Yugoslavia. His Feldpost number indicated that he was in *Jäger-Regiment 750*. He was also a radio operator, which might explain why he had the time to write daily entries. The photos showed he was young, and had dark hair. He was also thin, as most likely were other individuals his age serving in the German armed forces. His face looked carefree and innocent.

However, I immediately ran into problems with my translating. First, my knowledge of the German language was worse than expected. In fact, it was awful. I was overconfident in my abilities. Based on my prior experiences in Germany where I was competent in ordering beer and pretzels, finding my way to various locations, reading menus, and having very short conversations, I thought I could do this. If all else failed, I had a German–English dictionary… In addition, while the handwriting was legible, it was confusing. It did not resemble the Latin text or cursive that I was taught in grade school. I soon thought that this "simple" activity would become dead, and I was the proud owner of a few diaries I could not read and translate, along with a lot of photos. Fortunately, one of my retired colleagues was originally from Germany. I e-mailed some page scans of the diaries to Mary. In particular, I sent her some choice entries—those with a lot of details and one day in particular: May 8, 1945. The German surrender. Within a few days, she wrote back and said, "You're sitting on a gold mine here." But Mary also explained that the diaries were written in *Sütterlin* text. This style of writing was taught in German schools from about 1915 until about 1935 when even the Nazis determined that the text was too chaotic, subsequently requiring the more modern Latin-styled text when teaching writing in schools. Mary warned me that it would be almost impossible for me to translate. She was that type of person that never put perfume on her comments. She told people how it was. So much for an easy translation. Fortunately, Mary knew someone who could help—Bernie Siehling. I called Bernie and he was interested.

Bernie also had his own story of being a youth in Nazi Germany in World War II. He was born in Grand Rapids, Michigan, in 1930 into a family of German immigrants. In 1930, his father was killed in a car accident, which required his mother and him to move back to the family farm in Germany when he was just six months old. So Bernie spent his youth in Nazi Germany, as an American citizen, living on the farm with his extended family in the area. He and his mother never had any problems with the authorities as former Americans living in Nazi Germany, he said. Perhaps it was because his mother had married his uncle and was therefore a German citizen again. He recalls that during Operation *Varsity* in 1945, one of the last large offenses that involved the Allies crossing the Rhine river, one of his relatives serving in the Wehrmacht drove up to the farm in his *Kübelwagen*, the German equivalent of the US Jeep, and warned the family that the British would soon be at their farmstead. He then drove away, later becoming a prisoner of war in the hands of the Americans. He was correct. Soon after, a British Churchill tank drove into the family farm where the crew eventually got out of the tank to take a break. Bernie also has memories of how he helped hide the family's valuables and extra clothes by burying them in barrels around the farmstead to protect their belongings from potential looters. His family was fortunate that they were farmers and could live off what they grew and raised, since food was in short supply for many immediately after the war. He also reminisced about the many refugees that would show up at the farm looking for food. Rebuilding his nearby city of Borken, which was heavily bombed in 1945, was a post-war activity for young Bernie. As a teen, he and his classmates cleaned up the rubble and re-set cobblestones that were torn up by Allied tanks in their race to Berlin. Many of the adult men were dead from the war or still in prisoner of war (POW) camps waiting to be sent home. It was up to the young and the old to rebuild the town.

Bernie is the inquisitive type and enjoys his own research. During the war, he would watch Allied bombers fly over the farm. On one occasion, a B-17 bomber crash landed nearby. One of the crew members who bailed out of the dying bomber crashed through the roof of the Siehlings' chicken coop. Bernie recalls walking into the coop and seeing the flyer, in his sheepskin flying suit, hanging through the hole in the roof, suspended by the chute's shroud lines. While authorities took the now-POW away to captivity, Bernie never stopped thinking about what happened to the flyer. But he had a clue to the person's identity: he had taken a photograph of the wreckage of the downed plane that crashed close to their farm. About 60 years later, through his internet prowess, he identified the aircraft by its tail number. Eventually he also found the names of the crew through his internet searches. Then, he found the flyer that put the hole in the roof. Being the witty person that he is, Bernie laughingly explained that when the old flyer answered his phone, Bernie stated that he was calling to collect for the damage that this flyer had caused to the roof of the family farm in 1944. To this day, they still stay in contact.

After the war, when Bernie was an adult, he wanted to return to the United States, but US authorities in Germany questioned his allegiance and would not let him return. To prove his allegiance, they said that he needed to join the US Army. He could move back to the US after his stint in the army was over. So, Bernie joined the US Army—in Germany. Based on his fluency in German, the military designated him to be a translator/linguist and radio operator. The US army then sent him to Korea during the Korean War, even though he was fluent in German and had no working knowledge of the Korean language! Eventually, Bernie made it back to Grand Rapids after his service in the military. He married his sweetheart, Brigetta, who he met in grade school in Germany, convincing her to follow him back to America. They raised three children and now enjoy their retirement with their pet peacocks, serving as the Siehlings' security system, who strut and scurry around their secluded wooded property.

Bernie was a great help in the translations. He and Brigetta spent countless hours reading the diaries and translating them into English. In one of our many conversations we had while translating the diaries, Bernie asked the simple question: "Do you think Weber is still alive?" That was a good question. He would be in his 80s or maybe early 90s, so, it was possible that he was. A few minutes later Bernie was scouring the internet, and was then on the phone calling the town hall of the town in Germany where Weber lived in World War II. Fortunately, the town was small and the woman who answered knew the family. She told him that Weber had returned home after the war to Soviet-occupied East Germany, and lived and worked as a bookkeeper there his entire life. But he was dead. His wife was still alive but had Alzheimer's and was in assisted living. It was said that she would not be too useful in answering any questions. However, Weber did have a son who lived in Potsdam. He might be helpful. So, Bernie called the son and connected him with me. Through our e-mail conversations his son wrote that his father had never spoken about the war. In the post-war GDR—the German Democratic Republic, or East Germany—being in the German armed forces in World War II was something that was not readily discussed. In fact, World War II was not discussed by many Germans at all. It was widely felt that the 12-year period of the Third Reich was best forgotten. All Weber's son was aware of was that his father fought in Yugoslavia. He never knew that his father had kept diaries and he had never seen any photos of his father from the war. As with many veterans from the US, wartime memories were not shared. And, if shared, they were only with an intimate few who understood their fellow brothers in arms. How the diaries wound up in my possession will remain a mystery. Perhaps a junk picker found the diaries in the trash after the family cleaned out the home. From there, they eventually made their way all the way to the United States of all places, and were then sold by an online site.

But what his son did provide was a lead. This lead resulted in a multi-year journey of discovery, of not just one man's experience in World War II, but many. The lead was relatively simple. Weber's son gave me some contact information for one of his father's wartime comrades who lived in Munich, and who was still alive. From this, the question arose: how many more individuals are alive that fought in Yugoslavia during World War II? And this led to an idea—the collection of oral histories of those who fought in Yugoslavia. So, from this one contact, and the translation of one man's diaries, countless interviews were conducted with Germans, Ustaše, Chetniks, Americans, British, Australians, and Partisans who fought in Yugoslavia during World War II. Finding these persons was not too difficult. In most cases I simply asked if the person knew of anyone else that would like to talk to me. In fact, in one instance I found a US airman, a German Wehrmacht soldier, and a Yugoslav Royalist Chetnik who were all neighbors in the same retirement community. I guess time heals most wounds, but I'm sure they were still guarded in their conversations on what they did during the war—to avoid old flames ruining their barbecues.

To provide some context to all of these stories, and to fill in some time gaps in the diaries, this book also includes other source materials. They include the daily combat logs from the *118. Jäger-Division* that somehow survived the war. In my mind I imagine this division, in full retreat from the Soviets and Partisans, its German staff officers nevertheless worried that their divisional records would be destroyed—and preserving them at all costs. Bureaucrats at their best. This information allowed me to further pinpoint where units of the 118th were on particular days. In fact, as a radio operator, Weber most likely was one of the soldiers providing divisional HQ with the daily updates from the field that were included in the division's war diary. I also conducted my own interviews with veterans and used original photos and documents to build the story of Weber. Many of these photographs were taken by Weber himself and the captions on the back of them were very useful in identifying landmarks, places, and dates. I also re-traced his steps though Bosnia, Montenegro, Croatia, Hungary, and Austria where he fought. Signs of World War II are still found on the walls of many buildings, the landscape, and the collective memories of the people. All this information provides the reader with a better understanding of World War II in Yugoslavia.

And so, the story of one soldier's diary begins. But it is more than one diary. It is a story about World War II, and a civil war in Yugoslavia. This is the story of those persons that experienced the war, told in their words, and their interpretation of the war. Many needed and wanted to tell their stories to share what they felt was the truth about the war. Some felt that the history books were incorrect, or there was no written record of that particular event. Others took a more philosophical position. Gerhardt Hennes, who served in the German Wehrmacht, wrote in a letter to me: "It is important to keep a record of WWII, even though I do not expect that lessons will necessarily be learned!"[1] For many, it was the first time they shared their wartime experiences with someone; some wanted to shed the demons that they have carried with them for 70-plus years. For some, I had to promise that I would not share their names—perhaps out of the shame or embarrassment they felt for their actions. Others asked me not to write about them until they died. I have honored their requests. Many of these interviews included tears—it is never comfortable listening to an elderly person crying, assuring me that it was a "different time" and they are not that person that did those acts so many decades ago. But they did. Others, meanwhile, still carried intense hatred to this day regarding what happened in this theater of war—what Winston Churchill coined the "soft underbelly" of Europe—Yugoslavia.

CHAPTER I

1941

In 1939, Poland was conquered by Germany and the Soviet Union, dividing the country at the Vistula, Narew, and San rivers. The defeat of the nation took only 35 days.[1] Later in 1940, the Third Reich directed its efforts west, attacking Denmark, Norway, the Netherlands, Belgium, Luxembourg, and then France, getting closer to meeting Germany's goal of making Europe a single economic and political unit. The British Expeditionary Force (BEF) in France also experienced the German onslaught and was pushed to the beaches on the English Channel. Under Operation *Dynamo*, May 26 to June 4, 1940, over 300,000 Allied troops were rescued off the beaches of Dunkirk by a rag-tag fleet of fishing vessels and other small craft, and taken across the Channel to the safety of England.[2]

With the continent now under German rule, the next stop in 1940 would be Great Britain itself. The British rejected Hitler's demand to surrender, with Churchill eloquently stating that they would never surrender; they would fight on the beaches and the streets, whatever the cost, to protect their island. In the summer of 1940, the Germans started planning for an amphibious invasion, code named Operation *Seelöwe* (*Sea Lion*). Before the invasion could occur, however, Herman Göring's *Luftwaffe* (air force) would have to gain control of the British skies. It never happened. The four-month long Battle of Britain led to the permanent postponement of the invasion, and Germany's first defeat.[3] It was a signal to the world that the Germans could be stopped.

Now, in 1941, the Third Reich turned its attention to its true enemy, the Soviet Union. The Bolshevik "*Untermenschen*" ("subhumans") needed to be eliminated, the Nazis believed, and the plague of communism eradicated from the face of the earth. And Germany was the country to do it. Besides the elimination of communism and its leader, Joseph Stalin, invasion of the east served the German's practical needs. The Reich needed *Lebensraum*, or "living space," where ethnic Germans could readily settle and make it a suitable part of the world. The vast natural resources and farmlands in the east would also ensure the economic health of the Thousand-Year Reich, thus improving the lives of all Aryans.[4]

Before the Soviet Union could be invaded, Hitler needed to ensure that the flanks of the Third Reich were secure. To the west, the English Channel provided a natural barrier, and Britain was still licking its wounds from the British Expeditionary Force's loss in France, so it was not a concern yet. If anything, Great Britain was just a nuisance. To the south was Italy, an ally that would provide some source of protection to the Reich, even though Italian operations in North Africa were wavering on the brink of destruction with its failed invasion of Egypt in September 1940. In the battle of Sidi Barrani in December 1940, the British counterattacked the Italian advance into Egypt. The Italians lost 38,000 troops, compared to 624 British losses. It was a rout. The year 1941 was even worse for the Italians, but the bloodletting was staunched with the arrival of Rommel's *Afrikakorps* in February 1941, after which German forces, along with the Italians, pushed the British and Commonwealth forces back to Egypt.[5] However, one vulnerability that needed to be addressed by the Reich in 1941 was south of German-annexed Austria—Yugoslavia.

The Balkans

The Balkans was already a hotbed for war in the early 20th century. In the First Balkan War of 1912, Serbia and its Bulgarian, Greek, and Montenegrin allies formed the Balkan League, defeating the Ottoman empire, pushing the Turks out of Macedonia and almost all the way back to Istanbul. The subsequent Treaty of London carved up Macedonia among the victors, and Serbia doubled in size. Albania also broke away from the Ottomans and became its own nation. Soon after, in 1913, the Second Balkan War flared up when Bulgaria felt it had been cheated out of the land it should have received from the first war, attacking Serbia and Greece in an attempt to get it back. The war did not work out well for Bulgaria. Bulgaria lost more of Macedonia to the Serb and Greek victors.[6]

To the north, the Austro-Hungarian Empire butted against the Kingdom of Serbia. In 1908, the empire annexed Bosnia-Herzegovina, that it had been occupying since 1878. This outraged the Serbs who also had their eyes on it. The Serbs were now under even more threat of the empire's expansion into what they felt were rightfully their own lands.[7] On June 28, 1914, it all came to a head when Serb nationalist Gavrilo Princip assassinated Archduke Franz Ferdinand, and his wife Sofie, in Sarajevo during his trip to the province to inspect military troops.[8] In response, the Austro-Hungarian Empire declared war on Serbia; Serbia's long-time ally, Russia, declared war on the Austro-Hungarians; and Germany, an ally of Austria-Hungary, then declared war on Russia. Because France was allied with Russia, it came to Russia's aid. And because the United Kingdom was allied with France, they too were drawn into the war.[9] World War I would engulf all of Europe, destroy empires, and change the map of Europe forever.

The war did not go well for the Kingdom of Serbia. Out of all of the nations that fought in World War I, Serbia had the highest percentage of civilian deaths. It was estimated that about 840,000 Serbian citizens died, along with over 400,000 soldiers, about 12 percent of the Kingdom's total population.[10] Others estimated that total losses of the Serb population were as high as 20 percent.[11] In 1915, the country was over-run by the Austro-Hungarians, and the remnants of the Serbian government, along with many civilians and military personnel, and Regent Alexander and members of the royal family, retreated through Kosovo and Albania and were then rescued by the British on the Adriatic shoreline. The survivors, about 175,000 strong, were evacuated by the British to Corfu island in Greece, which became the location of the Serbian government in exile. Serbian troops from Corfu would later fight on the Macedonian front against the Bulgarians and Austrians.[12]

Discussions about the new Europe and the fate of the Serbian kingdom were already in play before the end of the war. In 1917, the federation of Slavs from the former provinces of the Austro-Hungarian Empire signed the Pact of Corfu with the Kingdom of Serbia, a declaration that all of the Slavs would form a single south Slav state after the war. Later in 1918, the National Council of Slovenes, Croats, and Serbs (in Bosnia and Herzegovina) was created in Zagreb, claiming to be representing the Slavic states in the crumbling Austro-Hungarian Empire. To protect the Slav states from the Italians, who were already invading land in the western part of the empire, the Council sought out the protection of the Serbs. Later in November, delegates from the National Council met with the Serbian government that recognized them and their request, which led to the annexation of the former lands of the Austro-Hungarian Empire that included Slovenia and Croatia.[13] Soon after the November 11, 1918 Armistice that ended World War I, the new Kingdom of the Serbs, Croats, and Slovenes was created by the Serbian monarchy on December 1, 1918.

The new empire was unstable from its beginning. Soldiers from Croatia that fought for the "Kaiser and King" in the Austro-Hungarian Empire were now living in the same nation as their centuries-old nemesis: Serbs that they fought against in World War I. The new kingdom also incorporated peoples of different cultures, ethnicities, and religions. Catholic Croats, who used the Latin alphabet and often spoke German, were now in the same kingdom as Orthodox Serbs who used the Cyrillic alphabet, spoke Serbian, and had different customs and norms than their Croatian counterparts. Many Bosnians, descendants of citizens of the Ottoman Empire who had lived in Bosnia and Herzegovina centuries earlier, practiced Islam and also had their own traditions and beliefs, and were often distrusted by the Serbs because of their Ottoman origins. Colloquially called the Kingdom of South Slavs, or Yugoslavia, the only commonality was that the people in the kingdom lived in the same part of the world.[14] It soon became a kingdom of distrust and dissension.

The annexation was not received well by the Croatians. Many Croatian citizens wanted an independent nation in the post-World War I world. Independence was part of the nation's long history. As far back as the ninth century, Croatia was independently ruled under the reign of Duke Trpinir,[15] while the first king of Croatia was King Tomislav, who reigned in 925.[16] The country was also traditionally allied with the Hungarians since the 1100s, not with the Ottomans and Serbs to the south.[17]

One particular group that opposed the merger with Serbia was the Croatian Peoples' Peasant Party (HPSS). Created in 1904 by Stjepan Radić and his brother Ante, the party politicized the peasant population, making them a powerful foe in Croatia and the new kingdom. The HPSS was threatening to the central government with its anti-coalition, and anti-centralization stance, and opposition to what it felt was Serb domination of the government. Opposition to Serb rule of the kingdom reached a crisis stage in 1921 when the now Croatian Republican Peoples' Party (HRSS) and Slovene representatives to parliament opposed ratification of the kingdom's first constitution. Regardless of their opposition, there were still enough votes by Serb and Muslim representatives in the National Assembly to ratify the Vidovdan Constitution.[18] The kingdom's new constitution, even though it gave voting rights to the peasants, and increased HRSS membership, also defined the kingdom as one unified state, stripping Croatia (along with other independent states) of its independent autonomy and giving the Serbs majority rule throughout the kingdom.[19] Angered about losing their status as an independent state within the new kingdom, the HRSS adopted a strategy of passive resistance to the new (in the HRSS's view) Serb-biased government.[20]

Because of the HRSS's actions, it was repeatedly under the scrutiny of the kingdom. Radić and some of his followers were harassed and repeatedly jailed for their revolutionary actions against the state. In 1924, the central government started placing further restrictions on HRSS activities, arresting Radić and some of his followers in 1925 for violating the kingdom's internal security law because of the party's association with the Soviets. After being released from prison, Radić was back in politics. He was made the minister of education in 1925, and then became a member of Parliament in 1927. On June 20, 1928, in a session of Parliament, Puniša Račić and other Serb MPs were publicly accused of corruption by Ivan Pernar and others from the now known (former HRSS) Croatian Peasant Party (HSS). On the floor of Parliament, Račić pulled out a revolver, shooting Pernar, killing two other MPs of the HSS, and mortally wounding Radić, who died a few months later. For his crimes, Račić was sentenced to house arrest in a villa in Serbia, which further outraged the Croats.[21] Vladko Maček then became the leader of the HSS after Radić's death, leading the HSS until 1941.[22]

With the kingdom on the brink of civil war over the Parliament assassinations, in 1929 King Alexander discontinued Parliament, banned all political parties, and imposed a royal dictatorship.[23] The political opposition was silenced and their leaders either fled the country or were imprisoned, including Maček of the HSS, who was jailed for six months in 1933 for inciting Croatian violence.[24] After the creation of a new constitution in 1931, Parliament resumed, but it was too late. Even though the king had made some reforms and concessions to appease the opposition, the new government was perceived as too pro-Serb by Muslims and Croats, and there was a movement for the kingdom to become a federation, regardless of the efforts of the king to appease the many factions.[25]

The HSS was not the only party wanting Croatian independence. There was also the Croatian Party of Rights (HSP). One of the persons active early in this party was Ante Pavelić, a devout Catholic and attorney from Bradina, Herzegovina, who was elected as the party's general secretary in 1918. Pavelić was effective in mobilizing students and nationalists for Croatian independence. In 1927, he was elected to the Croatian National Assembly representing Zagreb. His name and reputation for independence also extended beyond Croatia when he became known for defending Macedonian separatists belonging to the Internal Macedonian Revolutionary Organization (IMRO), who were also calling for independence from Serbian rule, and using violence to get their points across.[26] During this time, Pavelić was also meeting with Italian officials, seeking their support for Croatian secession from the kingdom, and giving promises to Italy that it could expand its sphere of influence into Croatia's Dalmatia region along the Adriatic coast, once he gained power, and Croatia became an independent nation.[27] Pavelić was also meeting with IMRO Macedonian separatists to coordinate their efforts to expedite the demise of Yugoslavia.[28]

Pavelić was not liked by the Yugoslav government for his actions. In July 1929, he was convicted in the Yugoslav court for treason, and sentenced to death, in absentia.[29] But Pavelić had already fled to Italy and the support of Benito Mussolini. In May 1930, Pavelić announced the creation of the Croatian Revolutionary Organization (*Ustaša Hrvatska Revolucionarna Organizacija*) or *Ustaša*, for short, whose ideology was based on fascist principles and Catholicism.[30] The Ustaša position was that Croatia should be independent and be entitled to all of its original territory; it was the Croatian's historic right that dated back over 1,000 years. Additionally, all Croats had the right to live in Croatia, and the Croatian peoples had been selected by God to defend Catholicism against Orthodoxy and communism. Other ethnic groups, especially the inferior Serbs, Jews, and Romas needed also to be eliminated from Croatian lands.[31]

Armed revolt and violence were at the core of Ustaša principles. One of the Ustaša publications from 1932 stated "the gun, bomb, and the infernal machine are the idols which shall bring back the land to the peasant."[32] Pavelić also had the support of some nations that wanted to see the kingdom's demise. In Italy and Hungary, Pavelić established training camps, schooling recruits in weapons and explosives use, while training subjects in Ustaša principles so they could lead others once they made it back to Croatia.[33]

To further build the movement, Pavelić appealed to Croatians around the world, built a large propaganda machine, and established a central command in Italy called the Nucleus, that coordinated Ustaša efforts in the kingdom. Through its network of local cells, the masses were educated in Ustaša principles and its followers increased in number. Direct actions including the assassination of government officials, and blowing up trains and government buildings were also occurring. Because of the religious persecution of Croatians, and the emphasis on Catholicism as an Ustaša ideal, even the Catholic Church was involved in the movement. Local priests spread the Ustaša ideals to their followers from the pulpit.[34]

One of their earliest successes that gained them some notoriety was the Velebit uprising. In 1932, about 20 Ustaša terrorists, some brought over by boat from Italy, along with some local Ustaše, attacked a police gendarme station in Brušane in the Lika district of Croatia, leading to a military response by the Yugoslav government. While the Velebit uprising was small in scale, it was a symbol of the birth of the Ustaša movement, informing the world of its cause and serving to further unnerve the kingdom, while also raising concerns in Belgrade about the abilities of the Ustaše, and the extent of their movement in the kingdom.[35]

The Ustaša also set its sights on King Alexander. In December 1933, there was an attempted assassination of the king in Zagreb that failed—the assassin hesitated in using grenades to kill the king because he did not want to kill the children that were surrounding King Alexander's vehicle. That night, police arrested the assassins, thwarting their plans to kill the king the following day.[36] When King Alexander was visiting Marseille, France on October 9, 1934, the assassins were successful.[37] The assassination was a joint effort between the IMRO and Ustaša, and was planned by Pavelić. The assassin was Vlado Chernozemski, a member of the IMRO.[38] Reminiscent of the 1914 assassination of Franz Ferdinand in Sarajevo, the king and his driver were shot in their vehicle. King Alexander died from the attack, while the driver lived. Chernozemski, the assassin, died in police custody that day from saber wounds. The Ustaša accomplices, Ivan Rajić, Mijo Kralj, Zvonimir Pospišil, and Antun Godina were later arrested and tried in France. They received life sentences, but they were released by the Germans in 1940, after France fell.[39] King Alexander's cousin, Prince Paul, became regent over the kingdom until the king's son, Peter II, would be of age to rule.[40]

The assassination was not an unqualified success for Pavelić and the Ustaša movement. Italy and Mussolini were accused by Belgrade of conspiring in the assassination. In response, Mussolini had Pavelić imprisoned in Italy, his training camps in the country were closed, and his followers were interred on the Italian island of Lipari, located north of Sicily.[41] Later, in March 1936, Pavelić was released from custody, but he remained in Italy under police guard, with the Nucleus still coordinating actions in Yugoslavia. Many of his followers went back to the kingdom to spread their Ustaše ideals and infiltrate the government to prepare for the return of the *Poglavnik* (or leader) to Croatia, when the time was right.[42] Belgrade still protested to the Italians for supporting the Ustaša. In 1937, Italy agreed with Belgrade not to support the Ustaša movement anymore. This was a lie.[43] It really did not matter. By this time, the Ustaša movement was very strong in Croatia.

Eleven-year-old King Peter II, Dowager Queen Maria and Prince Paul (right) at King Alexander's funeral in 1934. Prince Paul became regent until Peter, at the age of 17, was named king in March 1941. Peter and members of the royal family fled the kingdom following the German invasion, eventually making it to England where Peter would lead the Yugoslav government in exile. (*Bibliotheque nationale de France*)

The efforts of the HSS, Ustaša, and other pro-separatists in Croatia finally paid off. In 1939, Prince Regent Paul appointed Dragiša Cvetković the minister of health for the Kingdom, to the position of Prime Minister. Cvetković, was tasked by Prince Regent Paul to work with Macek' of the Croatian Peasant Party (HSS) to address the "Croatian Question" and broker a deal for Croatian independence within the kingdom. The resulting Cvetković-Macek' Agreement on August 24, 1939 resulted in the creation of the Banovina (or administrative subdivision) of Hrvatska (Croatia) that would have its own parliament and considerable administrative autonomy within Yugoslavia. The agreement also led to Maček being named as the Deputy Prime Minister of Yugoslavia.[44] Maček also remained as head of the HSS until the return of Pavelić and his Ustaša regime in 1941.[45]

Yugoslavia 1941

In 1941, Hitler wanted to expand his original Tripartite Pact—a mutual defense treaty that was created in 1940 between Germany, Italy, and Japan, and later Romania and

Hungary—to include Bulgaria and Yugoslavia. By incorporating these nations, Hitler would be reassured that they were on his side and the soft underbelly of Europe would be better protected from the Allies, especially the British, who already had a presence in Greece after Italy's failed invasion of the country in 1941. Including these countries in the pact would also allow Germany the transit of troops through Bulgaria and Yugoslavia to deal with the British threat in Greece. And then, with Greece's defeat, Hitler could concentrate on his invasion of Russia.[46]

On March 1, 1941, with pressure from Germany and promises of land from Greece, once the Germans conquered it, Bulgaria signed into the pact. The following day, German troops entered the country to prepare for their invasion of Greece. Yugoslavia, however, was reluctant to sign. The kingdom wanted to maintain neutrality, and if anything, align itself with the British, but the British did not have an adequate number of military forces to stop a German advance and protect Yugoslavia.[47] Hitler's overtures placed Yugoslavia in an unwinnable situation: refuse to sign the pact and face invasion by Germany and its allies, or sign it and face internal opposition from some of its highly fractious groups, including the Serbs. Joining the pact would further destabilize the nation, and ostracize it from the British.[48]

With no signs of support from the British, the Cvetković-Maček Yugoslav government signed the pact on March 25, 1941. Pro-Allied Serb elements of the Yugoslav military were not happy with this new alliance with Germany. Two days later, on March 27, Regent Prince Paul and his government were overthrown by a military coup. The 17-year-old King Peter II was declared to be of age to rule, and the new government led by air force general Dusan Simović renounced the pact.[49] Hitler was enraged with the Yugoslavs' actions. The nation would pay for its disobedience. Hitler ordered that Yugoslavia be attacked as soon as possible—and crushed. The invasion was appropriately named Operation *Strafgericht (Retribution)*.[50]

The German Invasion

On Easter Sunday, April 6, 1941, Germany, along with its Tripartite Axis partners, invaded Yugoslavia and Greece. German and Austrian troops entered from German-annexed Austria into Slovenia, while Italian troops entered the kingdom from the west. On April 11, Hungarian troops entered the Bačka, one of Hungary's old territories that had been taken by Yugoslavia after World War I.[51] Bulgarians, meanwhile, also entered from the east.

Ed Sakasitz ("Saki") was one of the many Germans who participated in Operation *Marita*, the invasion of Greece. Saki, an American citizen, moved back to Austria with his mother when he was two months old, and was drafted into the German Wehrmacht in September 1940, after serving in the *Reichsarbeitsdienst* (RAD). As an Austrian, Saki was proud to be in the German army. He said he thought about volunteering for the SS, but he did not meet their minimum standards—he was too short. He also thought about volunteering for the *Kriegsmarine* (navy); as a child, he had played in the various lakes around his village and had an interest in water and sailing. Later, he was glad that he did not join the Kriegsmarine, after seeing sunk ships during the invasion of Crete. Receiving his basic training in Bregenz, which is on Lake Constance in Austria, he recalls marching through Bregenz singing "Lili Marlene" and the Horst Wesel songs on the way to the shooting range: "We had to sing all the time you know… singing is duty. We didn't have to be nice singers, we just gotta be loud."[52] Saki was trained in using the Luger P-08 pistol, the standard infantry issue Mauser K-98 rifle, and the MG-34 machine gun. In late 1940, he was assigned to *Panzerjäger Abteilung 85*, a motorized anti-tank unit that was based in Salzburg. He was eventually assigned to manning the MG-34 machine gun in the German *Sd.Kfz. 251 (Sonderkraftfahrzeug 251)*, an armored personnel carrier halftrack. For the latter part of 1940, and spring 1941, Saki enjoyed his time around Salzburg and was preparing for what he thought would be the invasion of the Soviet Union. But that was delayed. Greece and Yugoslavia slowed Hitler's ambitions to the east.

In the invasion of Greece, Saki's unit was part of the German 12th Army. His unit was transported by rail from Austria where they rode in open flatcars with their equipment. He described their route:

> Hungary first… to Romania. In Romania, we stayed overnight in the towns, in big buildings, you know. I don't know, but I guess that they emptied some buildings for the Deutsche Wehrmacht, or something like that. It only took a few days to go through Romania, and then of course over the Danube River, and then we drove all the way down through Bulgaria and again stayed in little villages down there and eventually into Sofia. The last little town we stayed in Bulgaria was Petrich.

Yugoslav citizens, many of them ethnic Germans, greet their German liberators as they roll through the kingdom. Captioned on the back, the owner wrote "a German village by Belgrade." (Author's collection)

To attack Greece, German units had to pass through the Metaxas Line, a series of fortifications along the Greek–Bulgarian frontier. Named after Ioannis Metaxas, the prime minister of Greece from 1936 to 1941, the 155-km line of fortifications composed of forts, tunnels, machine-gun emplacements, anti-tank barriers, and trenches controlled key mountain passes. Combined with the rugged mountain terrain, it was believed that the line would stop or at least deter invading forces coming from Bulgaria. However, like the Maginot Line in France, it was easily penetrated and flanked by modern forces, including the Luftwaffe and panzers. Passing through the line was easy, Saki said, with little or no opposition. What resistance did exist was already taken care of by the lead forces. When his unit crossed the line, they had the opportunity to take photos of the destroyed pillboxes and other barriers. From there, it was an unopposed drive to the coast at Thessaloniki, on the Aegean Sea, that took them about a week. Saki said:

> When the war started on the Metaxas Line, I remember the Stukas, the German planes, the JU 87. They threw their bombs at the bunkers up there. And then the Gebirgsjager went up. Then, pretty soon the infantry started coming down with some enemy; they just gave up and surrendered. There was very little resistance going down to Greece. The Luftwaffe did most of the job. They bombed everything out there and they gave up. There weren't too many Greeks anyway. There were more British and New Zealanders where we were. And then from there, we proceeded going down to Greece all the way down to Athens. And from there, we then shipped to the island of Crete for the invasion.

He said that the invasion was easy and was deceptive on what war was really like. In his halftrack, he saw no combat at all. Even troops in his unit just walked along, occasionally getting alerts of enemy nearby that raised their level of awareness, but never led to any engagements. In most cases, he said that they could not keep up with the retreating enemy soldiers and there was little, if any, rearguard action to slow their motorized columns. What did slow their advance were the roads. Steep and narrow, often unpaved, the roads were not designed for a modern mechanized army. This oftentimes led to a slow mushy crawl of vehicles, horse-drawn equipment, and troops walking with the equipment. While at least comfortable in his halftrack, Saki said that on many days the marching troops alongside were making faster time than him. What troops they did encounter were prisoners that shuffled along the side of the road. The Greeks were disarmed and sent home, while the British and New Zealand troops were taken into captivity as POWs.

Later, Saki spent seven months on Crete, until being transferred to Russia in late 1942, where his unit fought near Leningrad. Now he was in a real war, he said, enduring the cold and the massive power of the Russian artillery. From Russia, his unit was transferred to Italy in 1944 where he became a messenger, driving a motorcycle. In late, 1944, he was wounded by artillery fire, getting hit with shrapnel in his legs and crashing his bike in the process. Placed on a hospital train, he would spend the rest of the war interned in neutral Switzerland.[53]

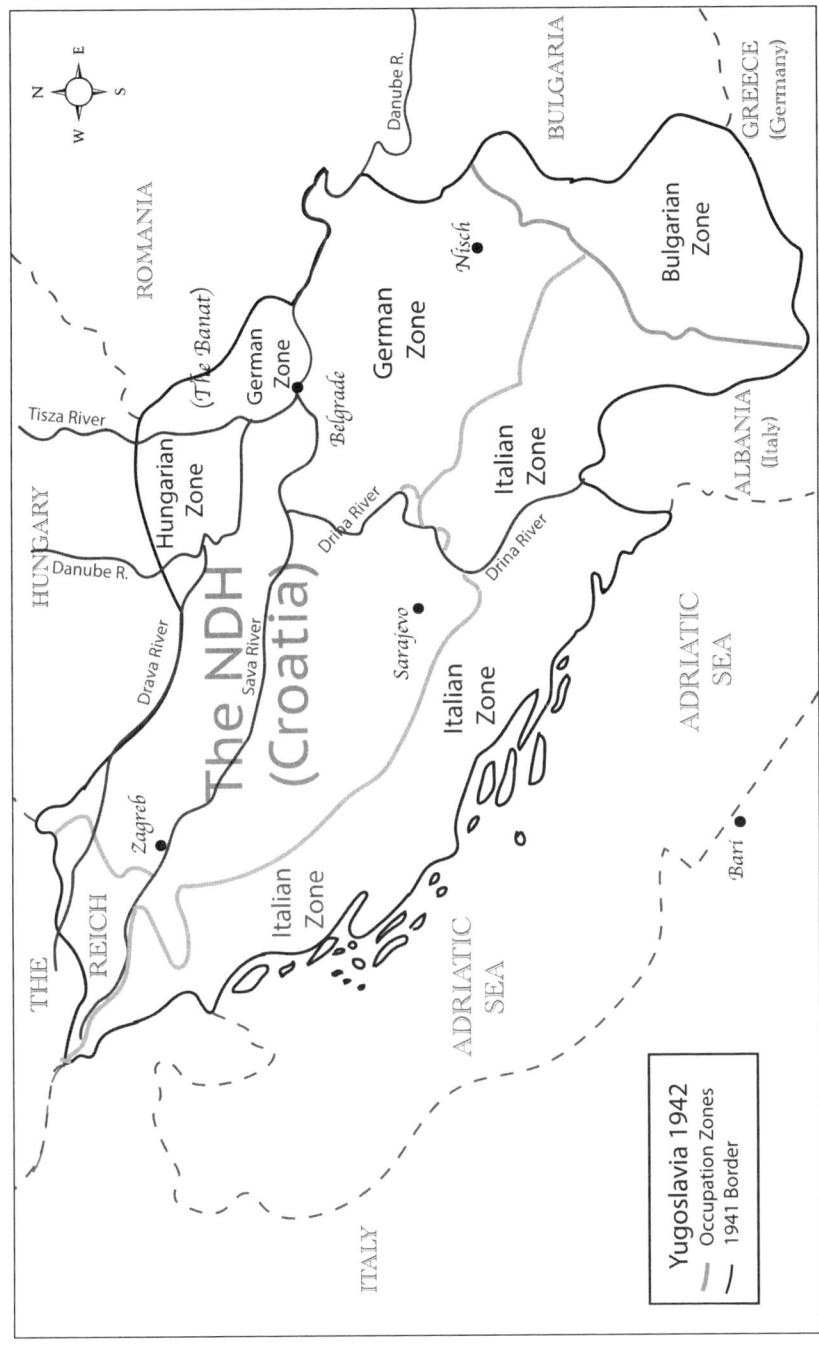

THE REICH

HUNGARY

ROMANIA

Tisza River

Danube R.

Hungarian Zone

(The Banat)

German Zone

Danube R.

Drava River

Sava River

Belgrade

The NDH (Croatia)

German Zone

Nisch

BULGARIA

GREECE (Germany)

Bulgarian Zone

Drina River

Drina River

Italian Zone

ALBANIA (Italy)

Zagreb

Sarajevo

Italian Zone

Italian Zone

ADRIATIC SEA

ADRIATIC SEA

Bari

ITALY

Yugoslavia 1942

Occupation Zones

1941 Border

* * *

At the same time that Axis units were entering the Kingdom of Yugoslavia from all directions, on Sunday, April 6, the capital city of Belgrade was awakened by the sound of German Stukas and medium bombers that pounded the city and terrorized the citizenry. Under the command of General Alexander Lohr, aircraft from *Luftflotte* 4, based in Romania, bombed the center of Belgrade for three days,[54] killing and injuring thousands, while destroying over 700 buildings and levelling about half of the city center.[55] Subsequent days also saw more Luftwaffe and artillery bombardment to further soften up the city for the arrival of the German infantry. To protect the city from the fast-approaching German army, Royal Yugoslav forces destroyed the bridges over the Sava and Danube rivers. On April 10–11 the Pančevo Bridge, or the King Peter II Bridge, over the Danube was blown. On April 11, the Royal Yugoslav army also blew both the Alexander and Railroad bridges over the Sava river.[56]

One person who experienced the raid firsthand was Zagortga Kellerman. Zaga, as she prefers being called, grew up in Belgrade. The daughter of a cavalry officer in the Royal Yugoslav army who died in 1939, Zaga, with her widowed mother and two sisters, lived in an apartment four doors down from the Hotel Moscow, which still exists today. She described her "pappa" as a democratically oriented man that was loyal to the king. On the day of the German attack, Zaga's family fled Belgrade by boat, traveling upstream on the Sava river to Šabac, to her grandmother's house. One of her uncles that was an aid to Regent Paul also left for the coast with the royals, and then traveled on to England. She had no love of Churchill for abandoning the Kingdom, referring to him as a "stupid elephant."

To slow the capture of the city of Belgrade, Royal Yugoslav troops blew the bridges over the Danube and Sava rivers on April 10–11. The left image shows King Alexander Bridge that spanned the Sava river, with a pontoon bridge next to it that was constructed by German pioneers. The right image shows the destroyed Pančevo bridge that crossed the Danube river. (Author's collection)

Later, the family returned to Belgrade and lived in their apartment near the Hotel Moscow. In the fall of 1941, living under the occupation became even more difficult. On Christmas Eve, the family were forcibly removed from their apartment to make room for living quarters for *Flakhelferin* staff, German female auxiliaries who assisted Luftwaffe personnel. An old friend of her father came to their rescue, moving them into the basement of his home that was near the city's royal park. With anger in her voice to this day, Zaga said that at least the Germans were honest. Soon after they were evicted, her mother requested their furniture and other personal property be returned to them, which it was.

Being 20 years old in 1941, she said that she did not live the normal life of a young woman. In her opinion, fraternizing with German men was unconscionable, although she qualified the remark to some degree by saying that "when you have a snake, you are polite to that snake…" She was a royalist, brought up believing in the king, and the Germans were the enemy. She did not have the opportunity to go to college, and because of the strict curfews the residents had, going out at night was not an option, due to the fear of getting caught by the German *Feldgendarmerie* that patrolled the city. Most of her time she played the piano with her mother, or read and socialized with her sisters. On occasion, they did visit her uncles and cousins who lived in the city for dinner; that provided some degree of pre-war normalcy. And they did frequent the royal park in the warmer months to socialize.

Besides losing their home, their privileged lifestyle basically came to an end. Zaga's mother no longer received her father's military pension. This was cut off during the Axis occupation. To get by, the family relied on money and food from her grandmother who owned property and businesses near Šabac. They also knew a riverboat captain that would smuggle food and other supplies to her mother when he made trips to and from her grandmother's. Daily activities also strained her dignity. She had to stand in line for coal and foodstuffs, choking up as she said, "Can you imagine the country of your great-great grandpa that you now have to line up for food? … It was a very hard time. I can't really tell you what is worse though, either the Germans or the communists…" When the communists re-took Belgrade in 1944, her life did not improve to a great degree. Now, she was considered a Royal Yugoslav collaborator and not a supporter of Tito. At the end of the war she remained in Belgrade, going to college and then working for the United Nations in the city. In 1947, she left Yugoslavia for good. Disgusted with Tito and communism, and being constantly harassed by Tito's secret police who thought she was a spy for the West, she moved to the US, becoming a schoolteacher in one of the many Serb diasporas that exist in America.[57]

* * *

On April 12, Belgrade fell to just a handful of SS soldiers from the *Das Reich Division* under the leadership of Captain Fritz Klingenberg. His unit having been tasked with reconnaissance of the approaches to Belgrade, and securing strategic locations along the way, he and six others managed to cross the Danube river by boat, capture some Yugoslav vehicles and soldiers, and work their way toward Belgrade, driving through Yugoslav checkpoints in their stolen vehicles and wearing enemy uniforms they had acquired. After a short firefight at Belgrade's city limits, they found their way into the city center, and raised the German flag. Soon after, the mayor of Belgrade and his entourage surrendered the city to Klingenberg after he bluffed them, stating that if the city and soldiers occupying it did not surrender, Belgrade would be further destroyed by the Luftwaffe. The mayor and military complied with his terms of surrender. The following night, forward elements of the *SS Das Reich* division entered the surrendered city, and Belgrade was officially in the hands of the German occupiers. Klingenberg was later brought before his superiors for disobeying his initial orders and taking Belgrade without permission. Supposedly, his response to the accusation was, "What was I to do, give the city back?" His indiscretions were overlooked, and he was awarded the Knight's Cross for his valor. Later, in 1944, his luck would end. Now a colonel, he was killed near Saarbrucken, fighting the Americans.[58]

Croatian troops were also involved in the capture of Sarajevo in 1941. Here, Croatian troops wearing traditional Royal Yugoslav uniforms, but now with their NDH insignia, pose with a Luftwaffe solider in Sarajevo. (Author's collection)

Belgrade was not the only target in Yugoslavia. The Luftwaffe pounded other cities and strategic locations, while ground forces plowed their way further into the kingdom, taking the major cities.[59] The Yugoslav military soon collapsed from the Blitzkrieg tactics. In some cases, entire units defected, as was the case of some Croatian battalions that were serving in the Royal Yugoslav military. Pro-Ustaša troops in the Yugoslav army also began revolting against their officers.[60] On April 15, Sarajevo fell, with German, Croatian, and Ustaša troops taking the city. The Ustaša immediately began atrocities against the Serbs, Jews, and Roma to the extent that the German occupiers complained about their brutality, raising concerns that it could lead to civilians further resisting the German occupation.[61] Citizens also sought their revenge against age-old rival ethnic groups. Now, it often was the Serbs versus the Muslims, and the Croats versus the Serbs.

Military personnel and refugees clogged the roads out of the kingdom, trying to get away from the Axis forces, in many cases moving toward the Adriatic coast to escape to Italy. The royal family was part of the exodus. King Peter II eventually made it to England where the provincial government of Yugoslavia in exile was established. Regent Paul was sent to live in Kenya.[62] Many of the citizens that got out of Yugoslavia first made it to the Italian zone along the Croatian coastline, away from the Germans and Ustaše. From there, they crossed the Adriatic to Italy, and resettled in other nations with the help of the Yugoslav government in exile.[63] Others would remain in Dalmatia until 1943. With the arrival of the Germans in Dalmatia in that year, they were forced out again, ending up living in refugee camps, such as the El Shatt refugee camp in Egypt. Located near the city of Suez, El Shatt was originally a British military camp that eventually housed over 20,000 Yugoslav refugees at its peak.[64]

The kingdom survived the onslaught for only 12 days. It was over fast. On April 17, the Royal Yugoslav military surrendered.[65] Now, the kingdom would be carved up. In the case of Croatia, the Germans wanted Maček of the HSS to be head of the new puppet state. Maček refused: he did not want to collaborate with the enemy. But the Ustaša seized upon the opportunity to rule. Already Pavelić, with about 300 of his supporters from Italy, had followed the Italian invaders and returned to Croatia. On April 10, one of his trusted followers, Slavko Kvaternik, formed a new government, declaring the Independent State of Croatia (*Nezavinsa Drzava Hrvatska*, or NDH) with Ante Pavelić as the leader—under the watchful eyes of the Germans.[66] As Poglavnik, Pavelić would be the prime minister and foreign minister of the new Independent State of Croatia that also included Bosnia and Herzegovina. Kvaternik, meanwhile, would be the commander of the Croatian Home Guard, known as the *Domobran*.[67] The rest of Pavelić's Ustaša followers who were interred in Italy on the Lipari islands soon returned home to their new country to begin their ethnic cleansing of Serbs, Roma, and Jews, while also fighting Chetniks and other "enemies of the state."[68] The Ustaša terror was swift in the new NDH. By

Surrendered Royal Yugoslav soldiers. The kingdom survived the German onslaught for only 12 days. On April 17, 1941 the war was officially over. Now a civil war would emerge and last for years. (Author's collection)

mid-July 1941, over 200,000 Serbs that lived in Bosnia and Herzegovina, now the NDH, were expelled to Serbia proper. Other state enemies, including the Jews and Roma, were also ordered to be destroyed, as the Ustaša started building concentration camps in the NDH.[69]

The rest of the kingdom was carved up by other nations in the Tripartite Pact. The Hungarians took the Bačka, an area in Yugoslavia that was bordered by the Danube to the west and south and the Tisza river to the east, while the Bulgarians took eastern Macedonia. Even the Albanians participated in the land grab. Albania took some of eastern Montenegro and western Macedonia. Ethnic Germans in the Banat in the Vojvodina, located in the north of Yugoslavia, became a special administrative unit of Germany. Serbia itself existed as a puppet state under the control of the Germans, who appointed General Milan Nedić, the former minister of war in the Yugoslav government, and an anti-communist, as the new leader of Serbia. Nedić was perceived by the Germans as someone they could easily control.[70]

Pavelić kept his word to the Italians on their ambitions for land in Yugoslavia. In May 1941, in the Rome agreements with Mussolini, the Italians got part of western Slovenia and the city of Ljubljana, and areas along the Adriatic which were divided into zones. The Italians were granted sovereignty in Zone 1, which included many of the islands in the Adriatic. They also had military and civil powers in Zone 2, an 80-km-wide belt of land from the Dalmatian coastline inland from Albania and north to Trieste, while in Zone 3, part of the interior of the new NDH, the Italians had military operational power over the Croatian regular army, known as the Domobran. A Ustaša presence was also prevented in Zones 2 and 3.[71]

The Partisans

The Italians and their repressive policies were immediately met with opposition. To counter resistance efforts, the Italians imposed the death penalty for anyone resisting or engaged in armed rebellion against them. Besides the executions, arrests, deportations of Croatians to Italy, and reprisals against the families and homes of suspected resistance fighters were commonplace. Soon, these resistance efforts became more organized under the communists, known as the Partisans, in the Italian areas of occupation.[72]

The Communist Party was nothing new to the Kingdom of Yugoslavia. The leader of the Communist Party of Yugoslavia (CPY) was Josef Brož, better known as Tito. Tito, a Croatian by birth, fought in World War I for the Austro-Hungarian Empire on the Eastern Front, and was taken prisoner by the Russians. While a captive, he was introduced to communism and soon became a devout follower, rising up the ranks, and being recognized for his fervor and leadership abilities in the kingdom by the home office, or Comintern in Moscow, that organized communism throughout the world. Living in Zagreb, the capital of Croatia, Tito and his followers clandestinely organized workers and students throughout the kingdom prior to the war. In 1928, he was arrested for possession of a handgun and grenades, and spreading communist propaganda in the kingdom. Sentenced to five years, he became a professional revolutionary in prison, smuggling in communist materials and educating other prisoners about communism, while training them in military tactics to prepare for the future Yugoslav revolution. Released in 1934, he remained in exile from Yugoslavia; he traveled to Spain for the Spanish Civil War, lived in Austria, and occasionally snuck back into Yugoslavia to further organize the communist movement. He would also visit Moscow many times before the outbreak of World War II, winning the admiration of the communist leadership, while navigating the coups and cut-throat ambitions of other party members to eliminate him.[73] Eventually returning to the kingdom incognito in 1939, he was named by Moscow as the general secretary of the Communist Party in Yugoslavia.[74]

The communists, like other opposition groups, were also active just before the 1941 invasion. Right after the coup of March 27, 1941, Yugoslav communists that had fought in the Spanish Civil War were smuggled back into the kingdom to help start the revolution. At the party's provisional committee for Serbia, a branch of the communist party of Yugoslavia, it was already decided that the monarchy had to be destroyed. For those members in the military, their task would be to cause confusion to speed up defeat, hide weapons, and identify officers that were sympathetic to the cause.[75] With the speed of the initial attack and defeat, the party was caught off guard, and they were in an odd situation. They could not fight openly against the Germans because Stalin and Germany were still allies under their 1939 Non-Aggression Pact. After the Germans attacked Russia, in June 1941, the pact became void, and the movement gained momentum with communist Serbs and Croats fighting against the Ustaše and Italians in the NDH.[76] Finally, on July 12, the *Politburo*, which made the day-to-day decisions of the Central Committee, ordered the people to fight against the German occupiers.[77] Because of Tito and the efforts of his followers, the communists were well positioned for the fight, immediately gaining ground against the Axis powers. Already, in 1941, national liberation committees were being established in areas called Republics that the Partisans had taken control of. Compared to other resistance fighters, such as the Chetniks, they were also more organized. From local brigades to units organized on a regional basis to give them an identity, they later became Proletariat army divisions led by military commanders.[78]

Unlike the Chetniks and other resistance groups that were present in the kingdom, the Partisans were a people's army. Ethnicity did not matter. All that mattered was the people defeating the common enemy—Germans, Ustaše, Italians, and others who did not support communism. The communists called for the equality of all Yugoslav peoples, controlling for and trying to eliminate any ethnic bias that existed in their ranks, and instilling hope for a new nation based on equality. Because the Partisan movement was not tied to an ethnic group, it offered its followers protection from the Italians, Ustaša violence against Serbs and Jews, and the Chetniks inflicting violence against the Muslims and Croats.[79] It worked.

* * *

One of the defenders against the German invasion of Yugoslavia was Milorad "Mike" Kristović, a young lieutenant serving in the Royal Yugoslav army in 1941. Mike was born in 1919 near the city of Užice in Serbia, which is located east of Sarajevo by about 185 kilometers, and about 210 kilometers south of Belgrade. He, his parents and his four brothers, he said, lived a simple but good life. He told me about how he ate out of clay bowls and used wooden spoons as a child, fondly recalling that his childhood home had low ceilings and smoked sausages that hung above their wood-fired stove in the kitchen. All of his clothes, he said, were made by his mother. And as farmers, they lived off the land. His father and grandfather also raised and sold horses to the army for extra income.

Mike joined the Royal Yugoslav military in 1936, attending officer school in Belgrade, where he studied engineering. "I was sworn to King Peter and wanted a career in the military," he said. Military service was engrained into the family. His grandfather served in World War I, and had told Mike about his retreat from Serbia into Albania and the starvation they experienced, to the point that his grandfather and other troops would take horse manure, wash it out, and pick out the undigested grains to eat. Mike's older brother was also serving in the Yugoslav air force when World War II broke out. His other two brothers were too young to serve. In 1938, Mike was commissioned as a second lieutenant and assigned to the Šabac area near the Sava river that divided Croatia from Serbia.

Mike explained that even before the war, there was a lot of political dissension and turmoil in Yugoslavia. He recalled that he was approached by a friend in Užice in 1940 and asked to join the communists, even though his friend knew that he was in the military. Later, when Mike was in Belgrade, he had the same thing happen. While in uniform, students would approach him and encourage him to join the communists. He said that there were also protests by the communists in Belgrade, and even in Užice, that were broken up by the police. Already in officer candidate school, they were told that the Croatians would be unreliable if a war broke out, and most likely it would be the Croats that they would be first engaged with. And Kristović also said that before the outbreak of the war, he was told by military commanders that it would be difficult for Serbia to repel the Germans.

The Royal Yugoslav army rapidly disintegrated after the invasion. With the major military communication hub in Belgrade destroyed, Royal Yugoslav units lacked a unified command structure. Units throughout the kingdom were on their own and

An artist's rendition of Mike Kristović when he was a Chetnik fighter. Unlike other Chetnik fighters he kept his face clean shaven when he could. His white shirt was made out of parachute silk. The slick silk helped prevent lice infestation. (Author's collection)

did their best to defend it against the Axis powers. On the first day of the invasion, Mike said that they did not even know that Yugoslavia had been attacked, because they had no radio communications with command. A couple of days later, they encountered German infantry reconnaissance troops, and soon retreated toward the safety of the interior of Serbia. His unit also disintegrated. He said that many simply decided to walk home, while others surrendered, or were later picked up as prisoners by the rapidly advancing Germans. For him, surrender was not an option. He ignored the government's order to surrender, and started moving to the safety of the center of Serbia to refit and regroup.[80]

Kristović and other Royalists heard that Colonel Draza Mihailović and a handful of other officers were setting up a resistance movement. Word had spread, in part, through British radio traffic about the Yugoslav resistance movement being organized in an area of Serbia called Ravna Gora, or "the Plateau," near the Drina river close to the Serb/Bosnian border.[81] Mike began his long march on foot with two others to Ravna Gora, relying on the local Serb citizens for food and shelter. Eventually, one decided to go home, so it was now just him and another enlisted soldier. Other supporters of the kingdom and crown also began filtering into the area, setting up camps in towns and villages that formed the basis of what would be called the Ravna Gora movement. Mihailović was named as the commander in chief of the movement by the Yugoslav government in exile.[82] Even though Mike was a Royal Yugoslav officer, and identified himself as one to this day, after Yugoslavia fell, he was now a guerilla fighter, known as a Chetnik.

The Chetniks

Historically, Chetniks were armed Serb citizens and nationalists who fought against Ottoman rule in areas including Macedonia.[83] In September 1903, the movement was institutionalized as the Serbian Revolution Organization, where citizens and soldiers alike were encouraged to fight against the Ottomans, to expand Serbia to what it considered its rightful territories.[84] Later, in the First Balkan War of 1912, Chetnik paramilitary forces followed along with and were used as auxiliaries in the Serbian army, sometimes fighting with the regular army. In other instances, Chetniks performed rear-guard actions, disturbing enemy communications, organizing local insurgents, and conducting raids and acts of terrorism against the Ottomans. These paramilitary groups often committed atrocities against the civilian populations and captured enemy soldiers. One of their trademarks was cutting off the noses and upper lips of their enemies—alive or dead—to further spread fear.[85]

Chetnik paramilitaries also fought in World War I alongside the Serb army. After World War I, the Serb government relied upon the Chetniks to act as security forces and fight against Macedonian separatists.[86] In 1923, Serb paramilitaries created the Organization Against Bulgarian Bandits, after 23 Serbs were killed in Macedonia.

By May 1924, the organization had over 10,000 members who were responsible for patrolling their communities. Later, in 1930, it was called the People's Self-Defense. To increase its power in the area the Yugoslav army distributed 25,000 rifles to its members, and other trusted citizens, who called themselves militiamen.[87]

The Chetniks also existed in other parts of the kingdom before World War II, where they committed atrocities against the Muslim populations in Bosnia and Montenegro.[88] In Croatia, their violence got so bad that in 1936, the HSS created its own militias in cities and the countryside to protect Croatian citizens from them.[89] The Chetniks even had their own associations. One such association, the Association of Serbian Chetniks, was created by Puniša Račić, the man who shot Stephan Radić and others in Parliament in 1928. Like their predecessors, the Chetniks were also recognized by the Yugoslav military. In the 1920s and 1930s, the Yugoslav military adopted guerilla warfare as part of its military strategy, and later in 1940, it created seven Chetnik battalions. These units even had their own insignia and uniforms that sported the traditional Chetnik skull and crossbones. When World War II broke out, members from some of these Chetnik associations and units would form the core of the Chetnik movement.[90]

This movement was highly fragmented, and the name "Chetniks" became the collective name associated with Serb resistance fighters, some that were not even associated with, or under the command of Mihailović.[91] Some Chetniks were independent local bands operating on their own initiative to protect themselves, their families, and communities from Ustaša atrocities.[92] Other Chetniks fell under Mihailović's central command, and followed his orders. This confusion over "Chetniks" would plague them throughout the war—who was actually following Mihailović and who was simply a Chetnik fighter. Mihailović's Chetniks also took a different position than other resistance fighters in the former kingdom. His strategy was to stockpile supplies and wait for the Allies to invade, and then collectively attack the Germans, basically following the tactics of other resistance fighters in occupied Europe. In the meantime, Mihailović needed to safeguard the Yugoslavs from their internal enemies—the Partisans, who were trying to overthrow the monarchy and install a new form of government.[93]

* * *

Mike said that most of 1941 was spent in Bosnia, fighting the Croatian Ustaša troops and Muslims who were on the Croatian side. He and his small unit wandered around eastern Bosnia, fighting near Višegrad, Banja Luka, and in the hills around Sarajevo. Then, they would return to the Ravna Gora area in Serbia to refit. On one of their missions in 1941, they attacked Muslims near Srebrenica in Bosnia, killing quite a few people, he said. But the enemy was also strong. In one fight with Ustaša forces, he hid in a tree for two days to evade certain death, if discovered.

Word even got home that he was killed in this battle. Eventually, he found some other Chetnik troops and made it back to Ravna Gora. On only one occasion in 1941 he recalled fighting the Italians. He said they had no military abilities: "Lovers and singers, that is all they are."[94]

In late 1941, Mike was promoted to the rank of captain and became a company commander. He said that in most cases, they never operated as a complete company. They were fighting a guerilla war, where fast attacks by small numbers of troops were the norm. Traditional troop maneuvers associated with taking large swaths of land or towns was not done in this war, he said. Like the other Chetniks, the fighters in his group grew beards as a sign of mourning for the loss of their king. Mike, however, did not. He told me that he was not yet able to grow a full beard, and instead he opted to maintain a relatively clean-shaven face throughout the war. But he did let his hair grow long, to the point that it extended down beyond his shoulders.

Mike also said the fighting had no rules. In Serbia, the villages and people were pro-Yugoslav. In Bosnia, the people were not pro-Serb. Many of the Serbs that lived in Bosnia had already moved back to Serbia proper to avoid Ustaša and Muslim atrocities, or they were forced out, or killed. He did not trust anyone in Bosnia. And he had no empathy for Muslims and the Ustaša. His mother's family, who lived in Bosnia, were massacred by the Ustaša in 1941. Some, he said, were beheaded. I asked him what they did with the Ustaše if they were captured. He laughed, drawing his finger across his neck: "You know what we did with them, you garroted them."[95]

* * *

On June 22, 1941, the Germans attacked the Soviet Union. Many of the units used in the invasion of Yugoslavia and Greece now set off to fight on the Eastern Front. Like many of their earlier campaigns, it seemed easy. In some cases, entire Soviet divisions were surrounded and taken prisoner on the German drive to take Moscow. The Reich's second-rate units, not quite prepared for or trained to be an invading force, soon occupied the former Kingdom of Yugoslavia to maintain order. It would not be an easy task. The Axis forces would soon discover that they had walked right into a civil war in the midst of their occupation.[96]

For young men, such as 17-year-old Gottfried Weber, who was eagerly waiting to serve, 1941 was an exciting year. Victory, not defeat, was a fact. The radio broadcasts and newspapers only had victories to report. The local *Kinos* (cinemas) playing the latest newsreels before feature movies showed the German war machine in action. Erwin Rommel, the Desert Fox, fighter aces, and Knight's Cross winners became celebrities in the minds of the public as they watched their exploits on the big screen. The Stukas screaming down and dive-bombing targets, modern tanks tearing across rivers and the dusty steppes, and happy citizens from defeated countries greeting their tired and dust-covered saviors as they marched on to complete the defeat of another country—were awesome sights to see.

The glamour of war was also validated by troops coming home on leave. Wearing their sharp uniforms that sprouted campaign ribbons and badges earned in combat, their stories made the young men envious and even more eager to serve. These accounts helped them dismiss what their fathers had shared with them about serving the Kaiser in World War I. Their fathers' stories of the horrors of war probably fell on deaf ears. After all, their defeated fathers were old, and they fought in an antiquated war that involved fighting from the trenches. This new war was one of *Blitzkrieg*, a lightning war that used modern aircraft and panzers to win. War could not come fast enough for many of them. Be it drafted in the Wehrmacht, Luftwaffe, Kriegsmarine, or volunteering for the SS, it did not matter. Gottfried just needed to get into the war before it was over.

CHAPTER 2

1942

The beginning of 1942 is a splendid time for the Third Reich. The cities and towns are buzzing with the sounds of victory. The national flag—red, with the white circle imposed with the black swastika—is proudly flown throughout the towns and in shops. News from the east is promising. Mother Russia is being bled dry. The Bolshevik hordes are in retreat and are surrendering en masse to Wehrmacht troops. In the north, the city of Leningrad is under siege. Army Group Center, meanwhile, is preparing for its spring offenses after being delayed by the cold Russian winter that literally froze the German Wehrmacht in its tracks. Further south, German forces are closing in on the Crimea and the Caucasus, while troops are eagerly racing further east in anticipation of reaching the Volga river, the traditional dividing line between Europe and Asia.[1] In the south, the Afrikakorps, led by the popular Erwin Rommel, is pushing into Egypt. The Reich cannot be stopped. It is a great time to be a German.

The diaries of Gottfried Weber begin in 1942. Weber lives in Waldenburg in the state of Saxony or Sachsen that borders Poland to the east, and Czechoslovakia to the south. On the German side is the state of Thuringia, a short distance to the north, and Bavaria to the southwest. Nestled in the district of Zwickau, a rural agricultural area, the town of about 5,000, including the adjacent areas, is surrounded by rolling hills, farm fields, and woods. The town itself forms a crescent or somewhat half-circle shape, following the upper ridge of the Zwickauer Mulde river that leisurely flows around the town. The river also divides the town, with the *Altstadt*, or old town, located on the south side of the river.

Dating back to the 1300s and known for its pottery, Waldenburg is a typical German town with narrow streets and cobblestones worn smooth from centuries of travel. Its well-manicured three-story stone and timber buildings painted in simple colors of whites and pastels line the streets. In 1942, with fuel being needed for the war effort, few vehicles are seen. Horse-drawn wagons are more present on the streets. The melodic clip clop of the steel-shod hooves on the cobblestones echoing against the buildings is reminiscent of the town in earlier days. The highest point and tallest structure in the town is St Bartolomäus' Lutheran Church that sits in the

Couples relaxing on the Mulde river near Waldenburg. (Author's collection)

center of town, its spire making the town easily seen from the adjacent farm fields and villages. Not too far from the church to the southeast, on Markt Strasse, is the *Rathaus* (town hall) with its clocktower spire and dual stone staircase that overlooks the Marktplatz. The building's four flag poles out front are adorned with Party flags and banners. About one block west from the Rathaus on the Carl-Wilhelm-Richter-Platz is the Gewerbehaus, one of the town's pubs that Weber and his friends frequent. Walking from the Gewerbehaus, about 100 yards to the southwest is the NSDAP (*Nationalsozialistische Deutsche Arbeiterpartei*, or Nazi Party) Headquarters, that a prominent Waldenburger had donated to the party. It's a large structure located at Hans-Schemm-Strasse 24, and Gottfried spends a great deal of time here. The district leader is Dr. Kurt Welcker, a local dentist, who has been part of the movement since 1923 when he was a student in Munich.[2]

The main point and perhaps pride of the town is the castle of Schönburg-Waldenburg, a palace complex that is the residence of the Schönburg family, descendants of Saxon nobility. Added to over the centuries, it resembles more of an estate than a castle. About three stories high with the exception of the square tower that is taller, its light tan and gray walls and red tile roof serve as another landmark for the town.

Not too far from the castle, across the river, is the Altstadt or old side of Waldenburg that is dotted with homes and factories. The Aldtstadt also has another Lutheran church on the Bahnhofstrasse, a street winding down to the train station that

Waldenburg today. In the center of the image is the city hall and town square. To the south is the old town where the Weber family lived. (Getty Images)

connects Waldenburg to neighboring towns of Glauchau to the west and the large city of Chemnitz to the east. Just south of the church is Weber's home. The landmark in the Aldtstadt is the large Grünfelder Park. Originally the summer estate of the Schönburg family, the English-styled park is a popular place for young couples to go for walks and to be away from the prying eyes of their parents and adults. The park is also a place for Gottfried to socialize and to go ice skating or play hockey with his friends on the large pond. At the Grünfelder is the Café Jacobi. With its outdoor deck that overlooks the pond, it is a great place to frequent with his friends, including Gotthard, Hartig, and Werner.

Being 17 years old, like millions of other German youths, Gottfried is in his third year of serving in the *Hitler Jugend* (Hitler Youth) or HJ. The HJ was a compulsory organization created by the Nazi Party to groom the nation's young men to be good soldiers and future leaders, ensuring that the ideology of the party continued for the duration of the Thousand-Year Reich. Originally in the *Jungvolk*, which was for youth over the age of 10, he graduated to the HJ at the age of 14. On entering the HJ, his unit or *Kameradschaft* was composed of about 15 boys who lived in the same area and went to the same school. These Kameradschaft were then grouped together as a platoon known as a *Schar*. About three to five Schars then made up the company or *Gefolgschaft* that organized HJ activities in the area. Gefolgschafts, meanwhile, were organized into *Banns* or regiments. Weber was in Bann 211 in the *Gebiet* or administrative district of Sachsen/Mitte.[3]

HJ activities included attending weekly meetings where youth were indoctrinated into the Nazi philosophy and one's duty to the state and *Führer*. Marching, singing, sports, hiking, camping trips, comradeship, and military activities including basic infantry tactics, compass reading, marksmanship, and weapons cleaning were other common activities of HJ units. Good manners were stressed. Many of Gottfried's HJ activities also included working at the Bann business office, and attending youth film hours where they watched movies like *Jakko*, a story about a troubled youth who joined the HJ, which gave him purpose in life. The underlying theme of the movie reinforced to those youth in attendance how great the HJ was to them—and Germany. Morning exercise classes, outdoor games, fire duty watch at party headquarters, collecting membership dues, maintaining roster reports, and operating the cash register at the local party headquarters were some of his other tasks.

The HJ uniform was constantly worn. The summer uniform consisted of a tan-colored long-sleeve shirt with shoulder boards, black corduroy shorts, wool socks, and black lace-up boots. On the upper left sleeve was the HJ district triangle number. Further down the sleeve near the bicep was the HJ armband. HJ members also wore a black leather belt with a silver buckle that was stamped with the HJ symbol and motto, "Blood and Honor," along with a leather black cross strap that was worn over the right shoulder and attached to the left side of the belt. Hanging off his belt on the left side in a black enameled scabbard was the coveted HJ dagger that often had the inscription *Blut und Ehre* or "Blood and Honor" etched on the blade. This knife with its chrome finish, and red and white enameled diamond badge with a swastika symbol embedded in the black grips, was perhaps the showpiece of the uniform. Unlike other items on the uniform, the knife was earned. HJ members had to pass tests and master the skills expected of a German youth to have the honor

A young man in the Hitler Youth wearing the summer uniform. (Author's collection)

of wearing it. There was also the winter uniform: a black jacket and pants with the summer long-sleeve shirt worn underneath it, adorned with all of the accoutrements that were worn on the summer uniform.[4]

In January and February 1942, most of Gottfried's activities were HJ-related. He was excelling in the HJ. Already in January, he was drawing up operations plans for HJ maneuvers. Later, on February 3, his new HJ leadership certificate was confirmed. Being the HJ-*Kameradschaftsführer*, or the local group leader, he now wore a red and white twisted lanyard, whose two cords were looped through his left shoulder board and attached to the button under the left sleeve pocket of his shirt. Besides typical weekly events, he was also in the HJ *Streifendienst*, or SRD, the HJ patrol service, a special unit within the HJ that was part of the 1936 Law of Hitler Youth. Found within each Gefolgschaft, SRD youth were selected by local HJ and SS leaders. Only those youth that were properly indoctrinated into the HJ, met the racial criteria of the SS, and were model HJ youth were selected for service in the SRD.[5] These select model members of the local HJ had state authority and were responsible for ensuring that local members stayed up to date on their dues, wore their uniforms correctly, and conducted themselves properly in public and in bars and other locations. Serving as the HJ police force, SRD members also assisted in security-related functions at HJ events, rallies, and activities. They also performed security roles at railroad stations and other locations as needed by the local police and HJ leadership.[6] If anything, these were the more radical and committed HJ members. According to the US Armed Forces Book on the Hitler Youth that was published during the war, it was reported that the "SRD works in closest collaboration with police authorities, including the Gestapo and its members, trained and supervised by SS, are regarded as eventual SS replacements."[7]

Get-togethers at the local Nazi Party headquarters were a common activity. The Nazi headquarters, by design, was the central hub of party activities in the town that coordinated official cultural, social, and of course, political events. Like many other towns throughout Germany, the local group or *Ortsgruppe* (unit) was responsible for recruiting new members. Potential party members completed an application that included their basic demographic information along with their address, occupation, and most importantly, a genealogy record to prove that they were full-blooded Germans. Membership was then approved in the main party office in Munich that issued a party number. This membership was then maintained in the master file of party members known as the *Zentralkartei* (ZK).[8] A membership card with the NSDAP number was then issued. On the back of the card were spaces where membership dues stamps were placed to prove that the person was a full-fledged paying member of the party. Loyalty to the party was reflected in one's willingness to pay dues. The area or Ortsgruppe also registered the person, and the party membership numbers, to maintain a local roster. Once a member, individuals could then proudly wear their NSDAP membership pin. About one inch in diameter, the disk resembled the party flag. Bordered in the national color of red, and with the words "*Nationalsozialistische Deutsche Arbeiterpartei*" in gold, with the black swastika superimposed over a white center, it could be worn on one's lapel. To personalize it even more, the owner could have his or her membership number engraved on the back. Every year on April 20, Hitler's birthday, these new members were officially inducted into the Nazi Party in a public ceremony. Later, members in good standing, those who attended meetings and paid their dues, would receive their official Red NSDAP *Mitgliedsbuch* (ID booklet). About the size of a passport, the book contained the owner's photo on the inside front cover and vital personal information on succeeding pages. In the back pages of the book membership dues stamps were affixed.

Participating in and serving the party was also time consuming for Gottfried. The local party oversaw some of the activities of the HJ and other youth organizations such as the BDM, the *Bund Deutsche Mädel*, the female equivalent of the HJ. These groups collected money for the annual WHW or *Winterhilfswerk*, a national collection drive to help the poor make it through the cold German winters. Like the Salvation Army bell ringers of today, these youth "can rattlers" would position themselves outside of public buildings and go door to door to collect for the poor. In exchange for their donation, citizens were given a small WHW "tinnie" pin that they could wear—probably as proof that they already gave and to repel the relentless youth from future solicitations. Relief goods such as food and clothing were also distributed by the HJ. Fridays at 8pm were the social evenings at the headquarters. At one weekly meeting in January, the Blitzkrieg invasion of Norway in 1940 and the battles around the northern city of Narvik were discussed. The following week, Gottfried attended a meeting on the Knight's Cross or *Ritterkreuz* holders, one of the highest military awards awarded for bravery in the field. Other weeks included guest speakers, such as Alfred Kurth, on leave from the front, who on February 20 shared his stories of Wehrmacht victories against what he described as the racially inferior and ill-prepared Red Army. In a later diary entry, Gottfied revealed Kurth's fate. Kurth was killed on the eastern front in September 1942. Besides social events, there were the official weekly party meetings at 8pm that concentrated on party business. These usually lasted an hour. Other nights included membership rallies. On January 30, his mother was sworn into the Party. In her honor, Gottfried gave a speech at the night's meeting.

There was some time for other things besides the HJ and the party. Photography was one of his hobbies. He also worked part-time as a bookkeeper in one of the town's factories. Snowshoeing, skiing, ice skating, and playing hockey at the local pond were some outdoor winter pastimes. Going to the state-controlled movies with friends and his older brother Georg, who was on convalescent leave from the front, was another common pastime. In January and February, they went to see movies including *The Comrades*, a story about Prussian resistance during Napoleon's occupation, *Comedians*, a story about actors in Weimar in the 1800s, *Quax, der*

Bruchpilot, a propaganda film about flying for one's country, and *Krishna, Adventures in the Indian Jungle*, which was about an elephant driver and his family, which he considered to be "rare nonsense." Other movies included *The Homecoming*, a story about ethnic Germans being discriminated against in Poland and saved by the German invasion in 1939, and *Wir Bitten Zum Tanz*, a story about some rival dance schoolteachers and their eventual comradeship. Of course, meeting friends at the Gewerbehaus, the Jacobi Café, and the Gasthaus in the town of Grünfeld were common social activities that sometimes resulted in a hangover the following day. He and his friends also roamed around the area—Oberwinkel, Penig, Grünfeld, Glauchau, Niederwinkel, Wolkenburg, Langenchursdorf, Polsterberg, Langenhof, Hellmannsgrund, Kallenberger, and Hübsch, oftentimes taking the train to get to some of these locations. One responsibility that he shirked was getting his truck driver's license. In January, he skipped his training. Later, in February, he canceled his truck driving instruction completely.

Having already registered with the local police, as all citizens were required to do, Gottfried received his notification to report for military service. On February 10, 1942, he went for his physical examination for the German Wehrmacht. At 8am he had his initiation, and from 9am to noon he had his medical examination and was determined "KV" or *kriegsverwendungsfähig*—fit for active service. He was also issued his military ID booklet called the *Wehrpass* (military passport) which recorded the owner's military service. The size of a modern-day passport, the inside of the front cover of the Wehrpass contained the owner's photo, while other pages contained additional biographical information, leaves taken, medical-related information, and any future awards earned while serving the Reich.[9]

To ensure that units on the front were provided troops in a timely manner, all of Germany was divided into military districts where elements of the German Replacement Army were located. It was the role of the German Replacement Army in each district to conscript and train new soldiers from within the district, while also sending wounded soldiers back to their front-line units when deemed fit for continued service on the front. Like other conscripts from the area, he was assigned to his local reserve unit that supported *24. Infanterie Division*. Since Waldenburg and Sachsen were part of the military district (*Wehrkreis*) IV with its headquarters in Dresden, he would be completing most of his training in the district, specifically in his recruiting subarea which was located in Glauchau.[10] He was then ordered to return home until he received his call-up orders for active duty. He celebrated this major life event by going to the movies and later went to play the card game Skat with his friend Fritz, who was on furlough from the front.

The RAD

Things moved fast for Gottfried. On February 21, he received his call-up orders for the *Reichsarbeitsdienst*. The RAD was a compulsory six-month labor service for young men that was completed before joining or being drafted into the military. Similar to the Civilian Conservation Corps in the US, the RAD was originally created to address the high unemployment rates among young males that existed in Germany in the 1930s. The RAD provided these young men with employment and job skills that could later be used for a civilian job. Later, the RAD was also found to have other benefits for the Reich. Its structure was ideal to initiate the youth of Germany into the culture, practices, and traditions of the military.[11]

German youth in the RAD were assigned to various units throughout the greater Reich to perform labor and construction-related activities. The motto of the RAD was *Arbeit Adelt* or "labor makes you noble." Work activities varied by the location of the RAD camps. They included building fortifications, such as the West Wall along the western border of Germany, and other military projects including bunkers and airfields throughout Germany. Other non-military projects included land reclamation and agricultural-related work to ensure that there was more tillable land to meet the growing food needs of the Reich. The common feature of the RAD, regardless of location, was that it was a paramilitary organization that had a rank structure and military-style training. Recruits called *Arbeitsmänner* (workers) lived in barracks, marched, sang, and trained in physical fitness activities, while realizing the importance of comradeship.[12] With this type of training, RAD recruits would be aptly suited for their basic training in the armed forces that soon followed their RAD service.

Unlike many German youth that performed their labor service requirements in Germany, Gottfried's call-up orders were to report to a camp in occupied Poland. To celebrate his call-up, he went to the movies and then to the Gewerbehaus to drink beer and socialize with friends. The following days he traveled on his skis to the surrounding towns of Niederwinkel, Wolkenburg, and Langenchursdorf to share his excitement and to say his goodbyes to friends. February 25 was his last day at work. On the 28th was his going-away party where he drank until 2am, followed by another day of drinking and celebrating with more friends at the Gasthaus in Grünfeld.

On March 2, he was on his way to his RAD unit in district XXXX Wartherland-Ost, that encompassed the annexed territory of Poland. It was a long two-day train ride. He went to the train station in Glauchau with Georg, who saw him off. From there, he went to Chemnitz, Dresden, Cottbus, and Frankfurt on the Oder. The following day, he entered the greater German Reich, the annexed territory of Poland, or formerly East Prussia that was lost to Poland after the German defeat in World War I. It was exciting. First stopping in Posen, he then made it to his final destination, the RAD *Lager* or camp near Krzewie, a small town in central Poland on the main rail line between Posen to the west and Warsaw to the east.

Upon arrival, he was assigned to the *2nd Trupp* (squad) and a bed in his barracks. RAD Lagers generally followed the same layout throughout the Reich. They were closed camps, meaning that all services needed for RAD recruits were found within the camp itself.[13] The camps were small in size; the standard complement was 216 men. About 180 were the *Arbeitsmänner*; the remaining 30 plus were the leaders and support personnel.[14] The Lagers were usually single-story wood structures with steel roofs. At the main entrance of the Lager was the guard house manned by an Arbeitsmann. Originally manned by a recruit and his spade, in 1942 in occupied Poland, there was now an armed guard with a rifle. It was enemy territory. Immediately visible from the main gate in the center of the camp were two flagpoles. Besides the national *Kriegsflagge*, there was also the RAD flag that had a solid red background with a round white center that displayed the rotating black swastika supported by two ears of wheat. Forming a chevron under the swastika, the wheat ears gave the impression that the swastika was floating above them. Around the flagpole was the square where the recruits would assemble for inspection and drill. Around the perimeter of the square were the camp buildings.[15] Each camp had three or four recruit barracks that opened into the parade ground. Each barrack was also split into three rooms. The 16 occupants of each room made up a *Trupp*, while the entire barracks formed the *Zug* or platoon. Three or four platoons, depending on the camp, formed the *Abteilung* (company). The Lager also included the general-purpose supply barracks, mess hall and kitchen, washroom and laundry barracks, the administration building and sick bay, the leaders' quarters, and latrine

An image of a typical RAD camp with the parade grounds surrounded by recruit barracks. (Author's collection)

barracks. Usually, between each building were flower beds that were tended and cared for by the recruits. Behind the group of barracks was a bicycle storehouse, an equipment storage shed, and a farm garden.[16] To ensure uniformity of appearance of the camps throughout the Reich, the buildings were constructed by one company that the RAD contracted with.[17] The camp and barracks were expected to be kept in pristine condition.

The following day Gottfried was issued his clothing and underwear. All RAD recruits were issued two sets of uniforms. First, was their *Drillich*, or work uniform, with lace-up shoes. Made of an off-white cotton denim material, this was the daily uniform for the RAD worker. Soon, the white denim material became washed out and stained in hues of brown-yellow or gray due to the dirty work the recruits performed. Because the men often worked with their tunics off, the tunics tended to be much cleaner in appearance than the pants. Nevertheless, it was expected that the recruits presented themselves well every morning at inspection and roll call where the *Drillich* was at least pressed, and relatively smart in appearance. Next, there was also the RAD dress uniform and hat. An earth-brown-colored tunic, it had dark brown collars with collar ranks, and shoulder straps. The entire uniform was trimmed out with a black leather belt with a silver buckle, and black jackboots. These uniforms closely resembled those that the recruits would soon be wearing in the armed forces. Each recruit was also issued a bread bag, backpack, canteen, gas mask, mess kit, sleep shirts, blankets, a mattress cover, underwear, socks, and a physical training outfit that included a white muscle shirt with the RAD emblem on it, running shorts and pants, and sport shoes.

One of the most important items issued to the recruit was the spade. The spade was the basic "weapon" for everyone in the RAD. These square-ended blades with short wooden handles were substitutes for the rifle. Ceremonial and symbolic in nature, recruits were responsible for maintaining the spade, ensuring that its blade was polished and gleaned in the sun. Like the rifle, which was the tool of the infantryman, the spade was the tool of the Arbeitsmann. It was expected to be kept oiled, clean, and functional. The spade, like a rifle, was kept in a rack in the recruit's barracks, where at a moment's notice it could be retrieved on the way out the door for battle, or in the case of the RAD Arbeitsmänner, surprise inspections, and marching drills in the camp square. Soon, in the recruits' life, this spade would actually be replaced by the rifle as they moved from the RAD into military service. While the tool changed, the underlying principle of caring for one's weapon did not. Spade inspections were also conducted by the leadership corps. Here, the spade had to be clean, rust free, and basically shining. Anything less would result in the recruit, and often his Trupp, being penalized for carelessness and not looking after another squad member. For this carelessness, they would receive extra physical and work-related activities that were often conducted in the mornings, which resulted in the Trupp missing their breakfast.[18]

RAD recruits liming up for inspection. (Author's collection)

The following three days Gottfried was getting used to camp life. In particular, he was being exposed to the labor perspective of the RAD. On March 8, he began his work in the afternoon, unloading irrigation pipes at the Krzewie train station. The pipes were to be used in the surrounding areas to ensure that newly resettled *Volksdeutsche* families (individuals who had an ethnic German background, but were not citizens of the Reich) who were given land in the Warthe had water for their crops. A lot of the work was very strenuous, to the point that he was "dead tired," "blown away," and had "sleep of exhaustion" on some days, based on his diary entries. The Arbeitsmänner also dug drainage ditches that most likely exist in the area to this day, installed pumps, and shoveled coal. To get to various locations, the construction crews traveled by horse carriage, or on foot, when they often marched in formation and sang. In other cases, the troops were assigned to the *Bauzug* or construction train unit that traveled along the rail line that ran east–west from Krzewie, or on the narrow gauge rail system that went north to Krosniewice and then to Ostrowy.

Many of the activities in the RAD were para-military in nature. The first week, Gottfried began his training in close order drill, and body posture. His training in the HJ helped, but it was still a struggle at times to march in formation, ensuring that the spade on his shoulder moved in unison with those of his fellow recruits. Unlike other RAD units that were stationed in Germany in 1942, his unit was also issued and trained in rifle use. He received weapons training in the second week. The unit was issued World War I-era model K-98 rifles. Longer than the current German World War II-issue K-98, the rifle was ideal for training and guard-related activities, but not for front-line troops engaged in modern warfare. The camp was in hostile occupied territory and the area was unsafe. Partisan attacks were already occurring around the camp. On Easter Sunday, April 5, Gottfried wrote that he had the most boring and saddest Easter in his life. Two German policemen were killed near the camp by partisans. On another occasion, he and a group of RAD Arbeitsmänner had to search the local woods where the night before, one of the guards heard a person calling for help. Of course, physical activities and sports were a common morning activity where the recruits would run or march through the surrounding areas and towns, singing as they went. Later in his service, he would also serve as an armed guard, protecting his fellow recruits who were working in the area.

Generally, mornings in the RAD were dedicated to physical fitness activities. Standards had to be met for the 100-, 200-, and 400-meter run, and long and high jumps. Recruits were also weighed and measured to ensure conformity to RAD fitness standards. The mornings also included basic military training, drilling with spades, and education in party-related topics. Afternoons were devoted to work that varied, depending upon one's assignment. Cleanliness and attention to detail were also stressed. Housekeeping chores were common activities. They included footlocker inspections in the mornings by Staff Sergeant Riegel. On his 18th birthday, Gottfried's inspection did not go well. His superior, by the name of Altenburger, dumped out his footlocker because he had accidentally left his key in the lock, "an unpleasant surprise," in his words. This, combined with the hard work he had that day, made him write in his diary that "it was the most miserable birthday in my life." Guard duty was very common. Almost on a daily basis, he had to perform guard duty for a two-hour shift. Barrack inspections were also commonplace at the camp, by his superiors and, in some cases, RAD leaders from the Gau and cities such as Stalno. In those instances where the barracks did not pass inspection, the recruits were denied breakfast the following morning. Instead, additional physical exercise was required. Recruits also slept on straw-filled mattresses. As part of the recruits' responsibilities, they had to re-fill the straw in their mattress bags. Pillows were the same: they too had to be re-filled with straw. Besides the barracks, the parade ground and surrounding camp areas had to be kept immaculate, where Gottfried had to often pull weeds and rake the ground smooth.

Kitchen duty was another assignment. Not too keen on the task, he wrote, "I am slowly catching on, but I am not crazy about kitchen duty," where some days were spoiled because of the amount of dishes (*verfluechte Scheisse* or "for fuck's sake") he had to wash. Common chores included carrying water for the kitchen, working in the supply room, and cooking. On many days these chores required getting up at 3am to fire up the kettles and begin the day's meals. Soon, he became adept at preparing meals that included sausage, *Rouladen*, which is rolled up strips of meat with bacon, pickles, and onions, potato salad, pudding, and cream of wheat. And, he had another inspection to be concerned about. Not only did his barracks have to be kept in order, but the kitchen was also inspected on a daily basis by the leadership corps. Kitchen duty, however, did have its benefits. Besides having free time in the afternoon because he got up so early, he had access to goods he could trade with the locals, including sugar, which was already scarce in 1942.

Free time was limited in the RAD, but it did exist. For entertainment and a break from RAD activities, going north to the town of Krośniewice to the movies was one activity. If not Krośniewice, he could go east to Kutno, a city of about 25,000 residents, that was about three kilometers away, to attend Wehrmacht shows and go to one of the local cafés, such as the Café Link. The camp itself also had entertainment nights where the mess hall served as a gathering place to watch movies including *Maskenball*, and *Bomma*. In some cases, he could have visitors. In April, his parents came to visit him at his camp. On some days, recruits had the afternoons off, where he and his comrades explored the area. On one day, they found some eggs and had dinner with a local Volksdeutsche family that had settled nearby. Other days, he would go behind the barracks, outside of the camp, and collect wild strawberries that grew in the short grass. Mail and packages were eagerly opened, while writing letters to friends and family was almost a daily activity. There was also a local *Bund Deutscher Mädel* (BDM). The BDM camp, basically the equivalent of an HJ camp for females, was a detour for Gottfried and his comrades on their way back from work details, and a place to visit and flirt with the girls when they had free days.

Extended leaves were also possible. In May, he went back home to Waldenburg on a five-day pass, his only five-day pass, to attend a wedding of his friends, Werner and Marianne. Traveling by express train, he was surrounded by wounded troops from the Eastern Front who were going home on convalescent leave. Making it home, he was back in his old routine, spending the evening at the pond, going to the Jacobi, and drinking beer. The day after the wedding, nursing a large hangover, he was back on his way to Krzewie. Later in September he got his second leave, a three-day pass to go home. After going to Krośniewice to pick up cigarettes, a valued commodity during the war, he was then on the express train back to Waldenburg to be with his brother Georg, and his friends. But there was one particular person that he wanted to see—his new love interest, Irmgard, who lived in Niederwinkel. His last night at home, he walked her home from Waldenburg where they kissed in her parents' garden.

Living with others in crowded conditions also led to some health issues. In March, scarlet fever swept through the camp. Gottfried was one of the many who were afflicted, which led him to have swollen tonsils, and the classic red spots all over his body. While the camp had a sick bay that treated some of common issues like stomach aches, to be properly treated, and isolated, he was sent by train to the Wehrmacht hospital at Kutno. Before long, many of his comrades were also admitted into the hospital. The food was not bad at the hospital. On one day his noon dessert was an éclair with whipped cream, something that was not available at home anymore because of wartime shortages. For entertainment, he and his hospital mates built a radio in their room. Finally, on May 11, he was released from the hospital. Traveling by horse from Kutno, he was back in camp that night.

Later in 1942 the RAD service was starting to get old for Gottfried. It was extending far beyond the six months' compulsory service. The summer turned into fall and Gottfried was still in the RAD. The weather was becoming cold and wet in Poland. So was his attitude toward the RAD. September 19 was his last day in the kitchen. He wrote that he had his fill of kitchen duty. Now, he would be performing orderly and guard-related duties in the camp. He was also starting to get tired of some of the other work he had to do around the camp, especially orderly duty for other troops' quarters, and washing windows in the officers' quarters. There was also inventory, running errands for the camp, and unloading potatoes. Guard duty was his primary task. It was miserable standing guard in the cold rainy weather that turned to snow in November.

In October, rumors started to circulate that they would soon be discharged from RAD service. He started counting down the days until his release from the RAD. He was also getting frustrated with his officers. One night in October, the officers had a party with guests from Krzewie, where he wrote that schnapps and real coffee flowed like a river. Frustrated with their actions, he wrote that it was a shame that the alcohol was being withheld from their comrades in Russia. Finally, on November 5, some of the Arbeitsmänner were released from service. Being in the guard detachment, though, Gottfried had to stay on, working in the kitchen again, and performing guard duty, until he finally got released from the RAD. Packing his bags on November 24, he was released from service on the 25th. Turning in his uniforms and equipment, he was back in his now loosely fitting civilian clothes that had been placed in storage at the camp. He returned to Waldenburg and settled back into civilian life, visiting, and socializing with those friends who still had not been called up to the RAD, or conscripted into the military. The circle of male military-age friends was getting smaller. Most of all, he got to spend time with Irmgard. But Gottfried was getting impatient for his call-up orders.

Basic Training

In mid-December, Gottfried was called up for his military service in the Wehrmacht. The powers-that-be did not let him enjoy the holidays with family and friends—there was a war on. During the war, every division had a replacement battalion at its home location, where the division, as needed, could request troops from this battalion to replace the injured and dead from its field units on the front. Because he was from Waldenburg, he reported to *Ersatz* (or Replacement) *Infanterie Bataillon 31* in Glauchau, not too far from Waldenburg, which was part of the 24. Infanterie-Division. This division had already seen action with the annexation of the Sudetenland in 1938, the invasion of Poland in 1939, and its current role on the Eastern Front, including the siege of Sevastopol and the Crimea.[19]

It was commonplace to train new recruits in replacement and training battalions close to their homes. By having soldiers from the same region, their shared values, cultures, and traditions would serve to maintain and build unit cohesion in their training, and hopefully on the battlefield. Being from the same area also ensured performance in the field. Knowing that one's cowardice or bravery in battle would get back home to friends and family, this practice served as a motivational tool to be a good soldier. As with his RAD call-up, Gottfried's letter was followed by drinking at his local hangouts, followed by hangovers, and saying his goodbyes to those male friends who were left in the area.

The first few days involved getting acclimated to military life. Assigned to the *Stammkompanie*, or reception company, for the first couple weeks, as part of his induction he was issued his uniforms and equipment and received his dog tags. His civilian clothes were boxed up and mailed home. There was no need for these civilian clothes; the life and identity that came with them were no longer part of him. His new attire would be field gray. His new identity was that of a *Soldat*, the best equipped and trained soldier that the world had ever seen.

During induction, he turned in his Wehrpass that now remained with the company. In his new uniform, and army haircut, he was photographed. No smiles. This front-facing headshot and upper torso photo was attached to the inside front cover of his newly issued *Soldbuch* (or soldier's book) that he would carry with him while in the field, and throughout his military service. Like the Wehrpass, the Soldbuch contained his personal information: name, religion, height, weight, etc. It also included pages on units that he was in, equipment issued to him, an inoculation record, leaves, medical issues, wounds, and decorations that he had earned. Another section was related to any disciplinary issues during his service.[20] Optimistically, he hoped it would remain empty. It was also hoped that the word *gefallen* would never be a word entered or found on the front page of the Soldbuch. If so, the owner would never be able to read it. He was dead, and most likely buried in a field grave in a remote portion of the Reich with a simple birch cross for remembrance. In these instances, the Soldbuch with half the dog tag, the other half buried with the soldier, would be returned to the next of kin with a letter from the commander, noting his comradeship, bravery in the field, and his sacrifice to the Fatherland.

These first two weeks were similar to his training in the RAD. He spent a lot of time enduring close order drills, uniform inspections, maintaining the barracks, and learning to be a German soldier. To assist in the training, recruits were also issued a book, *Der Rekrut*, which provided information on everything that the new soldier was expected to know in basic training, ranging from conducting oneself in public to weapons and military tactics.[21]

The early days in basic training went by fast, and it was soon the holidays. This was the first Christmas that he would be away from home. What frustrated him was that he was so close to home and yet he could not be with family and friends. This was done on purpose by the command. His new family would be his comrades, and it was important to understand this early on in the recruits' indoctrination into the Wehrmacht. While he now had a new family, he wrote that they still had their old traditions. The recruits were allowed to decorate the day room of the barracks, and they even had a tree. They spent the night singing Christmas carols and exchanging small gifts with one another. Gottfried had saved some letters to open that night, especially Irmgard's. He also opened a package that his family had sent him.

The command also treated them well. There was no drill or training on Christmas Eve and Day. Many of the command staff were on leave for the holidays, and there was only a skeleton crew of non-commisioned officers (NCOs) left to supervise the recruits. On Christmas Day, he wrote that they had a feast the night before. It included red cabbage and potato dumplings. Christmas was a day of rest, allowing each recruit to immerse himself in thoughts of home. While Gottfried wrote that he longed to be with his family and Irmgard, at least he was much better off than many of his comrades who were on the front. They were most likely celebrating their holiday in a trench or bunker, eating what meager lukewarm rations were brought up to them by the rear line cooks—if that. Thoughts of where they would be celebrating Christmas in 1943 also had to be on their minds. With any luck, he would be at home once the Bolsheviks were defeated.

CHAPTER 3

1943

1943 was a year of change for Germany. The Reich did reach the Volga in 1942, but now at Stalingrad, the German Sixth Army was being bled dry by the Bolshevik forces. It was also starving to death. In February 1943, the largest battle in the history of warfare was over with the Soviets as the victors. In North Africa, the mighty Afrikakorps under Erwin Rommel was being squeezed off the African continent by the British and the newly arrived Americans that were relatively green in their combat prowess. The Italians, meanwhile, were unreliable allies at best.[1] Times were changing. The Germans were no longer fighting for the expansion of the Reich and Lebensraum. They were now fighting to protect their homeland. The lists of the dead in the local newspapers were getting longer.

Infantry Training

Immediately after the first of the year, Gottfried was moved to another barracks and training company to begin his infantry training. All new recruits, regardless of their branch or later specialization, were trained in infantry tactics. The infantry was the heart of the army. Their first and foremost role in the military was infantry combat, as Gottfried would later discover. Most of this training was in the field, with limited classroom lectures. It was important to be able to perform in a realistic field setting. This consumed a large amount of his time in basic training. One of the most important weapons he was trained in was the rifle. Recruits spent the majority of weapons-related training mastering the infantry's K-98 rifle, the standard rifle issued to German military troops in World War II. Besides the K-98, recruits were also trained in the use and maintenance of the MG-42 machine gun that had recently entered service to replace the MG-34, which had a slower rate of fire. The machine gun was a critical element of any infantry unit. Its infantry support role and suppressive fire ensured dominance on the battlefield. It was a killing machine. Gottfried was also trained in other weapons including pistols as well as the MP-40, a 9mm machine pistol that was part of an infantry squad's weaponry. In essence, once he completed training, he could operate, clean, and maintain any weapon that he and his infantry squad or unit was exposed to.

Roles in the infantry had to be interchangeable to ensure victory. Recruits were also trained in compass reading, range finding, grenade, and mortar use. Gottfried also gained a good understanding of using field artillery, and its role in infantry assaults and retreats. Through all of this training, it was expected that recruits could perform well under fire, and understand their roles in combat. They were also trained in the responsibilities of individuals one rank above them. This ensured that the unit could maintain its combat effectiveness at all times, and in all situations, without relying on officers to guide them. NCOs were the primary leaders in the field. All of this training also ensured that the recruits' confidence levels were high. Knowing that they were better prepared, trained, and equipped than the enemy would lead to victory.

The days were long and nights were short. Typical days began at 5am with lights out at 9pm. By the end of the day, after training and drilling in the field, they and their equipment were often covered in fine dust, requiring everything to be cleaned before the next day's inspection. Besides the fine dust, there was the slop from the winter season, water stains, and mud. Lots of mud. The high hob-nail boots that were still being issued showed the wear of a day's march. These had to be polished black to perfection. All polish brush lines had to be straight with no cross hatching lines. Clothing had to be dried out and then brushed to remove the mud and dirt from the marches and field training. Like in the RAD, an emphasis on personal cleanliness was stressed. There was, however, time for comradeship. Singing was emphasized on marches. Every night, they would jointly clean their clothing, equipment, and especially their rifles, placing them in their racks for morning drill and inspection. Most of all, they looked out for one another to ensure that the eagle eyes of the NCOs' inspections the next day found no imperfections.

Nachrichten Training

After completing his basic training in February, Gottfried was sent to an *Ausbildung* (training) for advanced training. Based on where he lived, he was sent to *Infanterie Nachrichten-Ersatz-Kompanie 24* for signals training in the *Nachrichten* or communications company of the 24. Infanterie-Division. Other recruits he trained with would now be transferred to their March Company, awaiting their orders to be sent to the front. They were in the infantry and had no specialty. Because of his performance on the basic test for the military, or the aptitude he showed in basic training, Gottfried received a reprieve from the drudgery and danger of being an infantryman on the Eastern Front. Since he was selected for advanced training, he would spend another three months in the safety of Glauchau, but away from the friends he made in basic, and the front that was turning in the favor of the Allies.

Training in the Nachrichten Kompanie was intense. A strong motivator for passing the training had to be knowing that washing out would result in becoming a foot

Signals training in Glauchau. Here, recruits learn the basics of line communication. (Author's collection)

soldier. Gerhardt Hennes, who was a radio operator in North Africa, explained that the purpose of the advanced school was to provide recruits with the basics of the operations of all of the communications equipment found at the divisional and company level, and to gain an understanding of a radio communications network. The training often included wire communications, such as phones, and radio communications. Hennes said that learning the equipment was at first frustrating, especially when mastering the Morse code dahs and dits. The code itself was relatively easy to learn, but getting a proper rhythm when sending Morse and developing the ability to translate the incoming messages took a lot of practice.[2] And, there were also the coded messages that Gottfried himself complained about in his diary. Received messages had to be decoded, while sent messages had to be encrypted, which took a lot of time. In the field, time was one's enemy. And, the codes would change, requiring that radio operators knew what codes were required for that particular day. Once Gottfried and his squad had mastered the basics of equipment use, they then went out on practical exercises in the area. In Germany in February and March it was cold, wet, and snowy, but the training most likely served its purpose. He now understood his role in the radio communications network and how critical the radio was in modern warfare. More practical hands-on or field training would come later when he was sent to his company.

It was good that he was close to home and Ilse, his new love. It is unknown where he met her and why Irmgard was no longer in the picture. Ilse was originally from Dresden, but now living in the area with extended family. Besides his time with Ilse, he also had many days off where he could go home to Waldenburg and visit his family in his new Wehrmacht uniform, most likely going to the party headquarters and talking with HJ youth who were envious of his ability to serve. On some days Ilse would take the train to Glauchau, and when he could, they would meet in one of the city's cafés and walk in the park, holding hands, and steal a quick kiss. He was in a much better situation than his comrades in the 24th who were now on the Eastern Front fighting near Leningrad.[3]

The *III. Jäger-Regiment 750*

Having completed his communications training with the 24. Infanterie-Division, he was transferred to the *3. Bataillon/Jäger-Regiment 750* in late April 1943. Soldiers in the 750th were originally from the military district of Salzburg. However, as part of the 15th wave of recruitment throughout the Reich, in 1941 each Wehrkreis was required to raise another regiment for the war effort. To build the 750th and other regiments, some troops from the *136, 137, 138, and 139 Gebirgsjäger-Ersatz-Regiments* were given to the 750th. Instead of going to Norway, Poland, and Russia, like prior troops from these regiments had done, soldiers from these Ersatz regiments were destined for occupation duty in the Balkans. But *Wehrkreis XVIII-Salzburg* could not get enough troops from its area for Jäger-Regiment 750 and so it looked to other Wehrkreises. One was Wehrkreis IV where Gottfried was from. Wehrkreis IV subsequently became the feeder for 3. Bataillon of Jäger-Regiment 750 which was composed of the *11–15 Kompanies*.[4]

Jäger-Regiment 750 was part of *718. Infanterie-Division* that was created in April 1941. *Jäger-Regiment 738* and *Artillerie-Regiment 668* were also part of the division that took part in anti-guerilla operations in Serbia and the Independent State of Croatia (NDH). The operational zone of control for the 718th was the Drina river in eastern Bosnia, the Sava and Bosna rivers to the north, and south to the Italian demarcation line.[5] Throughout 1942 the division was operating in this area, engaging in tough fights with the Partisans, while being suspicious of the Chetniks who were also operating in the area. The 718th's divisional records show that in many cases, it was just small numbers of German soldiers garrisoned in towns who relied heavily on local militias and German forces to control the growing threat of resistance throughout the area. In those situations where an operation was planned or the occupiers were attacked with a large number of fighters, *Kampfgruppen* were sent in. These were ad hoc combat groups composed of Croatians and Germans, sometimes with panzers and artillery, if available, that would engage the enemy in force. The division was also experiencing problems with its Ustaša ally. The 718th was interested in pacification in their zone of control. However, Ustaša terror and the slaughter of Serbs throughout the area, combined with Bosnian Muslim militias that formed to protect themselves from the Chetniks, led to a lot of instability in the region. This resulted in the Partisans becoming stronger as the citizenry gravitated toward them for protection.[6]

A funeral procession in Sarajevo, 1942. Already in 1942 the Germans and their allies were seeing greater numbers of dead from the growing resistance threat. The Wehrmacht cemetery in Sarajevo in 1942. This was destroyed after the war. (Author's collection)

In April 1943, the division was renamed *118. Jäger-Division*. Still headquartered in Sarajevo, the unit's change was simply not a number: it received better equipment and troops to deal with the insurgency. Unlike most traditional infantry divisions in the Wehrmacht, *Jäger* divisions were light infantry divisions. These Jäger divisions were composed of two infantry regiments, instead of three that were found in other infantry divisions. They also had an artillery regiment that was equipped with smaller 75mm mountain howitzers that allowed for mobility in the tough Yugoslav terrain that they fought in.[7]

Gottfried's orders were to report to the headquarters unit of the 750th in Sarajevo. After a short leave at home to say his goodbyes, he most likely went by train to Prague, and then to Vienna. The troop train was crowded with replacements for his division and other units, along with supplies and equipment bound for the Balkans. From Vienna, he went south, crossing into Slovenia and then into Croatia. Most likely traveling south from Agram, the capital of Croatia, his train then entered Bosnia, now part of the Independent State of Croatia (NDH) that was created by the Pavelić regime in 1941. Crossing into Bosnia from Croatia it appeared that the land had sprouted long narrow asparagus stalks. Now, the skyline was spiked with minarets. These rocket-shaped Muslim towers were everywhere, pointing up into the heavens to carry messages to Allah from the believers on the ground. In the background stood the tall craggy dark mountains that the Germans were fighting in and for, and trying to hold. As the train rolled on, all of Bosnia appeared to be just mountain after mountain in the reflection of the rail coaches' windows. These mountains were not like the sunny Alps back home in Germany and Austria. Their dark colors cast an ominous and foreboding shadow over the valleys and towns below their peaks. For many young Germans on the train, this was most likely the first time that they were venturing outside the Reich. Their view of the craggy and mountainous landscape from the slow rolling train had to be quite different from the snowy Alps with their green meadows they were accustomed to. For some, it had to increase their anxiety of the fear and death that they would soon be encountering.

To prepare him for his new unit, Gottfried was issued new clothing and boots. The high black jackboots associated with the German soldier were now exchanged for more functional combat boots. Already in 1943 leather was getting scarce, and most likely the traditional jackboots were no longer practical in modern-day combat. The new ankle-high boots had steel cleats around the edge of their soles to grip rocks, and were constructed of thick brown leather. The boots were stiff and heavy, and because they were low in height, Jägers now wore laced canvas gaiters that wrapped around their boots and the lower pant legs to prevent debris from getting into their boots, while also protecting the pants from wear and making them look neat in appearance. The old pony fur packs that German troops had used earlier in their invasions in Poland, the west, and Russia, no longer existed. Instead, Gottfried was issued a more functional and larger canvas rucksack that contained his equipment and personal items. His old rectangular shaped overseas cap, which could fold flat and tightly fit on his head, was also replaced with the M-43 field cap. Made of wool, it was can-shaped with a flat top and a short brim to shield his eyes from the sun. Sewn on the left side of the cap was the silver metal Jäger device that consisted of an acorn that dangled from the base of three oak leaves, connected by their stems. On his right sleeve, he wore a cloth Jäger patch, signifying that he was in an elite unit. On the left arm at bicep level was his oval signal blitz that he had sewn on. Woven into this patch was the Z-shaped lightning bolt or signal blitz that designated his specialty as a Nachrichten troop. The color of the blitz was light green, which was the *Waffenfarbe* or the distinguishing color of the Jäger troops. He looked good.

Men in Gottfried's division were also different from his replacement battalion peers. Most of the men in the 750th and the 118th were older than him. The average age of the unit was over 30, and because of their age and concomitant abilities, they were considered inferior in quality to normal front-line troops.[8] The majority were also from Austria. Their mannerisms and German Bavarian dialect were much different than what was spoken at home. If not from Austria, there were even some troops from Czechoslovakia—in some cases, former Czech military personnel who were absorbed into the German military after the 1938 annexation of the Sudetenland also became part of 3. Battalion.[9] Gottfried had little in common with many in the division. Fortunately, some men from 3. Battalion were from his region of Germany, which helped him to cope with being away from home.

One Austrian that was part of the newly formed 118. Jäger-Division was Rudy Wagner. He was a radio operator in *2. Batterie* of Artillerie-Regiment 668. This regiment also followed in the footsteps of Gottfried. An Austrian by birth, Rudy explained that he became a radio operator because radios at the time were relatively new and interesting for young men. They were perhaps equivalent to the keen interest that modern-day youth have in computers and technology. Rudy was introduced

Left to right: The Jäger sleeve patch worn on the right arm; the Jäger hat device worn on the left side of the hat; a photo of a young Jäger wearing the Jäger hat device and sleeve patch. This Jäger saw combat as evidenced by his infantry assault badge, silver wound badge, and Iron Cross Second Class ribbon sewn into his buttonhole. (Author's collection)

to radios at the age of 15 when he learned Morse code and radio use in the Hitler Youth. He was in a special group of the HJ—the Nachrichten or signals HJ. He said: "Morsing was very easy for me. My father was privately a musician. It was in my blood." He also volunteered for the Wehrmacht:

> The decision was easy for me. As a normal soldier you were put into a local infantry regiment. A deadly job is a Panzergrenadier. If you offered your service to the Wehrmacht as a volunteer, you were allowed to choose your section of the army by yourself… You should know that the year before, I fell in love with a South-Tirolean girl living near Innsbruck. I actually ran away from home and spent some weeks with her in the Tirolean mountains. I always liked mountain climbing too, spending summer vacation every year in the Alps. So quite naturally I asked to become a Funker in a mountaineering regiment in Innsbruck. For the next three months our love was saved. Here, I also came in contact with radio equipment for mountaineering troops as we used it during mountain exercises. When my three months were over, our commander made a lucky decision for me. Until now, I was designated to the Gebirgsjager, that means to the mountain infantry. Gebirgsjager for example, occupied Norway and Narvik… Now, as they were preparing to build a fighting division in Sarajevo [118. Jäger-Division] they sent me to an artillery regiment. They were perfect artillerists, but they had no Funkers. In this way, some of my comrades and me were sent to Sarajevo, and switched in this way from a Gebirgsjagerdivision to a Jager division with less army tradition.[10]

Rudy was not assigned to the 118th communication headquarters like Gottfried was. He was out in the field, close to the front lines, and serving as the crucial link between the field and headquarters. He said:

> The battery was always 10km or more behind the first line. Quiet, save mostly. The observer and the ballistic expert, and mostly an artillery officer had to join together with the second Funktrupp (also of 2 men, and 2 cases) and send back his continuous orders for the cannons' shooting directions, the quality of the grenades, and so forth. It's called "Vorgeschobener Beobachter"—advanced observer. For every battery [four cannons] belonged a Funktrupp and a Fernsprechtrupp. The Funktrupp was under the order of one Funk-Unteroffizier of two units of two men each. Each unit had one complete portable radio. The two groups divided their work for fairness. One of them had their bunker near the battery, the other one had two possibilities: In peaceful stable situations, the Observer (Beobachter) belonged to the B-Stelle (Beobachtungsort), normally on a hilltop with a good view in the direction of the enemy. In his company were the two radio operators. During a battle involving more than a B-Stelle, there was the VB—that means the group of two operators and the Observer on an advanced site, very often in the middle of their own fighters… Whenever possible, the Funktrupp was put under some shade, not because of an easy life, but to save the equipment… Communication was not often in speech, but in Morse code, that means Morsing in speeds up to 100 words per minute. Those who could not fulfill this became Fernsprechers—the phone operators. These persons had to lay phone cables and were always on their legs, even in the middle of the battle and up front, because they had to produce a communication line between the front soldier and his staff for orders. As the wires were damaged in battle, they were continuously on their way, flat on the ground to repair it. Being a radio operator was much safer.[11]

He also described the equipment that he carried:

> It consisted of two aluminum cases, each one about 20kg. One was the sender [emitter], the other contained the rest that means an Anodenblock (like a box containing single batteries).

An early war photograph of the Torn.Fud2 (*Tornister Funktrupp d*) radio in use. This was the standard portable backpack radio used by the Wehrmacht in World War II. Both Rudy Wagner and Gottfried used the same radio. (Author's collection)

I think it was altogether about 110 volts. Further, it contained a Sammler, that's a container with plates in acid, like in cars. Contrary to the Fernsprecher, as a Funker, we had to connect by radio to the artillery observer and the battery itself. Its current of a few volts served for the basic circuit in the electronic tubes. The rest was an antenna, of about three meters or more and separated into pieces, the Morse equipment, and Kopfhorer [head phones]. If you count 20 kilos for the case, 7 kilos for the gun, some more kilos for ammunition, gasmask, and hand grenades for destroying the equipment in case of a hopeless situation, you know this is what we carried up and down the mountains… Our Tornisterfunkgerat (radio backpack) we named Dora or Berta. The Dora (D) or Berta and others meant the model of radio equipment."[12]

Wagner was in Sarajevo a couple months before Gottfried, arriving just after Easter, along with other comrades from the Vorarlberger or western Austria and the North and South Tirol regions of Austria.[13]

Sarajevo

Headquarters for the 118. Jäger-Division was located in the former capital of Bosnia, Sarajevo. In 1943, the city had a little over 100,000 citizens—a big city for the Balkans. Founded by the Ottoman Empire in the mid-15th century, the city was historically on a trade route between Istanbul and Europe.[14] Laying in the Sarajevo plain in the Dinaric mountains, the city runs in an east–west direction, following the Miljacka river that almost splits the city in two. The river in most seasons looks more like a shallow trough with stone-walled sides. With cofferdams to widen the river's flow of water, it winds through the downtown area. The main part of the city rests in this river valley. Over the years, the city had grown up the sides of the mountain where the neighborhoods, defined along religious and ethnic lines, climb up hundreds of feet from the city floor. In the mornings, a smoggy haze hangs over the city from the many chimneys spewing white and gray snake-like smoke columns from their hearths into the lazy breeze of the valley.

Sarajevo was an important rail and air center for the Axis powers. Just west of the city was the country's major rail depot and marshalling yard that served as the rail connection for the entire country and the southern Balkans, including Greece. Since Sarajevo was on one of the main rail lines for the Balkan route, if not the primary one, it was a transportation hub for troops and supplies going down to Greece, and even to Africa when the Germans were there. The rail line also carried raw materials going back to the Reich. Bosnia was rich in bauxite, the metal needed for the production of aluminum. Iron, copper, and other raw materials were also mined in the Balkans and shipped back to the Reich by rail.[15] In 1944, this rail line would be a prime target for Allied bombers.[16] About 7.5 kilometers to the southwest of the city center was the Sarajevo-Butmir Luftwaffe airbase, now the international airport for Sarajevo. Originally an alternative air strip for the Royal Yugoslav air

Images of Sarajevo. Clockwise: The Miljacka river running through central Sarajevo with city hall in foreground; a view of Sarajevo with city hall in background; the central bazaar; one of the many minarets that dot the city. (Author's collection)

force, this was the main airbase for the Luftwaffe. It was still under construction in 1943. In addition to Sarajevo-Butmir, the main Croatian airbase for the area was Sarajevo-Rajlovac, which was the pre-war civil air base for the Yugoslavs. This base was larger and had many more permanent structures than Butmir. Like Butmir, it was on the west side of the city, close to the Miljacka river.[17]

All of the government buildings and major hotels were used by the Ustaša and Germans. In general, the Ustaša were responsible for domestic affairs, including policing the city and terrorizing the citizens, while the Germans were in charge of military operations throughout Bosnia.[18] The city itself was bustling with troops in transit, and those who were quartered throughout the city. Some were in the Jajce Barracks on the east side of the city. Built by the Austro-Hungarians, the barracks is easy to see on the city's skyline. On the west side of the city is the relatively modern and largest military base in the Balkans at the time, the Filipović camp, now the grounds of the University of Sarajevo.[19] Because housing was tight, Gottfried was most likely billeted in a school in the city. While schools were still in operation, it may have been a Serb or Jewish school that was no longer needed since these "Untermenschen" were ripped from the social fabric of Sarajevo. Other troops were also billeted in private homes throughout the city.[20]

Life was tough for citizens. They were in their third year of the war and people had to do whatever they could to get by. One person, Egor, was a fortunate thief and black marketeer. Working for the railroad, in the initial confusion of the invasion in 1941, he and one of his friends cleaned out a boxcar of wheat flour that was parked on one of the sidings in the large Sarajevo marshalling yard. Being a long-time Sarajevan, his parents had endured the hell of living in Sarajevo in World War I, and the starvation. Their stories probably led to him to be prepared for a similar situation in 1941. Hiding bag after bag of flour in the homes of trusted friends throughout the city, he used and bartered the flour throughout the war. This kept him and his family alive in a city that was experiencing constant food shortages.[21]

In early 1943, Sarajevo had to be amazing to a young German who had really never left the homeland. Not only was a foreign language spoken, but the Cyrillic alphabet was used. The culture and the traditions of the people living there also had to be mind boggling. The city was a melting pot of Muslims and Catholic Croats, Jews, Orthodox Serbs, and Roma that made up the tapestry of the crossroads of humanity, impacting the culture and architecture of the city. But the purges by the Croatian Ustaša and deportations of Jews by the Germans had eliminated most of these "undesirables" from the city. Most Sarajevans were proud of their multi-cultural and multi-confessional city. While historically the city was dominated by Muslims, Sarajevo had established its own civic identity based on individual religions, cultures, and tolerance toward one another. This civic consciousness and solidarity were based on a shared and collective value system that had evolved over the centuries, leading to Sarajevo being a unique political and cultural center in the Balkans. The

Sarajevans were proud of this to the point that city and religious leaders teamed together to protect Serbs, Jews, and Roma from the Ustaša regime and its repressive laws.[22] On an individual level, Muslims and Christians who lived in the city also hid and helped Jews to escape. Many of the Jews that escaped the initial slaughter in 1941 had fled to the Italian zone of occupation along the Adriatic. The Italians were much more tolerant and actually rescued many, housing some of them on the many islands in the Adriatic, and later transferring them to displaced persons camps in Italy. Serbs, meanwhile, either converted to Catholicism to appease the harsh Ustaša regime and stayed in Sarajevo, or fled into Serbia proper, away from the Croatians, and possibly joining up with the Chetniks or Tito's Partisans to seek their vengeance on the German and Croatian occupiers. Muslim refugees from the Bosnian countryside, fleeing from the war and Chetnik forces, replaced the Jews and Serbs, further straining the meager food supplies in the city, while creating a housing crisis for the city leaders.[23]

The city in 1943 was also a mélange of the new and the old. In Novo or New Sarajevo, many of the structures had been built by the Austro-Hungarian Empire. Other modern structures were built after World War I when Sarajevo and Bosnia became part of the Kingdom of Croats, Slovenes and Serbs, later to be the Kingdom of Yugoslavia. This modern and cosmopolitan part of the city had geometrically designed streets with multi-storied stone and concrete buildings that one would find in modern cities throughout Europe. Here, the streets were paved and had concrete

One of the many Jägers who had their photos taken at the Lisac photo studio in Sarajevo. (Author's collection)

curbs, a stark comparison to the ancient parts of the city. A tramcar system was also found in this part of the city. One of the first in this part of the world, it rolled down the recently renamed Pavelić Street. Modern businesses and shops could be found here too. One common stop for soldiers was the Foto Lisac photography studio on Pavelić Street where soldiers could have their photos taken alone, or with their comrades. Often printed on a postcard-size format, they were mailed home to loved ones using the German *Feldpost* system. Since Gottfried had a camera, this new city, with all of its quirks, was a great place to continue his photography.

Gottfried saw a lot. Five times a day, the city's mosques called the devout Muslims to prayer. In some cases, the church bells and call to prayer loudspeakers mounted on the tops of minarets competed with one another to assert their dominance in the city. The German occupiers were unaccustomed to these calls to prayer, which must have created much background noise not heard in their Christian hometowns, and perhaps waking Gottfried multiple times during the day when he tried to sleep. Veiled Muslim women walked the streets covered from head to toe in their hijabs. Sometimes in all black, others wearing all white, or even colorful striped cosmopolitan patterns, they walked fast and with a purpose, avoiding eye contact with men and nonbelievers. Some even wore modern shoes with heels with their hijabs. Occasionally, reluctant and scared Muslim women were forced to pose for photos by inconsiderate soldiers. These photos would later be shared with families and friends back in the proper Reich. Their husbands, meanwhile, stood out of the picture frame, seething with contempt for the actions of these foreigners, while nevertheless still maintaining a cordial smile for those soldiers who violated their wives, religious beliefs, and local customs. But a camera shot was less painful than a bullet. These actions were more fuel for the fire of hatred that existed toward the occupiers.

Photographs taken by German soldiers provide insight into what Sarajevo was like in 1943. Muslim men, considered to be "brothers" of the Croatians and subsequently protected from the Ustaša purges that targeted the Jews, Serbs and Romas, wandered the streets in their red or gray fezzes, wearing their traditional white baggy shirts and dark ornamental vests, often trimmed at the waist with a large scarf wrap. Their pants were often baggy with leg wrappings from the knee down, and their footwear were simple leather shoes or clogs. Other Muslim men blended their religion and a Western look, wearing overcoats and suits with white shirts and ties, topped with fezzes. Curious flocks of children ran throughout the bazaar area, oftentimes outnumbering the pigeons. Dirty, barefoot, and sometimes dressed in rags, they trailed after the soldiers, chattering and begging for sweets and money. Other residents of Sarajevo continued on with their domestic chores and work, ignoring the new occupiers. Perhaps in their minds the Axis forces were simply another occupying force in the history of the ancient city, who would soon be gone. Maybe the Sarajevans were used to this. First were the Ottomans, then the Serbs, followed by the Austro-Hungarians, and now the Germans.

The old town bazaar in the Ottoman district, dating back centuries, was a tourist attraction for the Germans and Gottfried. Smelling of a sweet combination of coffee, tobacco, spices, and grilled *ćevapi* sausages as one walked down its narrow streets, it still bustled with the locals doing their business and socializing, along with German soldiers who were taking in the sights. Homemade German flags, the black arms of swastikas not quite wide enough, angled off many of the rooflines of the small shops, flying above awnings made of sagging cloth or decrepit wood and rusting corrugated metal. Gottfried's photos show that some of the shops, dating from the 1800s or earlier, are barely the size of a large room. Their bulky wood doors hang open on old rusty hinges, revealing the contents of the shop to passers by. Eager shop owners, meanwhile, lean against the frames of their shop doors, trying to make the place "enemy friendly" by speaking in clipped and broken German with a heavy Serbo-Croatian accent. Other owners sit on stools, staring at the ground, ignoring the occupiers. Leery soldiers shoot glances at one another regarding the honesty of the merchants and the quality of their products. At some shops, metalsmiths hammer out souvenir cups and vases from disused brass shells that were left behind after the invasion to their audience of occupiers. Hand-woven colorful rugs with geometric patterns hung over old wooden doors in the adjacent shops.

The bazaar's many cafés catered to the locals and occupying soldiers, including Gottfried. Real coffee was still available in 1943, most likely imported from Turkey. And it was strong, unlike the substitute coffee that he was used to back home. Local men, sometimes of military age, which had to make a German soldier wonder, lazily sat in their café chairs across from weathered old men with bushy moustaches, watching time slide by. Maybe some were counting the number of German troops and recording their unit numbers that were found on the cyphers attached to their shoulder boards. This information would later be shared with their friends in the hills around Sarajevo. Perhaps two years, or even two weeks earlier, they had fought against the Germans. Maybe they were still loyal to King Peter and were Chetniks. Or they were among Tito's Communist Partisans. Who knew? It was tough to tell friend from foe in Sarajevo. Smoking from their hookahs and drinking the strong Turkish coffee, they exchanged suspicious glances with their most recent occupiers as they walked by.

Gottfried took many photos. One photo he took was of the Sarajevo city hall. Built by the Austro-Hungarians in the late 1800s, it is a castle-like structure and one of the largest buildings in Sarajevo. With German flags mounted high on its walls, it ominously looks over the city on the other side of the Miljacka river, keeping an eye on this occupied area of the world. The city hall has a dark history. A thousand feet to the east, on the corner of the Appel Quey and Franz Joseph Street, is where Gavrilo Princip successfully assassinated Archduke Franz Ferdinand and his wife Sofie, after their driver took a wrong turn on the way to the hospital to visit those wounded in the earlier botched attempt on the crown prince's life by members of a

Serb nationalist group called the Black Hand.[24] An old photograph of the site shows that the building now houses the Foto Enisa photography studio. On the corner of the modern-looking building is a glass-encased bulletin board displaying photos. The dirty outline of the plaque that was mounted higher on the building's wall that marked the assassination site can still be seen. The plaque itself was removed and presented to Hitler, a huge Serbophobe, as a war trophy.[25] It is a pretty nondescript location for an incident that cost the world millions of lives. Other photos he took included a shot of the Latin Bridge—nicknamed the "Bridge of Death," this is just across the street from where Franz Ferdinand was assassinated—and the Catholic Sacred Heart Cathedral located in the business district, along with many street scenes.

* * *

Gottfried was assigned to 3. Bataillon/Jäger-Regiment 750 (III./750th) of the 118. Jäger-Division in Sarajevo. The 3. Bataillon would basically be his permanent unit throughout the war. Usually, a signals battalion was composed of about 400 personnel. Within the battalion were headquarters units, a telephone operating company, the radio company, and a signals supply column.[26] Gottfried was assigned to the radio company. The textbook number of personnel in the radio company was about 162 individuals and about 50 different vehicles.[27] According to his lifelong friend,

An example of a typical German Nachrichten convoy of Henschel radio trucks. This image was taken in France in 1940 by a radio operator in Signals Regiment 521. Later, this unit participated in the invasion of Greece in 1941. (Author's collection)

Richard Wachter, who was also a radio operator in the III./750th, they actually had fewer personnel in their company; Wachter recalled that the company had about 120 personnel. Of these, some were assigned to vehicles, while others were found in stationary or relatively fixed positions in towns where the particular company was located. In many cases, these radio operators were not permanently assigned to one company. Instead, they were moved around to meet the needs of the battalion and division.[28] This is what Gottfried would be doing.

Because he was assigned to the motorized headquarters company, one of the first things that he and other radio operators had to do was to get a military driver's license. At this time, most German men probably did not have a driver's license, since vehicles were not that common in the first half of the 20th century. In his two-week crash course he took in Sarajevo, Gottfried learned how to drive small vehicles such as the Kübelwagen, the German equivalent to the US jeep. Radio operators also had to learn to drive the larger communications trucks in case the assigned driver might be out of action. Training had to be difficult. The roads surrounding Sarajevo, if they could be called roads, were narrow, paved with crushed stone, if that, and had tight turns, and blind spots that made it difficult to see oncoming vehicles. In many cases, the roads today are still too narrow for opposing vehicles to pass one another at the same time, requiring one of the vehicles to find a wider part of the road, in order to allow the other vehicles to pass. Fortunately, in Bosnia at this time, opposing road traffic was very most likely rare, except for mules and wagons. Upon completion of the course, Gottfried now had his official German Wehrmacht driver's license called a *Führerschein*.

Field Training

His time in Sarajevo was over, and now he was placed in field training, working his way through Bosnia. Being assigned to the headquarters communications company, he had the luxury of being in a motorized unit. Most of his comrades relied on the tried and true transportation system of the Jägers—their feet. Mules, meanwhile, carried the heavy equipment and supplies. Because the Jäger troops were constantly on the move, oftentimes roaming the hills in hunter groups, the radio was the most critical type of communication for troops in the field. Two-man teams composed of a radio operator and an assistant, who carried the batteries and radio equipment, were attached to units in the field, using their *Tornister.Fud2* backpack radio, or a field radio, to communicate with the company.[29] The radio was a means for coordinating patrols and attacks against the enemy, and calling in artillery and aircraft to support the ground operations. They had to be in constant radio contact with their company commanders who organized the fight. Depending upon the need and situation, messages could be sent in Morse code, or by voice. However, the range of these radios was limited.

To learn the intricacies of the radio in the field, Richard Wachter told me that new staff were paired up with seasoned radio operators. Gottfried's unit's role was to serve as that critical link between field units and company headquarters, and between division headquarters and the field. They would receive radio messages from the field, and if necessary, pass them on to company headquarters. On a daily basis, all of these units in the field also had to check in with the company headquarters. Then, the company radio operators passed messages to divisional headquarters. In operations, meanwhile, commanders would use the radios to communicate orders to subordinates. Subordinates in the field received instructions and issued orders.[30] On some days, Wachter said that the radios did not work well. In the hilly and mountainous areas around Sarajevo, reception at times was limited. If not the reception, at times, the radios themselves would give him fits, where the batteries would unexpectedly die or a radio tube would fail.[31]

To maintain radio communications with their short-range radios, the Germans basically followed after the field troops using mobile radio trucks made by Henschel or Krupp. These trucks were equipped with receivers that were much more powerful in range, and were effective in receiving and sending messages to headquarters and artillery and air units that provided support to the ground units. Boxy-looking things, the trucks' rear compartment had large windows and a back door. It looked like a work shed on wheels. The crew size of these vehicles included two drivers and radio operators working in shifts. Crammed in the back of the van were at least two radio operators, sitting at a folding work table with their radios in front of them, surrounded by additional equipment and supplies. One operated the receiving unit, scanning the frequencies. The other was sending messages to units who were assigned a particular frequency.[32] Photographs show that the trucks at times were part of a larger communications column. Parked in a safe and secluded area, the radio antenna masts that were mounted to the rear of truck were raised when the trucks were parked. The scene around the surrounding area often showed troops loitering around the vehicles, eating, relaxing, and waiting for their shift on the radios.

As a radio operator, Gottfried was fortunate. He was in a vehicle, and he was not fighting the enemy directly. As explained by Richard Wachter, the radio teams "were not involved in the fight. Our task was to maintain the radio connections… we were still able to leave our vehicles and the devices in time and we were always very lucky."[33] Not being frontline troops, they were only lightly armed with their rifles, the MP-40 machine pistol, and handguns. But in Bosnia there was really not a front line, and the enemy specialized in hit-and-run tactics. The enemy was everywhere. Basically, the Germans owned the cities and rail lines to some degree, but the enemy—whether it be the Chetniks or Tito's Partisans—owned the countryside, and the night. The best the Germans could do was to keep the roads open and to protect the rail lines from sabotage, and fight back when they could. As explained by Otto Kumm of the 7th SS, the Germans always needed to keep the pressure on the Partisans to keep them on the run and off balance. If not, they could regroup and become a formidable enemy.[34]

But they did have another means of controlling the enemy: terror. The commander of Serbia, General Franz Böhme, issued an order that for every German soldier killed, 100 civilians would be executed. Men were often executed in firing-squad fashion. Women and even children were often shot too. For every German soldier wounded, 50 civilians were executed. The same policy applied to missing German soldiers. In many cases, this order was followed by commanders in the field. Other German commanders thought the order was too extreme, and ignored it. Furthermore, the enemy were not considered soldiers or insurgents. Instead, they were labeled as bandits by the Germans. Bandits had no protections under the Geneva Convention or modern rules of warfare. The policy in combat was straight forward—ruthless brutality. Any house that had shots fired from it was burned down. When communist Partisans were captured, there was a short interrogation, followed by a summary execution. Any persons found carrying messages, ammunition, or fleeing or resisting the Germans were also executed.[35]

In some cases, this practice of terror did work to curtail the actions of the enemy. Mike Kristović, a Royal Yugoslav officer fighting with the Chetniks, recalled that they still targeted the Germans. But now, they tried avoiding killing or wounding any German soldiers. Instead, they would blow up strategic targets such as roads, bridges, and railways. Fighting in Bosnia and Serbia, he was concerned about his fellow Serbs. When in the NDH, however, attacking Germans directly was commonplace. Now, his second enemy, the Croats and the Partisans, would bear the brunt of his troops' actions and the German reprisals. The Partisans, according to Kristović, did not care at all about German reprisals against citizens. In his opinion, they were more ruthless with the Germans, which led to a lot of innocent civilians being executed.[36]

* * *

While the city of Sarajevo had to be strange to Gottfried, so too was Bosnia itself. One thing Gottfried wrote about was the dirty whitewashed villages that lined the roads. In many cases, these villages were simply a row of small homes on each side of what they called a road in Bosnia. These homes were low in height and had straw thatched roofs. He wrote that he could barely stand upright in many of them, and they smelled like a barn because the peasants shared their quarters with farm animals. Many of the villages that he went through were destroyed from previous battles or German retaliation, displaying burned-out roofs with char marks rising up from glassless windows. And the toilets in some of these places, even in the larger towns, were not flush toilets like back home. There were simply holes in a concrete slab or wooden floor that one had to squat over. How archaic, he wrote. And then there were the Roma. The Roma basically no longer existed in Sarajevo because of Ustaša and German atrocities. But out in the countryside, they were still encountered by the troops. Gottfried wrote about how dirty they looked. But he also commented about some of

Troops from Gottfried's unit flirting with a scared local girl taken in Bosnia or Montenegro, 1943. Note the lightning signal blitz and "F" or *Funktrupp* banners. (Weber/Author's collection)

the younger women—how attractive they were. Roma women, who with their long inky-black hair and hardened cheek bones looked as rugged as the mountains that bore them, were definitely off limits. Their presence, however, most likely reminded him and other troops of the girls they left behind, making them yearn even more to be holding their pure and wholesome Aryan blonde-haired and blue-eyed girls for whose race and lifestyle they were fighting for. Women with golden blonde hair, the color of wheat shimmering in the harvest sun, were almost non-existent in Bosnia. He was homesick. He complained in his diary about not being able to be with Ilse.

The Chetniks

Mike Kristović and the Chetniks were not too far from Sarajevo and Weber in 1943. Like the earlier years of the war, in 1943 Mike said that they were constantly on the move, fighting the Ustaša and Partisans in eastern Bosnia. They avoided Germans. They were too well organized, had superior weapons, and would unleash harsh reprisals against the local civilians for the injury or death of any German soldier. In most cases, the Chetniks roamed the countryside in small bands and only entered towns when they verified that they were pro-Serb by sending in an advanced patrol. Then, they would often march into the town in formation, sometimes carrying the Yugoslav or Chetnik flag as a show of force and to try to build their movement, recruiting locals for the cause.

Chetnik fighters pose for a photograph, somewhere in the German zone of occupation, 1942. The Chetniks had a tenuous relationship with the Axis forces: sometimes a needed ally and other times an enemy. (Author's collection)

In 1943, the Chetniks were relatively strong in some parts of the former kingdom. The Italians considered the Chetniks in Zone 2 to be "Anti-Communist Volunteer Militia" and demanded that the NDH recognize them as such. The Chetniks were also successful in spring 1942 in routing the Partisans out of east Bosnia and sending them west. In eastern Bosnia, Serbia, and Montenegro itself, the Nedić government provided weapons to the Chetnik fighters; German commanders also set up truces with the Chetniks to collectively fight against their common enemy, the Partisans.[37] In the Italian zone of the NDH, in 1943, the Chetniks controlled large areas, including cities such as Mostar. Herzegovina, near the coast, was a recruiting ground for the Chetniks where their numbers of followers increased because of Ustaša and Partisan terror and the failure of the Italians to intervene.[38]

Mike said that most of the men in his unit were farmers and part-time fighters who needed to tend to their fields in the spring and be back for harvest in the fall. For larger operations, they would go and recruit these farmers. Mike said that they knew where they lived, so they would stop by their homes on the way to the fight. Oftentimes, when the mission was over, they would part ways, with the full-time fighters going on their way to Serb-held areas, and the volunteers going back to their farms. In the winter months, operations for both sides slowed down. Most of winter 1942 they were quartered in villages and towns they controlled in Serbia, living with Serb families or in their barns or outbuildings. When in Bosnia, they quartered themselves in Serb-friendly homes that remained, or in those of the Croatians, Muslims, or other enemies who were since evicted or dead.

Food and supplies were always limited throughout the war, even in 1942 and 1943 when they were receiving aid from the Allies. Early in the war, they received supplies from the Ravna Gora command in central Serbia. Later, any extra supplies they pilfered on their missions would be brought back to base and redistributed to other Chetnik groups. They were ordered not to eat a lot because a stomach wound with a full gut would lead to infection and death. The Serb people they relied upon were poor and hungry too. Mike always knew that demanding large amounts from the locals could turn their loyalty away from the Chetniks and to the Partisans. For their enemies, however, be it the Partisans, Ustaša and their Home Guard units, or the Muslims, pillaging by Mike and other Chetniks was commonplace.

They always used captured weapons and supplies, or what they got from the British drops. On one occasion in 1942, they highjacked a German supply train heading to the Eastern Front. The fight was easy. Mike's brother, who had joined him at Ravna Gora in late 1941, and two other fighters, nicknamed the "black trio," took the train crew hostage and then approached the Germans who were taking a break, eating sandwiches on the side of the track. With guns leveled on them, Mike said that the Germans were given a simple choice: surrender or die. The Germans surrendered. The rest of the Chetniks who were hiding in the nearby woods showed up with oxcarts and hauled away the weapons and supplies to the hills. The Germans were stripped of all of their equipment, especially their boots that the Chetniks always needed, and locked in a boxcar. The black trio performed the rearguard actions, making sure that the rest got far away, before leaving the Germans and train crew to fend for themselves.

This was their standard modus operandi in 1942 and 1943: take Germans prisoner, steal whatever they could, including the soldiers' boots and other personal equipment, lock or tie them up somewhere, or hold them captive until the main group got a large lead, and then let them go, leaving them to fend for themselves—barefoot, and even sometimes naked, to ridicule them even more—and let them run for the closest town or village where there was a German garrison. In Mike's opinion, the Germans and Ustaša were spread too thin. They never owned the countryside throughout the war, just the towns and cities where they were garrisoned. The countryside was the domain of the Chetniks and Partisans who brutally fought for it. Mike said that the fate of captured Partisans were different from their German prisoners they took. The Partisans were killed on the spot. Before they were executed, however, they were stripped naked to avoid any holes and blood stains on their clothing that the Chetniks took with them.

Not all enemy engagements were successful. In one story Mike shared from 1942, his unit's mission was to dynamite a small wooden bridge to prevent Ustaša and German vehicles from patrolling and infiltrating the area. While in the process of setting the charges, they were surprised in the early morning by a Ustaša patrol. Even though the patrol was small with only a couple armored vehicles and about a dozen soldiers, it was deadly. They scattered to the other side of the bridge, trying to defend it, but they were seriously outgunned. He described the German machine guns the Ustaša had: "...so fast, that the bullets flying in their direction were like sand going through one's fingers." Before they knew it, the Ustaša had shot their way to their side of the bridge, and the troops in a truck following disembarked and outflanked them. Soon, 18 of his men were dead, and the rest were forced to retreat into the woods. To avoid capture, he covered himself with leaves and moss.[39]

If not the Ustaša, Partisans were also a threat. In another battle Mike recounted, they were ambushed by a patrol. They had to scatter and soon they became disorganized, and it led to hand-to-hand combat as they were trying to seek cover in the structures around a bridge. Mike himself came around a water wheel and was stabbed in the neck with a bayonet. One of the fighters with him shot and killed the Partisan, but Mike's neck wound was relatively serious. Even though his skin has aged from 10 decades of life and sun, the long scar is still visible on his neck.[40]

Operations *Weiss* and *Schwarz*

To assert their presence and gain the countryside, in early 1943, the German command initiated Operation *Weiss* (*White*). Planned in phases, the operation was designed to capture Tito and eliminate the Partisans in the areas north and northwest of Sarajevo. To achieve this, units of the 118th and other German units, such as the *7.SS-Freiwilligen-Gebirgs-Division "Prinz Eugen"*, along with the Italians and Croatians, would slowly surround the enemy, tighten the perimeter, and destroy them in the process. To do this, the Italians would primarily hold their positions near the line of demarcation, while German, Croatian, and even Bulgarian forces would encircle and destroy the Partisans from other directions. *Weiss I* officially ended on February 18, 1943, and it was somewhat successful. Approximately 8,500 Partisans were killed, compared to 355 Germans. More importantly, the bauxite-producing areas were cleared of the enemy. But many Partisans escaped through the weaker Italian lines into Montenegro and Herzegovina. To deal with this issue, Operation *Weiss II* began in mid-March and included more Italians from Montenegro.[41] The goal of this campaign was to eliminate the Partisans in southeast Bosnia, who had established their own government called the Bihać Republic. To accomplish this, the 118th, 7th SS, and other German units attacked from one direction, while Italian and Chetnik forces attacked from the other. However, the Partisans made it out of the encirclement in their famous feint at the Neretva river, where they purposefully blew up the Neretva river bridge, their primary means of escape from the Germans, nevertheless still using it to get away. After their successful retreat across the river, they moved into the eastern parts of Bosnia and closer to Sarajevo.[42]

Immediately following *Weiss I* and *II*, Operation *Schwarz* (*Black*) was initiated in May 1943, to keep the pressure on the Partisans. Gottfried made it into

Prinz Eugen troops pose with a tall Chetnik fighter somewhere in Bosnia. (Author's collection)

the field at the end of *Schwarz*. In this operation, German forces would move into Montenegro and Herzegovina from the north and the east to destroy the Partisans. Also included in the campaign were Croatian, Bulgarian, and Italian forces. Similar to *Weiss*, the goal of Operation *Schwarz* was to encircle and destroy the Partisan troops. To achieve this, the aim was to isolate the Partisans near Mount Durmitor between the Tara and Piva rivers in northern Montenegro.[43] Besides eliminating the Partisan threat, *Schwarz* also directed that the Chetniks, another threat to the Germans, be disarmed and captured. This was out of the Germans' concern that if there was an Allied invasion in the Balkans, the Chetniks would side with the Allied invaders. This created some conflict with the Italians, who considered the Chetniks to be reliable supporters. They were reluctant in supporting the German orders and treating the Chetniks as adversaries, instead of allies.[44]

In total, about 127,000 Axis soldiers attacked an estimated 22,000 enemy combatants during *Schwarz*.[45] As part of the operations, German forces had pushed close to the town of Foča where Chetnik and Italian forces were blocking the Partisan fighters. To stop the Axis ring from closing and preventing their escape, the Partisans attacked Foča but failed to break through there. From there, they fought their way into the Sutjeska valley in Montenegro and escaped. While this was a Partisan defeat, their breakthrough was nevertheless considered a tactical success, based on the prowess and will of the Partisan fighters.[46]

Fighting throughout the area was intense. One of Gottfried's comrades from 3. Bataillon/Jäger-Regiment 750 (III./750), Herbert Trappel, wrote about what he called a typical way of fighting the Partisans during *Schwarz*. Trappel described how he and his fellow troops, while young in years, had a zest for action and displayed a great deal of bravery when rescuing their wounded comrades. During *Schwarz*, Partisan units would break through the German lines. The Germans would then chase after them, and oftentimes, the Partisans would simply evaporate into the wooded hills. In the more mountainous areas, the Jägers used artillery to defeat the Partisans. Trappel also wrote about the abandoned huts along the way and how calm and quiet some of the areas were after the battles: "There were no more living creatures to be seen... We stand shaken before our dead comrades, deprived of their uniforms and weapons, they are mute accusers against the madness of this war. The only thing left to do was to lay them down for the last time..."[47] The Partisans would strip the German dead of their uniforms and equipment. Everything was needed in their fight against the Germans and Chetniks.

One Chetnik involved in the fight with the Germans was Lothar Pankosk. Originally from Agram, Croatia, Pankosk was in the Royal Yugoslav army in 1941. After his unit surrendered to the Germans near Belgrade in 1941, he was transported to a POW camp in Austria, where he then volunteered to serve in a German auxiliary force in Croatia. From there, he defected to the Chetniks, fighting both Tito's Partisans and the Germans. However, in Operation *Weiss*, he and his Chetnik unit supported elements of the Prinz Eugen division, fighting the Partisans at the Neretva river. Later, during *Schwarz*, he was also supporting the German attack and was wounded by the Partisans, and sent to a German hospital to recover. After *Schwarz*, however, many of the Chetniks were disarmed by the Germans. Because of this, after his stay in the German hospital, Pankosk then began fighting against the Germans again. Later, in 1944, he was back again fighting with the Germans; his group of Chetniks was assigned to the Prinz Eugen Division in their attempt to capture Tito in Operation *Rösselsprung* (*Knight's Move*) in January 1944.[48]

In all, *Schwarz* was successful for the Axis powers, to some degree. The Germans captured 4,000 Chetniks and their commander, Major Đurišić, in Montenegro.[49] Another 7,500 Partisans were casualties of the battle, about one third of their force.[50]

Prinz Eugen

The 118th was not alone in its fighting against the Partisans in Bosnia. There were Croatian troops from the *Verstärktes (kroatisches) Infanterie-Regiment 369,* some Bulgarian allies, Wehrmacht troops from other divisions, and the SS Prinz Eugen Division. The SS Prinz Eugen division would repeatedly cross paths with Gottfried and the 118th throughout the war.

Already, Germany was feeling the shortage of military-age personnel and started to look to the occupied areas that had Volksdeutsche. In the Balkans there were many Volksdeutsche who had settled the area over the centuries. One particular group were the Danube Swabians, individuals who migrated from Austria and Germany in the 1600s and 1700s, following the Danube river downstream and eventually settling in the area known as the Vojvodina, a region in northern Serbia that is bordered by the Sava river to the south, and Danube river to the east. Over time, the colonists' culture, architecture, language, traditions, and agricultural practices assimilated with those of the Hungarians, Serbs, and Romanians who lived in the area. It was an economically vibrant area that was distinctly Germanic in nature to the point that a dialect of the German language was spoken.[51] When the Germans invaded in 1941, photographs show Volksdeutsche in their traditional native dress, greeting the soldiers and giving them bread and salt, a sign of lasting alliance and prosperity.

Historically, the area was the outermost region of the Hapsburg empire, where the Christian settlers protected the empire from the invading Turks and from the threat of Islam.[52] Within the Vojvodina, there were three geographical areas: the Bačka, which was Hungarian, and occupied by the Hungarians during the war; Syrmia, that was part of northeast Croatia; and the Banat, part of Serbia. During the war, the Serbian part of the Banat was occupied by the Germans.[53] The other part of the Banat, not in the Vojvodina, was located in western Romania. After the German invasion, the Serbian Banat area was declared an autonomous administrative area by the Germans under the pro-German leader Josef Janko, who was elected in 1939 as the official leader or *Volksgruppenführer* of the Volksdeutsche. They were allowed to govern themselves under the careful eye of the Reich, elevating their status in the region.[54] Janko and his government administrators were most likely banking that the Germans would be the victors, and that the Volksdeutsche would be rewarded with some degree of independence in the new Reich for their undying support.[55]

From the Banat region, the Germans recruited ethnic Germans for the 7.SS-Freiwilligen-Gebirgs-Division "Prinz Eugen." Created in 1942, the division was named after Prince Eugene of Savoy, an Austrian military war hero, who is credited with ousting the Ottomans from the Banat and the city of Belgrade during the Austro-Turkish war of 1716–18. Prince Eugene ended hundreds of years of Turkish aggression against the Hapsburg Empire. The subsequent Požarevac Peace Treaty of 1718 between the Hapsburgs and Ottomans allowed for the settlement of more Germans into the area. The treaty also created the boundaries of the Vojvodina at the Danube and Sava rivers.[56] The name "Prinz Eugen" had a lot of symbolic meaning among the Banaters. It was a name that denoted freedom, unity, and nationalist fervor among the Volksdeutsche. He was the George Washington of the Volksdeutsche. It was perhaps the correct name to inspire a new generation of ethnic Germans to fight for their ancestral homeland.

The leader of the new Prinz Eugen division was Artur Phleps, a Romanian Volksdeutscher himself who fought for the Kaiser and King of Austria during World War I. Until 1941 Phleps commanded a mountain corps for the Romanian army, and then joined the *Waffen SS*, fighting against Russia. Phleps rapidly rose up the SS ranks. In January 1942, he was ordered to create a Volksdeutsche unit from the Banat in Serbia, which led to the creation of the Prinz Eugen division. Phleps was responsible for building the division from the ground up. Traveling throughout the Banat, Phleps re-opened old military barracks and recruited officers for the division. Many of the officer corps in the division were ethnic Germans that were transferred from other SS divisions. Some Croatians also served as the original nucleus for the division. Originally, a great deal of the equipment for the division was second hand and spoils of war. Tanks were taken from occupied countries such as Czechoslovakia and France, and rifles were often World War I or Yugoslav surplus. To incite individuals to join, it was promised that the Prinz Eugen division would only be deployed in Yugoslavia; members of the division were assured that their service was directed at protecting their homeland against the enemy, be it the Partisans, Chetniks, or anyone else that threatened the Banat. There were many volunteers for the division, but not enough, even though Heinrich Himmler personally appealed to the Banaters to join. To build the division to capacity, service for Volksdeutsche men between the ages of 17 and 50 became compulsory. It no longer was "Freiwillige" or a volunteer division, but the word still remained part of the division's name. Later in 1943, as an incentive to join, Prinz Eugen soldiers received German citizenship for their service.[57]

Recruits from Prinz Eugen came from all areas of the Banat and from all walks of life. Erwin Ellmer was a Volksdeutscher and Banater who joined Prinz Eugen. Ellmer was born in September 1923 in Gross-Betschkerek, a major urban center in the central Banat district about 50 kilometers north of Belgrade. Unlike most soldiers in the unit, he came from a more privileged background. His father Johann was a medical doctor, and Erwin listed his occupation as a student in his Wehrpass. He also spoke German, Hungarian, and Serbian. While he identified his religion as Catholic in his Wehrpass, it appears that anti-Semitism and religion was not an issue in his family. His father had re-married in 1938 and his stepmother, Elisabeth, was Jewish.[58] Called up for service on April 25, 1942, he was first placed in *Gebirgs-Artillerie-Regiment 7* for basic training in the city of Gross-Kikanda. After basic training, he was sent to the 1st Battalion and promoted to the rank of *Sturmmann* (senior private). Fighting the Partisans in Serbia, he got frostbite on his toes, leading to a period of hospitalization and rest from the front. In April 1943, he was promoted to the rank of officer cadet and fought the Partisans in Croatia. In May and June, during Operation *Schwarz*, he found himself in Montenegro fighting the Partisans.[59]

Michael Fingerhut was also drafted into Prinz Eugen. Born into a Catholic family on July 6, 1920, he was from Sigmundfeld, which was located in the central Banat district in the Vojvodina. His father's occupation was listed in his Soldbuch as a farmer. Like most of the troops in Prinz Eugen, he also identified his own occupation

The faces of Prinz Eugen. Top: Erwin Ellmer's photograph from his *Wehrpass*. Bottom left: Michael Fingerhut's recruit graduation photo. Bottom right: Hans Preuss's photo and *Wehrstammbuch* or soldier's file. (All Author's collection).

as a farmer. He was called for service on May 7, 1942, and for his basic training he was sent to SS *Gebirgsjäger-Ersatz-Battaillon* in Pantschova, Serbia. Moving on to Belgrade for a short time period and assigned to *Ausbuildungs-Bataillon 7*, he was then sent to the *SS-Pioneer-Ersatz-Bataillon* (engineer) school in Dresden. From there, he went to the *SS Gebirgsjäger-Regiment 13* where he served as a *pioneer* (engineer), was issued his standard K-98 rifle, and was later given permission to carry a Czech model 27 pistol that he picked up from the battlefield. After a 20-day leave back to Sigmundfeld in April, 1943, that was granted to him for his one year of service, photos of him show that he and his unit were in Mostar, in Dalmatia. Later in 1943, his unit also secured the Adriatic coastline from the Partisans.[60]

Others came from the far reaches the of the Banat. Another conscript was Adalbert Lallier from the northern Banat, close to Hungary. Lallier and his brother "joined" Prinz Eugen based on the time-honored "God and Country" theme that is used by soldiers in many nations. Lallier explained that the Catholic Church approved of them joining. And, because they were Volksdeutschers, they were morally obligated to protect Western civilization from the Soviet hordes. Most importantly, their father, a prominent figure in town, and a believer in the Austrian monarchy, forced them to join. Drafted in June, 1942, he and his brother were some of the first inductees into Prinz Eugen. He recalled that the basic training involved a lot of physical training, running, and instruction in weapons that ranged from pistols to mortars. He also received ideological lectures related to Nazism in his basic training. He estimated that about 80 percent of his fellow recruits were from peasant stock. He was rapidly sent to Bosnia where he first was a mule handler. From there, he became a truck driver, and was then trained as a radio operator.[61]

There was also Rudy Hansinger. In his home outside of Milwaukee, Rudy told me his story, explaining in his older age that his memory was failing: "My story is in my brain and my heart and I can't spit it out." Rudy was born in 1926 in the Banat near the town of Gross Gaj, about 60 kilometers north of Belgrade. His family settled in the area in 1770. He explained that originally his village was in the Austro-Hungarian Empire. With the breakup of the empire after World War I, his home was now in Serbia; other relatives were just across the border in the Romanian Banat. At the age of six, his family moved to Belgrade where he attended a private school, learning German. "You had rich people, ministers of high things. I was one of the poorest in there. I remember I would come to school with a piece of bread and butter… my dad came with seven children. If you lived in Serbia [as a Banater] you were an enemy because of the First World War. My dad was treated OK because a Serbian officer married my aunt. And, he being an officer could get a job for him at a military quartermaster base for the Serbian army. He was working there in Belgrade as a Schwabo [a nickname given to Banaters]."

At the age of 16, in 1943, Rudy was in the equivalent of the German RAD labor corps. He explained that they were called *Deutschen Jugend*, and they wore a round swastika on their uniforms. The square-styled swastika was reserved for the real *Reichsdeutsche*. It made him wonder why they were different, because in his mind they were all Germans. Like the German RAD, he worked on all types of projects, living in farm stalls, animal shelters, or a Gasthaus on their travels throughout the Banat. Also, like the RAD recruits in Germany, they were issued spades and had to march. Wehrmacht officers led them. He described it as a pre-school for boot camp.

He was called up for duty into Prinz Eugen in October 1943, after completing his labor corps training, and turning 17. He had no choice. He was conscripted. Out of curiosity, I asked if I could see his blood group tattoo that many SS soldiers had under their left armpit. The tattoo existed in case the soldier lost his dog tag that was imprinted with his blood type. He explained that he never got one, due to the fact that for his physical, the medical staff for Prinz Eugen were not available. Instead, he went to the *13. Waffen-Gebirgs-Division der SS "Handschar"* unit located in Belgrade for his physical. Because Handschar was primarily composed of Muslim recruits, he explained that this unit did not receive blood group tattoos, because Islam prohibited marking one's body.[62]

He was ordered to report to Weisskirchen in the Banat for basic training, the same barracks his father was at for his basic training in World War I. Basic training was an 8- to 10-week crash course, he said. Recruits were only trained in small arms and used World War I-era rifles. A lot of the training involved running on

Prinz Eugen recruits receiving rifle training near the Nera river at Weisskirchen in the Banat. (Author's collection)

the sand dunes near the Nera river, just south of town. On some days, they would have to do their runs wearing gas masks—in his opinion, to make them tough. One day after returning to their barracks, he saw a familiar face. It was his father. He said: "I went out there and here he was standing there thinking about the past. He was not proud. He was worried. He was sad." In Rudy's opinion, "Everyone knew the war was coming to end in '43. You couldn't say too much, or you would be sweeping mines."[63]

While most of the recruits in Prinz Eugen were from the Banat and were Volksdeutschers, others in the division were Germans, and came from the Reich itself. One "true" volunteer for the SS was Hans Preuss. Originally from Berlin, at the age of 17 Preuss was inducted into the RAD and had his medical physical on July 9, 1942, where he was determined fit for service. Like all German soldiers, he had to affirm that he was not of Jewish blood. On August 2, 1942, he signed an affirmation that he was not of Jewish blood and was instructed about the concept of the Jew. But, he never made it to the RAD. Instead, he volunteered for the Waffen SS, and on October 30, 1942, he found himself in basic training with the *SS Totenkopf Infanterie Ersatz Bataillon 2* in Warsaw. He was now a grenadier and was sent to the SS driving school located in Schröttersburg in Central Poland (now Płock) from December 12, 1942, to May 5, 1943. The SS had taken over a Catholic seminary for the driving school, kicking would-be priests and nuns out in the process. After spending two weeks in a hospital in January for an appendix operation, he returned to driving school, earning his driver's license for motorcycles (I), trucks (II), and cars (III). On May 6, 1943, he was transferred to the *7. SS Panzer-Ausbildung Ersatz Regiment,* a training and replacement unit for the Prinz Eugen division. Finally on July 7, he was sent to the division's Gebirgs-Artillerie-Regiment 7 in Bosnia. Just completing Operation *Schwarz*, he joined his unit in its normal area of operations to the north and east of Sarajevo.[64] Later, in August, along with Croatian Infanterie-Regiment 369, his artillery unit moved to the city of Mostar in Herzegovina, after the Italians had basically abandoned the city. From Mostar, he then participated in some of the coastal operations at the end of 1943.[65]

Foča

Gottfried took a lot of photos in 1943. One of his first stops during Operation *Schwarz* was the town of Foča, which is located at the juncture of the Ćehotina and Drina rivers, about 80 kilometers southeast of Sarajevo. Photos that he took of Foča show that the Drina river is shallow in some spots. One of the photographs shows a picturesque image of women doing their wash along the banks of blue-green Drina. Another photo shows the Prince Carl Bridge over the river whose center span was blown by the enemy to slow the German advance.

Foča was a town that had a dark history in World War II. In August 1941, the Italian army allowed Chetnik Serbs to take over the Ustaša-held town, where depending upon the source of information, the Chetniks killed between 300 and 1,000 Muslims, and raped Muslim women in retaliation for the Muslim forces who had committed their own atrocities against Bosnian Serbs throughout the area in 1941.[66] The victims were taken to the bridge over the Drina river where their throats were cut and the bodies dumped into the river.[67] Later in the winter of 1941/2 after the successful Operation *Trio I* by Axis forces, that pushed the Partisans out of eastern Bosnia, Foča became a stronghold for the Partisans, to the point that it was the headquarters for Tito in 1942. The area also became part of the liberated area that the Partisans called the Foča Republic, an area between Goražde and Foča, between eastern Bosnia and Herzegovina. In May 1942, Operation *Trio II* was carried out by the Germans who attacked Goražde then moved south and retook Foča, to

Foča 1943. Top: Gottfried's unit along the Drina River. Bottom left: one of the destroyed bridges at Foča over the Drina river with Mount Durmitor looming in the background. Bottom right: German troops taking a break along the Drina. (Author's collection)

The bridge over the Foča river in 1943, and now. (Author's collection)

wipe out the enemy that was pushed out in *Trio I*, while the Italians moved north. Fighting through the Italian lines, the Partisans successfully escaped their pincers, moving back into northwest Bosnia and Montenegro.[68]

Sixty-plus years later when I went through the city retracing Weber's steps, the same bridge that Weber took a photo of in 1943 still lies on the river bed. In

One of Weber's stops on the way to disarm the Italians after their surrender in September 1943 was Višegrad. In the background is the Mehmed Pasa Sokolović bridge that spans the Drina river, which is now a UNESCO World Heritage Site. (Author's collection)

its place is a temporary span, if more than 60 years can be defined as temporary. Surprisingly, some Muslims are still living there with their Serb neighbors, having returned after the 1992 war. Many of the minarets in Gottfried's photos are also gone. A local Muslim cleric told me that they were blown up by the Serbs in the 1992 Bosnian civil war to erase the Muslim culture in Foča. When I showed one of Weber's photographs to one of the Serb locals to help identify some landmarks, in broken English he described the Muslims as rats that needed to be killed. He would not help. The ethnic hatred is as deep as the ravines in Bosnia, and the scars of the last war are present on the people and landscape. At a gas station along the Drina river, just outside of Foča, part of the parking lot was an old Muslim cemetery. The alabaster headstones were poking out of the river slope as if they were screaming for help. Back home, I told this story to a Croatian friend who was originally from Sarajevo. Knowing the area, he looked at me with a surprised expression on his face and said, "That place is the heart of darkness. I can't believe you went there."

From Foča, Gottfried went to Goražde and then eventually to Višegrad, the headquarters of 3. Bataillon/Jäger-Regiment 750 at the time. He was now out of the communications convoy and placed in a fixed location. But he would soon be on the move again, thanks to the Italians.

The Italian Surrender

The Italians were becoming more of an unreliable ally to the Germans than they were at the beginning of the war. Things were not very stable back in Italy. The Allied forces had already invaded Sicily in May 1943. Later, on July 25, Mussolini was dismissed as prime minister by King Victor Emmanuel II, and arrested. King Emmanual replaced Mussolini with Marshal Pietro Badoglio, who reaffirmed Italy's allegiance to Germany, even though Italy was in secret negotiations with the Allies for a surrender. The Germans, however, knew about this through their contacts in the Vatican.[69] Signed on September 3, and brought into effect on September 8, the Armistice of Cassibile called for the immediate surrender of all Italian territory, the immediate withdrawal of Italian troops to Italy, and the guarantee of free use of all airfields and naval ports in Italian territory by the Allies that would be protected by Italian forces until the Allies took over those functions. The armistice also required that Italy use its best endeavors to deny, to the Germans, facilities that might be used against the Allies.[70] Italian troops were also ordered to remain armed and be prepared to fight against any violence directed at them. Later on October 13, the Italian government officially declared war against Germany, based in part on Germany's "arrogance and ferocity" that included compelling Italian troops to disarm, attacks against troops, and violence against Italian citizens.[71]

It was a scramble for the Germans to secure the Italian zone of control along the Adriatic. The surrender left a huge power vacuum in Dalmatia. Immediately, Gottfried's bataillon and other units raced into the Italian zone of control, and especially to the coastal areas where both Partisan and Chetnik forces were fighting for, and gaining territory. One of the greatest concerns that the Germans had was that the Italians were basically abandoning their garrisons and giving away all of their supplies and weapons to the enemy. These supplies and weapons would subsequently be used by the "bandit" forces in their fight against the Axis powers.

Dan Cupković, a Chetnik Serb from Knin in Herzegovina when the war broke out in 1941, told me about the Italian surrender. When the Italians surrendered, he explained that it was a free-for-all. In Knin, the Italians basically handed out arms, equipment, and supplies to him and other Chetniks. They took as much as they could carry and wanted, to the point that they needed trucks and gasoline to move more. The Italians readily gave him and his fellow Chetniks those too. They drove their hoard into the hills, hiding the arms and equipment, and kept going back for more. They did this for days until they had cleaned out the local garrison, all with the tacit support of the Italians. On one of their last excursions, they were captured by the advancing Germans. I assumed that this was a dangerous situation to be in, but he explained that it was not. They were held for a few hours and after the Germans figured out who they were, then they were let go—to collect up even more weapons and supplies to fight the Partisans. He also told me that the Chetniks

Italian troops surrender to German troops, Knin, 1943. (Author's collection)

A Chetnik fighter poses for a photo in Knin, 1943. In the background are German soldiers. (Author's collection)

Left: The Đjurđevića Tara River Bridge near Pljevlja in 1943. The Partisans blew one of the spans in 1942, forcing Weber's unit to use a pontoon bridge to cross the river. Right: The Partisan threat was always present in Montenegro. Here, an NCO and officer from Weber's unit interrogate a suspected Partisan. (Weber/Author's collection)

were not alone in their scramble for equipment and supplies. The Partisans were also competing for the same resources. With the free-for-all, they now had a de facto truce that they would not fight one another—for the time being.[72]

The 118th acted fast. On September 9, Gottfried and his unit started their march in a southerly direction from Višegrad. One of the first stops his battalion made was in Prijepolje in Serbia. Then they crossed into Montenegro, which was in the former Italian zone of control. The vehicle convoy stopped in Pljevlja, in the shadow of Mount Durmitor, one of Tito's strongholds, and then to the Tara river bridge. Over 500 feet above the Tara river canyon, the photo taken by Gottfried shows that one of its spans is missing. It had been blown up by the Partisans in 1942, so they had to take a long detour and finally cross the Tara on a pontoon bridge built by German pioneers. Next was Savnik. After a short stay in Savnik, they then made it to Nikšić in Montenegro. Already in May 1942, during Operation *Schwarz*, the SS Prinz Eugen division had taken the city, leaving a trail of atrocities in its wake, but it was now in Italian control with the Partisans and Chetniks fighting in the region.[73] In Nikšić is the large white church, the Cathedral of St. Basil of Ostrog, that is just east of the rail station. It stands out in stark contrast to the smaller buildings in the area. Another photo taken near Nikšić shows a lot of Italian soldiers milling around equipment. When I shared Gottfried's photos with Rudy Wagner, who was on the same route to the coast as Gottfried, he provided more information on Gottfried's journey. Rudy Wagner explained to me that Nikšić at the time was full of Italians, divisions of them. And they would not surrender to the Germans:

> They did not want to go into a prisoners' camp, but defend themselves. So, one morning the commander of our division went together with his officers in his jeep right into the center of town to the Italian headquarters, and said: surrender, or look up the hills. There our cannons are ready to destroy you all. All of the Italian divisions surrendered at once.[74]

Top and bottom left: an Italian garrison somewhere near Nikšić in 1943. Bottom right: a surrendered Italian soldier walking with a Knight's Cross recipient from Weber's unit; on the back of the photo Weber highlighted the point that the officer was a Knight's Cross holder. (Author's collection)

Driving the same route in the 21st century as the Germans did in 1943, the landscape changed rapidly from Bosnia to Montenegro. Bosnia was filled with heavily wooded areas and hills. Montenegro, in comparison, was dry and dusty, covered with rocks, and there were fewer trees. Many of the stretches of roads on the way to Nikšić were simply treacherous, and in some cases terrifying. Many of the roads were not fully paved, only consisting of crushed rock as a base. In other situations the roads were narrow, and single laned, carelessly snaking their way through steep river gorges. At the time of my trip, the US Department of State recommended not driving at night in Bosnia and Montenegro, due to the fact that the darkness would impair one's vision of upcoming curves, while overall road conditions could lead to serious accidents. Guard rails in most cases were non-existent on these roads. One stretch of the road was collectively named the "Death Road to Nikšić" by my wife and good friend Martin Super, a son of Croatian immigrants, and my translator on the trip. It was simply terrifying. The

Montenegro in the fall was hot and dry. A German motorcycle with an NCO riding on the back passes burning structures on their race to the coast. (Author's collection)

road on the driver's side hugged a high rock wall. On the right-hand passenger side was a deep river valley gorge, with no guardrails to prevent the compact Opel from sliding off the road. Two vehicles could not pass as the road was very narrow in most parts, but this was not an issue because we were the only ones on the road, perhaps a clue that the locals in this remote part of the world avoided driving on it.

The 118th headquarters and Gottfried stayed a few days in Nikšić before they moved south to Danilovgrad, then to Podgorica, and then Cetinje. They finally made it to the coast area at the end of September, stopping at Kotoro, a large port in Montenegro that had to be secured. From there, they went in a northerly direction to Trebinje, near the coast.

Most of his journey through Montenegro involved the radio column meandering its way down to the Adriatic coast, supporting the troops. Gottfried, like others, often bivouacked in four-man tents that were constructed by lacing together their camouflage *Zeltbahnen*, multi-purpose triangular-shaped canvas tarps that could serve as poncho, ground sheet, or tent quarter. On some occasions they were delayed by blown bridges that had to be repaired by the pioneers before they could move on. There were also hit-and-run skirmishes with the Partisans in the countryside, and some organized resistance by Italians in those cities where they

Images of Weber's stops in Montenegro. Top to bottom: Cetinje; looking down on Kotor; the building used as the headquarters in Podgorica. (Weber/Author's collection)

had garrisons. However, many Italians gave up without a fight or defected, serving as German helpers, known as Hiwis. In September and October it was also hot in Montenegro. Still in a wool uniform, the journey was very uncomfortable for the troops. Photos show a rocky, dusty, and inhospitable terrain as they worked

Left to right: One of the many switchback roads in Montenegro that the unit had to take on its way to the Adriatic; a radio team somewhere in Montenegro huddling under what shade they could find in the hot, fall sun. (Weber/Author's collection)

A squad from the 118th poses somewhere on the Adriatic coast. (Author's collection)

their way down to the Adriatic coast. At least Gottfried was in a vehicle. Other comrades such as Rudy Wagner had to walk, carrying his radio and other equipment on a mule. Rudy explained that because his rifle was so heavy he would hang the sling over the back of his neck, hanging the rifle in front of him. By doing this,

While the 118th was going through Montenegro, other units including the Prinz Eugen Division were working their way south too. Somewhere near Mostar, 1943, Michael Fingerhut (left) of the Prinz Eugen Division relaxes with two of his comrades. (Author's collection)

the rifle sling served as a yoke, and he could then relax his arms by draping them over the rifle's stock and muzzle. He also complained about the thirst and the heat.[75] Another one of his comrades described the march as traveling "through the cruelly ragged mountains, through deep gorges without bridges, in the great heat of southern countries and the constant fighting with the devious Partisan, the embarrassing disarming of the fallen confederate [the Italians were originally allied with the Germans], which did not even go without a fight… The protection of the coast is the most critical, so this march was no less exciting than arduous. It cost a few drops of sweat."[76]

The division then moved into the Dalmatia area along the coast. Another of Gottfried's comrades, Wilhelm von Tyrus, described Dalmatia in derogatory terms:

> … it is a very special area. It is populated by a very wild people who are used to robbery and murder. It is consistently covered by mountains and forests with large rivers and pastureland. The only livelihoods are from cattle and sheep, apart from those few who live on the sea coasts who differ from the rest in their way of life and language. They use the Latin dialect while the rest use the Slavic dialects and wear barbaric clothes.[77]

Along with units of the 118th, the Prinz Eugen division also mobilized for the coast. Already occupying some cities in the Italian zone of control, elements of Prinz Eugen moved from Mostar to the coast, seizing the port city of Split on September 27, capturing 202 Italian officers and 9,000 men from the Italian *15th Infantry Division "Bergamo."* Per the Führer's orders, all Italian officers were to be shot. On the 28th, three Italian generals were shot, followed by another 45 officers on the 30th, after their summary court martial.[78] Prinz Eugen also moved down into Dubrovnik, seizing the ancient walled city that was also a stronghold of the Italian army.[79]

Korčula

In late 1943, with the coast relatively secure, the German high command determined that the islands off the Adriatic coast needed to be taken away from the Partisans. They were serving as Partisan strongholds, especially after the Italians had vamoosed the islands, leaving a great deal of their arms and supplies in the process to the Partisans. These islands could also serve as jumping-off points for a potential Allied invasion. To prevent any potential toehold on the Yugoslav mainland for the Allies, Operation *Herbstgewitter (Autumn Storm)* was created by the German high command. Gottfried was involved.

The first phase of the operation involved clearing the Pelješac peninsula, a large finger-shaped peninsula that angled out from the mainland. On October 23, the Prinz Eugen Division led the attack on the peninsula. From the mainland town of Ploče, a short distance away by water, various units landed at towns and coves along the east side of the peninsula. Prinz Eugen also attacked north from Ston, which is located on the southern end of the peninsula.[80] At this time, Gottfried was at the town of Metković on the mainland and then Ston on the peninsula, moving with the 750th and other units. The attack was successful: the Partisans were caught by surprise. After a three-week battle, they abandoned the peninsula. Some of the Partisans from the *13th Dalmatian Brigade* that was on the peninsula fled by boat to the island of Korčula, while other units fled to the mainland.[81] The Pelješac was now controlled by the Germans.

After the peninsula was secured, the second stage of the operation came into effect. The primary goal of this operation was to prevent the enemy from using the southern islands of Mljet, Hvar, Brač, and Korčula, from Split to Dubrovnik along the Adriatic coast, as a possible landing site for an invasion of the Yugoslav mainland. Of these islands, Korčula was the largest, being about 32 kilometers long and six kilometers wide. Heavily forested, and mountainous with a few towns and many inlets to hide boats and receive supplies from Italy, it was the ideal Partisan stronghold.

The strategic value of Korčula was also recognized by the allies. While the Germans were attacking the Peljesac peninsula, Fitzroy Maclean, a British officer with the Special Operations Executive (SOE), and the personal representative of Winston Churchill to Tito, crossed over to the island of Korčula by boat from the Yugoslav mainland to assess the situation for the SOE. Spending time at the actual town of Korčula, he described it as a prosperous area full of fishing boats in the harbor. In his words, the "whole place had a holiday air that was most agreeable," even though there were Luftwaffe attacks in the harbor area. The island was also buzzing with Partisan activities. With the mainland in German hands, supplies from Italy for the resistance were now being ferried to Korčula and the mainland by British and Partisan boats.[82]

On December 22, Gottfried's unit and elements from the Artillerie-Regiment 668, along with some other German Wehrmacht, Croatian, Kriegsmarine, and Luftwaffe units, attacked Korčula. Like other islands, after the Italian capitulation, Korčula and others in the Adriatic became Partisan strongholds.[83]

The attack on the island of Korčula was nothing like the D-Day invasion in France. The German invasion force used a ragtag fleet of vessels, even including wooden schooners that were taken from local fisherman for the cause. It looked more like a scene out of a 19th-century pirate novel than a 20th-century landing. Troops were on the decks of schooners, waiting to disembark on the island. Rudy Wagner recalled that on his boat there was a steel platform-like crow's nest above the landing craft deck, where they had placed a machine gunner that was spraying the landing area. Across the Pelješac peninsula near Orebić were other guns of Artillerie-Regiment 668, covering the landing areas with their deadly fire, while the Luftwaffe provided some air cover. Wagner was disappointed with the invasion. He said he should have earned the Iron Cross Second Class for his bravery during the attack. But it was revoked because his radio partner left their radio outside of their billet the day before the invasion, and it was subsequently destroyed in a rainstorm. As part of their punishment, Rudy had to attend radio refresher training in the town of Korčula after the island was secure.[84] In his memoirs, he wrote of an unforgettable experience when in the town. The sisters in the cloister of the Franciscan monastery allowed one of his comrades in his unit, Pater Celestin, a trained organist, to play their organ. On a return trip to Yugoslavia after the fall of Tito in the 1990s, he wrote that the organ was still there.[85]

Gottfried was part of the invasion force that was responsible for taking the town of Korčula, which is on the east side of the island. He was with the 15th company for the invasion. While technically not permanently assigned to the 15th, staff from headquarters units were sent to various groups, as needed, or for specific operations.[86]

It was relatively easy. Invasion craft departed from Orebić on the Pelješac peninsula, crossing the narrow Korčula channel that is about three kilometers wide at that point. Gunners at Orebić used the Bokar tower, also known as the Kanalevic Tower, located on the northwest part of the town, as an aim point for their artillery during the invasion.[87] The company landed to the west of Korčula town. By noon on December 23 the town was in German hands. Even though Gottfried was not on the first wave of invading troops, it was still dangerous. During the invasion he was

The town of Orebić as seen from a schooner leaving the island of Korčula. Orebić is where Weber and his unit staged for the invasion of Korčula on December 22. (Author's collection)

struck in the thigh by what appeared to be a mortar fragment. The wound was not severe enough for him to be taken off the island to be treated, nor for convalescent leave home. A medic or the company doctor pulled the fragment out of his thigh, cleaned it, and stitched it up. It was relatively minor. The wound, however, qualified him for the German wound badge. Equivalent to the American Purple Heart, since this was his first combat-related wound, he would receive the award in black, which was for one or two combat injuries. For those soldiers who received more wounds in the course of the war, the silver grade was awarded for three to four wounds, and a gold existed for those who received five or more wounds or were killed in combat. This badge was worn on his upper left-hand tunic pocket.[88]

For other units that invaded the island, it was a little more difficult. Frans Werner was with 14. Kompanie of 118. Jäger-Division that landed on the south side of the island in the early morning hours of December 22. Landing about 11 kilometers to the west of the town of Korčula on the southern coast, he explained that the invasion began about 5am with the shooting of white flares by the invasion craft as they sprayed the beach with machine-gun and 20mm cannon fire. His company initially experienced little resistance from the Partisans; the machine guns on the shoreline were rapidly silenced. From the landing, and during the first day, some of the company progressed toward the town of Korčula, while others moved westward toward Postrana and Kampus, securing the main road that ran across the center of the island. The following day, 118. Jäger-Division's third battalion linked up with the first battalion at the town of Pupnat, at the center of, and the highest point on the island. There were so many troops there that Werner described it as an anthill of troops. The troops also had four tanks that joined the column. From there, they moved west toward Čara where they met some enemy resistance that was eliminated by the tanks and pioneers. The 24th was basically a repeat of the 23rd. Advancing toward Smokvica, located on the west side of the island, the company got some resistance from their flank on hill 303 and in front of them on hill 160. This required them to storm the hill and engage in hand-to-hand combat with the Partisans.[89]

On Christmas Day, the battle for the island was basically over.[90] The Partisans had already started evacuating the island during the nights of December 24 and 25 from Vela Luka and Prigradica, on the west side of the island, moving troops and refuges to the islands of Hvar and Vis by boat. It was not an organized evacuation.[91] By the 26th the entire island was in German hands. According to the German Navy War Diary, the Germans took 212 prisoners and captured 21 small coastal vessels, four motor boats, and 160 other boats.[92] The Germans themselves had 52 dead, 264 wounded, and 32 missing in action. The Korčula channel was also back open to shipping.[93] The losses to the Partisans were large in the island campaign. About 1,150 Partisans were killed. It was considered one of the greatest defeats of the Partisans in Yugoslavia in World War II.[94]

There were other Allied forces on the ground on Korčula. One American on the island during the invasion was Sterling Hayden. A movie star who became a second lieutenant in the Marines and then an Office of Strategic Services (OSS) operative, Hayden had an interesting military career. He used his civilian passion of sailing to run weapons from Italy to the Partisans on the Yugoslav and Albanian coastline, while also rescuing downed Allied aircrews and transporting them back to Italy in his boat. In his new position as OSS liaison with the Partisans in the Dalmatian islands, he was sent on a reconnaissance mission to assess the German offensive, the state of the Partisan resistance, and to determine if Korčula was still a suitable location to drop off supplies from Italy.[95] Making it to the island on Christmas Day, he and three Partisans were ambushed by German troops while surveilling the island by jeep. The driver was killed, and Hayden and the two other Partisans fought their way out.[96] Escaping to the island of Hvar by small boat on the 26th with other refugees, he then met with Partisan leaders on Hvar, surviving two different air attacks from the Luftwaffe's Stukas while there. From Hvar, he then crossed over to the island of Vis on a schooner loaded with refugees. Finally, on New Year's Eve, he left Vis and returned to Bari, Italy, in a small boat and during a winter storm, to deliver his intelligence report. For his bravery in this mission, he was awarded the Silver Star.[97]

Jim Botica, a 20-year-old resident of the town Račišće on the island of Korčula, was also on the receiving end of the German invasion. Botica joined the Partisans after the Italians left the island. He carried one of the many rifles that the Italians had left behind. He had no uniform to wear. He and 10 other Partisans were assigned to an Italian artillery field piece that they towed around the island with mules, occasionally sending rounds over to the Pelješac peninsula that was now in

German hands. According to Botica, the Partisan units were soon destroyed and on the run. Soon after the invasion, they abandoned their field piece, dismantling it to prevent it from being used by the Germans. He and some other Partisans were also fired upon by German aircraft which resulted in their pack mule being killed, forcing Botica and the others to scatter to the hills. He also recalled that when the Germans invaded, they were ruthless, throwing grenades into homes and killing many innocent civilians, and forcibly removing residents from their homes. After the invasion, when things calmed down, he returned to Račišće, reuniting with his family. But he and about 25 other young men were soon arrested by the Germans, first transported to Korčula town, and then sent across to Orebić on the mainland. For months, he was a forced laborer, building German fortifications along the coast, until he escaped. He then rejoined the Partisans in their fight against the Germans in Herzegovina and Montenegro, where he and his fellow Partisans ambushed German supply trucks and mined roads. Toward the end of the war, he went back with the Partisans to Korčula, and reunited with his family on the island.[98]

The Royal Navy was also on the island during the invasion. Ken Gadson, a Royal Navy officer on a British motor torpedo boat (MTB), was hiding in one of the island's coastal inlets. Starting his war by fighting the Axis powers off the coast of North Africa, he was then sent to Bari, Italy where his unit prowled the Yugoslav coast targeting German supply ships and fighting with E-boats, the German equivalent to the US PT Boat. The MTB tactics included attacking supply ships and German E-boats by night and then hiding in the many island inlets during the day, carefully camouflaging their MTB with netting and branches. He recalls the German attack on Korčula:

> I remember Christmas Day and two of us we were hiding in one inlet in Korčula, the largest island just off the coast and another MTB or MGB—I don't know—was around the corner in another inlet. Now we've had a rough time. We hadn't had much sleep… dispirited because we knew that Jerry was coming and it was Christmas Day. So we posted the usual chap up on the hill. He was a bit thick. And we had a sort of Christmas Day party. We had too much rum and all sort of fell asleep, and I think the skipper as well. The guard came down from the hill at dusk and said, "I've been blowing my whistle all afternoon and nobody's taking my notice." And of course the import of that sort of fell on us all and we just cut everything and ran and warned the other boat… So we both came shooting down towards the sea. The Germans were on both sides of the inlet. I think it was an attempt to capture us whole… there was shooting and banging going on as we were going down like a mini fjord… and you know bangin' on both sides of the fiord with parts and things flying off the boat and Jerry's ready to stop us getting out. And, when we got to the sea there were E-boats waiting for us. It was a grand slamming match. It was obvious that we were outnumbered. I was on the bridge and the skipper said: "Get smoke quick." We had a sort of a color gas thing on the stern; one of our mechanic's job was to release some sort of acid onto the sea, and it created smoke. And we did that in desperate circumstances, you know, and the skipper called for that and nothing happened. We didn't know if the chap had been shot and killed or whatever… Anyway, I don't know if I said I would go or he said you go, but I went. I ran down to get the chap. He was no longer there. He was down in the engine room.

There's nothing brave about what I did. It was our salvation. Of course there were searchlights on us and all those things… I was sent flying. I picked myself up and it was difficult to get up. And I'll tell you some detail because this is interesting. I'd been hit for the first time with a bullet in my shoulder—my right shoulder, and I didn't feel a thing. I realized it when I sort of went to use it to get up. It is almost like an elation because you always wonder what it's gonna be like if you get hit and how painful it would be. And you know now it's not so bad. And I went down… by then I was hit again. I was hit several times and was trying to get back to the bridge… I just obviously passed out. My boat doubled back into Korčula… no people were killed, but others were wounded, but I couldn't talk. I got one in the face… the bullet in my face knocked my teeth out, so I couldn't talk. It might have been a first aid person that looked at me, and he said to take us ashore and leave us [to the Germans]. I mean it's obvious that the whole of the island was taken by the Germans… With the Germans there was no prisoner taking, none at all. You can understand it, so back we went to the boat.

The skipper then decided to cut and run, and obviously signals are going to and from the Admiralty in Bari and they said make a run for it… and of course naturally you was thinking that the E-boats were waiting for us, lickin' their lips. Fortunately, a storm grew up, and I can remember that because it took us 14 hours to get back to Bari. The weather was so bad. I don't

The town of Korčula in 1943 and today. Across the Korčula channel is the Peljesac peninsula and the town of Orebić. (Weber/Author's Collection; iStock/Getty Images)

Weber posing for a photo in the villa where he was posted. (Weber/Author's collection)

know whether their E-boats are very seaworthy or what, or if they do not like rough weather, but they were not there… I had to be tied down and so did the others, you know, to stop us rolling about. Of course once we got to Bari, we went straight into hospital… and that was the end of my war. But the boat picked up ammunition and supplies and went straight back into the fray.[99]

After the invasion was over, Weber's unit was garrisoned outside the old town of Korčula. The town itself had some damage from the German attack, but it was pretty well intact. Dating from the 10th century, the town was known as the birthplace of Marco Polo. An ancient walled and thumb-shaped town, it extends into the Adriatic and is surrounded by water on three sides with a large quay on the north side that has been used for centuries for trade, making the city a wealthy location along the Adriatic coastline. The old walled town itself is small, about 100 buildings, with narrow cobbled walkways so tight that some can only be walked by foot. The old stone buildings and their ornate architecture show that it was an important center for the Venetian trade in past centuries.[100] Beginning in the late 1880s, the town of Korčula and the island itself was a tourist destination.[101] Hotels such as the Hotel Korčula and the De La Ville lined the waterfront,[102] while the port was a destination for steamships carrying tourists over from the mainland. Compared to other areas where the 118th was fighting, Korčula had to be a resort.

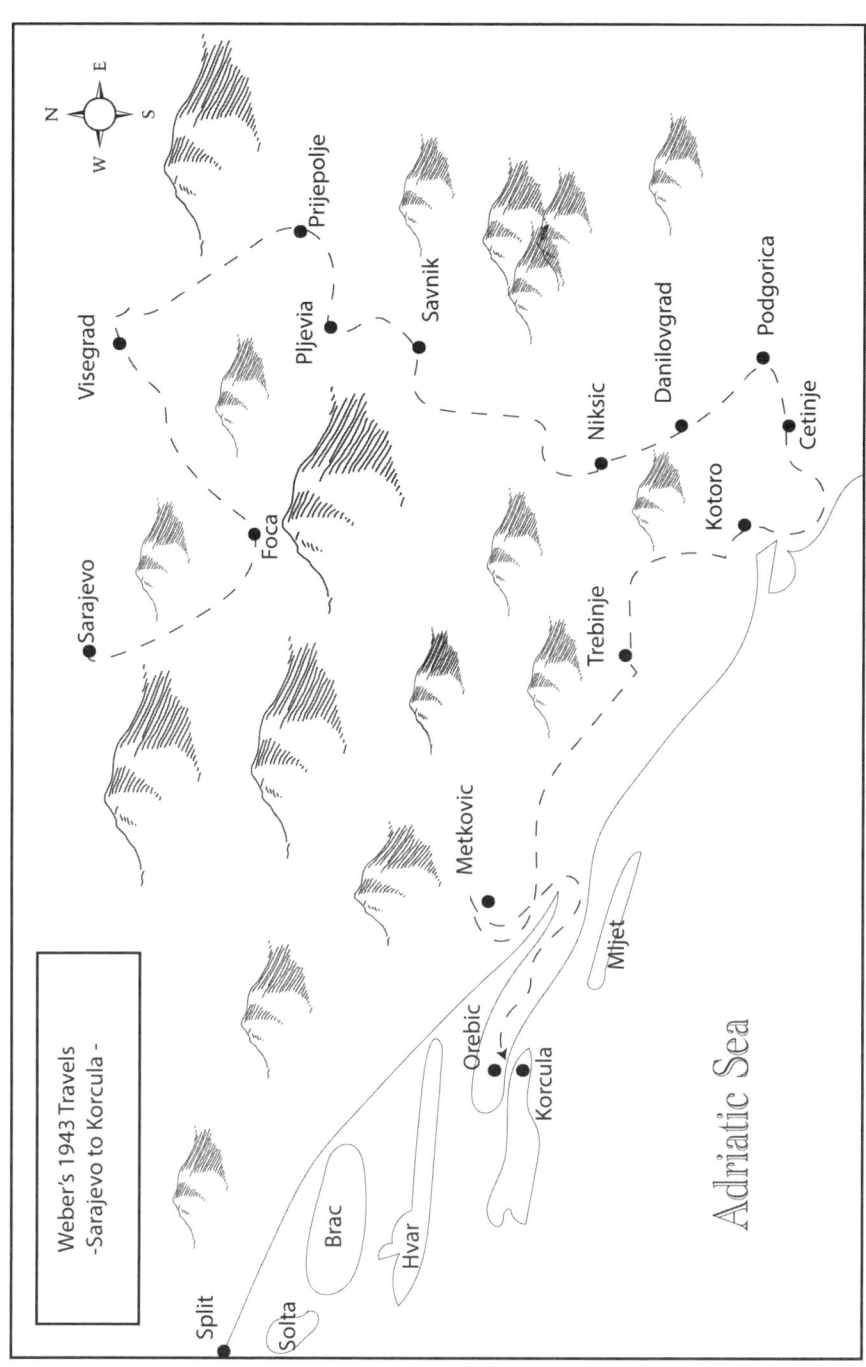

Weber's 1943 Travels
-Sarajevo to Korcula -

Photos of Gottfried show him standing at the gate to the old city and sitting on the ancient seawall. Not much has changed in Korčula since 1943. It was easy to find the exact location of these photos when I re-traced his steps. Weber wrote that operational headquarters set up its radio communications center in one of the town's palaces. While there are actually eight palaces in the old town that are adjacent to the ancient Cathedral of St. Mark,[103] he was actually in the former nuns' monastery on the west side of the town, outside of the old town walls, and near the harbor of Korčula. He was also billeted in one of the houses near the old town, that he called "millionaires' housing," just a short walk from the monastery.

Now, he was no longer on the road, but on an island in the Adriatic that was under German control, and relatively safe. Things were looking pretty good for Gottfried and his unit at the end of 1943.

CHAPTER 4

1944, Korčula

In 1944, the Germans were in a desperate situation. Italy was basically lost and partially occupied by the Allies fighting their way up the narrow mountainous country. The Soviets were bowling over the Germans on the Eastern Front, penetrating into Poland, and the anticipated invasion of France to open up a second front, that Stalin desperately needed, was in play. Some of the German allies including Finland, Romania, and Bulgaria who jumped on the Axis bandwagon in the victory years, in hopes of being rewarded for their allegiance after the war, were teetering in their loyalty to the Reich. In the air, the 8th Army Air Force in England and the 15th in Italy were strategically bombing targets by day, while the British were fire-bombing the Reich by night.[1] It was not safe to be a German anywhere. In the former Kingdom of Yugoslavia, the civil war between the Chetniks and Partisans was in full force. The Partisan movement against the Germans was also getting stronger, thanks to the help of the Allies sending vast amounts of supplies and equipment to Tito's forces by air and sea. The twilight of the Thousand-Year Reich was approaching.

* * *

In January, Gottfried found himself on the island of Korčula, in the town of Korčula. The first month involved unloading equipment from the docks and getting everything organized in the radio command center that was located in a monastery. Unlike the radio equipment found in his truck in 1943, this equipment filled an entire small room, comprising a complete radio system that was staffed by many Nachrichten troops. He wrote that the monastery itself was beautiful. His housing was also excellent. Being in the headquarters unit appeared to have its privileges. For the first month, the troops were limited by orders on what they could do in and around town in their free time. While the Germans supposedly had the island, surrounding area, and town, there was still potential danger from the Partisans. It was still too dangerous in January, 1944, to explore the area. January also brought him a surprise: leave—his only one during the war. While only a few days and not

Weber on leave in Zagreb, January 30, 1944, posing for a photo in the Josip Juraj Strossmayer square. Behind him is the bust of the Croatian writer August Šenoa, that is still there. (Weber/Author's collection)

long enough to get home, he was able to go by train to Zagreb. Out of the combat zone and into the relative safety of the interior of the NDH, a photo of him shows that his leg injury did not limit his mobility. Gottfried explored the city's parks, slept in a warm bed, and had relatively good food to eat.

In February, his housing quarters were moved to a bombed-out hotel where he and his new roommate, Raymund, had to cobble together furnishings for their room by combing through the town's wreckage for any salvageable items. While not as good as the millionaire's villa, the old hotel was still a good place to be in the early months of 1944. And, he was probably much better off than most German soldiers serving in the former kingdom. Over on the mainland the winters were much colder and the enemy was stronger. Gottfried had a good place to sleep, was decently fed, and the area was relatively safe.

Even though they were in the mild Adriatic climate, the winter months on the island were cold. He wrote that it was cold, damp, and rainy, requiring him to go collect firewood to heat his room. Sticks and logs were relatively easy to find on the heavily wooded island, if they wanted to risk venturing out in the occupied territory. Other sources of firewood that he and his friend Suppan and his roommate Raymund collected included wood scraps from the bombed-out buildings. Or, to make collecting even easier, there was the occasional theft of firewood from the wharf

The communications command center located in the monastery in Korčula. (Weber/Author's collection)

Left: Weber, still in his wool uniform, poses near one of the dock torches in Korčula town. Right: the same area today. (Weber/Author's collection)

area where German supplies were received from the mainland. On many days, he and Raymund split the firewood in an attic room in the hotel where they were billeted.

* * *

Weber and the 118th were not alone on the islands in the Adriatic in 1944. In their race to secure the Italian occupation zone in late 1943, the Germans occupied the southern islands of Brač, Hvar, Mljet, and Šolta. The one island they did not get was Vis. Located west of Split in the Adriatic, Vis is the furthermost island from the Yugoslav coast and was a strategic location for the Allies, particularly the British and the Partisans. This island soon became a thorn in the Germans' side. The Germans would regret not taking it.

Vis served as a jumping-off point and hub for Partisans and the British to attack German garrisons on the outlying islands, and reconnaissance activities and raids on nearby islands including Šolta, Brač, Hvar, Miljet, Korčula, and locations on the mainland. Vis also served as a supply hub to the Yugoslav mainland. Supplies would be shipped from Italy to Vis, and finally by small craft, often under the cover of darkness and away from the nightly E-boat patrols, to the Partisans fighting on the mainland. Vis also served as an emergency landing strip for damaged Allied aircraft returning from their bombing missions. The gravel runway was short enough for a landing, but not large enough for bombers to take off from again. Those aircraft that made it there were simply pushed to the margins of the field and scrapped. Crews, meanwhile, were taken back to Italy in C-47 transports or by boat. A squadron of British P-40 Warhawk fighter planes, referred to as Kitty Hawks by the British, also operated from the airstrip. Vis also became the headquarters of Marshal Tito in 1944 when he was forced from the mainland by the Germans in their failed attempt to capture him at Drvar.[2] The cave where he lived and worked is now a popular tourist attraction on the island.

The commander of Vis island was originally Colonel Jack Churchill. Born in 1906, "Mad Jack" graduated from the military war college in 1926 and then served in Burma, retiring from military service in 1936. When war broke out in 1939, he re-enlisted in the British army as a second lieutenant and was sent to France with the British Expeditionary Force. In France, he was soon recognized for his aggressiveness, use of guerrilla-type tactics, and riding into battle on his motorcycle with his claymore sword, bow, and bagpipes. As the legend goes, on one occasion while rescuing a wounded British soldier in France, Jack impaled three Germans with his sword and beat another to death with his bare hands. This action earned him the Military Cross for bravery. Mad Jack believed that an English soldier was not properly dressed for battle unless he carried a sword.[3]

His aggressive and effective tactics, and perhaps lunacy, in France caught the attention of the British high command who subsequently selected Churchill to lead the newly formed commandos, becoming second in command of No. 3 Commandos. On December 27, 1941, Jack led the attack against the German garrison and fish oil factory at Vågsøy, Norway which earned him another Military Cross. What was expected to take days, Jack and his unit accomplished in two hours.[4] Churchill then became the commanding officer of No. 2 Commando after the March 1942, raid on St. Nazaire that destroyed the drydock, preventing the repair of German ships there and forcing them to run through the English Channel for repairs in Germany. But the attack was costly. Out of the 612 commandos that were on the raid, 215 were captured and 169 were killed. After this raid, Bob Bishop, a No. 2 Commando veteran, recalls that "Jack propined several unpublished raids [that do not exist in the history books] to this day across the channel to France which further gained the attention of the British High Command."

Churchill then took the No. 2 Commandos into Sicily, where according to Bishop, "he really came into his own at Salerno." Here, Jack, again with his sword in hand, along with one of his corporals, captured 42 Germans during the invasion. From Salerno, the No. 2 Commando moved into the Apennines and then to Vis where Mad Jack became the commander of the entire island garrison. Because of all of the responsibilities related to administering the island, Jack's younger brother Tom, a brigadier general, soon took over command of the island, allowing Mad Jack to do what he did best—planning and participating in raids, leading his troops from the front, and rallying them in battle by playing his bagpipes.[5] Bob Bishop perhaps sums up his old commander in a simple, but precise manner: "Oh yeah… Jack was one of the greats."[6] Mad Jack Churchill's exploits on the Adriatic islands left a lasting impression on the soldiers of 118th too. In 1971, he was the guest of honor

"Mad Jack" Churchill playing his bagpipes to veterans of 118. Jäger-Division at their 1971 reunion in Graz, Austria. (Author's collection)

at one of their many reunions that were held in various cities throughout Austria. Old hatreds now gone, the former enemies shared their military comradeship over drinks. Mad Jack left his longbow and sword at home, but he did bring his bagpipes.

Bob Bishop No. 2 Commando

Bob Bishop was another Allied soldier on the island of Vis. Stationed there from January to June 1944, his No. 2 Commando unit came to the island in landing craft infantry (LCI) vessels from Bari. Originally drafted into the British army, Bob interviewed for the commandos and was accepted, training to be a commando at Achnacarry Castle in the rugged Scottish highlands. Bishop said that training was hard.

No. 2 Commando was also billeted in the fishing village of Komiža on the western coast of Vis. Bob described the town this way:

> There's some sort of a waterfront street there with maybe World War I buildings three to four stories high and some alleyways—two back from that. There was one church which was disused by the time we arrived; still a priest in it, but he didn't do anything on account of politics, and there was one jetty there where two motor gun boats were tied up—MTBs and sundry schooners. Shortly after we got there, a Bofers gun anti-aircraft battery arrived and set up on the side of the harbor... The No 2. Commandos were housed pretty much anywhere where you could find room for us. Some were in shelters on the west and north side of Komiža, a few were in some of the disused houses in Komiža town itself. We were all pretty much all taken out of Komiža later on because the Luftwaffe arrived and bombed Komiža rather heavily in retaliation for Šolta... they knew we were there. It was in retaliation for causing trouble, I suppose.

The No. 2 Commandos kept busy:

> We [No. 2 Commando] were stretched to the limit on the island. There was the boarding party, there was the raids, the reconnaissance, patrols where you would be dumped somewhere like Hvar town for example, on the western end of Hvar island and stay there for two weeks or something, and then they'd come back and pick you up. As soon as you get back, you'd be in line for something else—extremely busy. We had to not only mount these offensive operations... we had to look after prisoners that the Navy, our own boarding parties, and from Partisans if we could get them [German prisoners]. And we had to administer the island too, and we even had to help build an airfield on the place, a strip I should say which was quite hard work. We were very very busy... many many many tasks.

Besides work on Vis, No. 2 was busy harassing 118. Jäger-Division on the islands and other German forces in the Adriatic. According to Bishop:

> Jack was instructed to be aggressive as soon as we possibly could and we didn't have anything [to get us around] so Jack looked up the schedules of pretty much all of the Partisan fishing boats to see where they were going. So, he asked if they mind dropping us off and if they could be nice enough to pick us up on the way back. You know, the night cruise. The raids were a success and Jack never wanted to be known to change a winning system... Some [of the boats] were on their last legs, others weren't too bad. We put on what we could and some kind of ridiculous thing about it was that the vessels that were available limited the size of our operation... We did the best we could with them. One thing about the commando creed is improvisation, a quality that has to be acquired.

Boarding raids were another activity for No. 2. For many of their boarding raids on German shipping, the No. 2 Commandos were basically modern-day pirates, concealing themselves on Yugoslav fishing boats and then boarding German supply boats. Bishop said: "I can remember many a night going out on them seeing their shape on the horizon, ducking down—while two or three Germans prowled the deck… so we got alongside—unfortunately for them." After taking control of the vessel, the boat, crew, and cargo were hauled back to Vis. The Germans became POWs and were sent to Italy, while the spoils were distributed to the troops on the island and sent to the Yugoslav mainland to supply the Partisans.

Besides the occasional "pirate loot," food on Vis for Bishop was simple and limited. He explained:

> … the Partisans were given a lot of American flour and other supplies brought over from Italy, but they kept it to themselves and they had a poor initiative to share. They set up bakeries on Vis and baked loaves… yummy real nice white bread, and we got nothing… We just had the old British army mainstay—hardtack biscuits. However, the Partisans were not averse… they would sell a loaf for 2 packs of cigarettes. Oh, corn beef too. A can of corn beef between two men a day plus the package of these hardtack biscuits, and a dry ration of tea. And if you were lucky, a can of condensed milk. Protein and other needs came from sharing a can of corned beef with another guy.

British troops have tea with a Partisan fighter on Vis. The island of Vis was an Allied stronghold in the Adriatic that served as a supply connection to the mainland and a jumping-off point for island raids. (National Army Museum)

The island was also crawling with Partisans. In many, if not most cases, the Partisans accompanied the commandos on the island raids, Bishop recalls:

> They came with us on several operations... If they decided to make their mind up to do something, they were brave and put up with all kinds of hardships, and there was the lack of training of course. There was a complete lack of fire discipline and they made all kinds of noise when they shouldn't, and stuff like that. Signals was very poor. Their signals was really limited to runners... poor devils... They had a child-like political philosophy, and there was no other opinion other than what they had. Unfortunately, it was heavy duty communist stuff and I can't blame them for that, I suppose. They were the ones who were doing all the work.[7]

An American on Vis: Andrew Mousalimas

The Americans were also on Vis. One American was Andrew Mousalimas, who was part of what was known as the "American Group" or the American Operational Group in the OSS who were Greek-Americans and Greek nationals who volunteered to rid Greece of the Germans. Mousalimas, the son of Greek immigrants, grew up in Oakland, California. In 1943, at the age of 18, he and two of his Greek high-school buddies heard about the formation of the 122nd Infantry Battalion that was created by President Roosevelt at the request of the Greek government in exile. The battalion was looking for Greek-American volunteers. Being a first-generation American and fluent in Greek, he and his Greek buddies jumped at the chance to serve in a unit that was slated to fight in the proposed invasion of Greece. The battalion was mixed with young Greek-American volunteers fresh out of high school, and older street-wise merchant marine Greek nationals who volunteered for service in the US army after being stranded in America.[8]

The unit was trained at Camp Carson, Colorado. Mousalimas recalls that the training was hard. They would go on 25–30-mile hikes in the mountains: "We go out and train all week and bivouac; we would come back on Saturday and he would give us one day off." Because of this rigorous training, Mousalimas said that his later OSS training was a breeze. In September 1943, Mousalimas, along with his unit, was sent for specialized OSS training to the Washington D.C. area. They first trained at Area F, the Congressional Country Club in Bethesda, Maryland that was converted to a military training site for the OSS. Living in tents in view of the posh white clubhouse, Mousalimas said that they used the greens as targets for their mortar training. They literally blew the place up with their mortar and live machine-gun training.

> We were in Group 4. They called us the Jitterbug Group. Unlike other groups that were 50/50 Greek immigrants, most of us in our group were Greek Americans, and we were young. We did a lot of hand to hand combat and a lot of dismantling mines, going into his buildings and trying to find out, you know, if there was any booby traps in there... They had a Frenchman there that worked for the underground and he would say: if you don't like it here, you go back to your mommy. He taught us knife fighting. Almost every night we went out hiking—not far... just far enough to use our compass.[9]

He was also trained in weapons in "Area B," now the site of Camp David. After completing their training in December, 1943, they left for North Africa, departing by boat out of Newport News, Virginia, crossing through the Straits of Gibraltar, and following the North African coastline. They stayed in Cairo for a couple of weeks and then crossed over to Italy in early 1944. Mousalimas said: "I probably spent more time on ships than some Navy guys did… 31 days going there and 4 days on the HMS *Staffordshire* going from Alexandria to Taranto, Italy, which was the worst ship I had ever been on—a miserable ship." All four units of the American Group, about 75 troops total, then crossed over to Vis from Bari in small craft that resembled gunboats. This would remain as their base of operations until they moved on to Greece, later in 1944.

Mousalimas and his unit were billeted in Komiža on the northwest side of the island, right near the wharf.

> They put us in a billet on the side of the mountain, and it was kind of nice, you know. We ate pretty good… The people were wonderful. We had a woman right next to us. God, she couldn't have been more than 35 you know, but anybody over 30 looked old… I'm only 19. She would wash our clothes, underclothes, whatever… and wouldn't take anything—just a half a bar of soap. You know, that GI soap. That's all she wanted. We tried to give her something, she didn't want anything… just a half a bar of soap. We met a Serbian Orthodox family there… weren't too many Serbians there, and we got very friendly with them and we would take them… don't ask me how we got the flour, I won't admit anything… but we would take them flour and they would cook for us once in a while, whatever she can cook, and we got very close to them. On Easter Sunday she had an old goat that had probably gave final birth and we sneaked out 4 bags of flour, and we bartered. We got that little goat and then my squad and 4th Group barbecued it for Easter Sunday, for Greek Easter.

Mousalimas also said:

> Vis had a lot of troops… It was loaded with Partisans. The Partisan women were dressed in their regular army uniforms, and Tito put out an order that if a Partisan woman even stopped to talk to an American or British soldier, she would be sent to the mainland. I found out later that five or six guys did make out with the girls, but we were pretty honorable. Like I said, we wouldn't talk to them because we knew damn well that the girls would have to be sent over. And they were gorgeous—big strong looking women, big buxom women. We had a great relationship with the male Partisans too. They would kid us on how the Russians were doing all the fighting. We would sit there drinking Rakija [plum brandy] and they would go "živeli Roosevelt" and we would take a drink. Then we would go "živeli Churchill." They were pretty careful not to bring Stalin in until the third živeli, even though they were communists. And you know, we had a nice time. They were big strong, big fit bruising guys. I don't know if you know but these Yugoslavian guys are pretty good-sized guys, and hell, by the third živeli were all through!
>
> Anyway, we did a lot of training there and we walked around a lot. They had vineyards on the island and I don't think they have anything else that I can remember—it was pretty rocky… There was the airfield there just beyond Komiža and we would go there once in a while when American planes with American airmen would land there and we would bring them in for a couple of days and then send them back to Bari. Americans were always surprised to see Americans [on the island] there 'cause they say it's always only British and Partisans. Guard duty was another task. The only bad part was that once in a while we would have guard duty on the beach in one of these kind of a huts there… I don't know what the hell it was… and

British troops line up for inspection in Komiža, 1944. Komiža was one of the towns on the island of Vis where British and US troops were garrisoned. (National Army Museum)

we would sleep there. And boy, it was cold, and the rats was as big as cats. We would go to sleep, and in the morning we would see rat droppings all over us… didn't bother us at all.[10]

German air raids were an issue. Because of Luftwaffe raids and other alerts of German or friendly British aircraft flying over Komiža, Mousalimas and his group had too many sleepless nights. They decided to sleep outside of town. So, after 4 or 5pm, they would have chow and then go up to the side of the hill, outside of town, where they had dug some trenches. Locking their equipment in their billet, they would take only their rifles, ammunition, and a blanket to sleep with, returning to the town in the morning. Even though he felt that the bombing raids were inaccurate, they were now at least safer—although uncomfortable.[11]

Life as a Radio Operator

On February 18, Gottfried wrote that he was now familiar with the equipment to the point where he could work independently. But, there were still some days where he missed a signal which resulted in a reprimand from his superiors. He was not the only one that missed calls. He writes of others getting in trouble too, and having to talk to the command staff. In some weeks, he was on night duty with the radios, working from 10pm to 2:30am. In other cases, he had to work until 7am. He also had the day and afternoon shifts too. All of the radio staff were rotated in what appeared to be a bi-weekly basis. He was getting into his routine of ciphering, and making sure that he had the correct codes for the day to properly encode and decode messages. Some of the coding and decoding was frustrating for him. On some occasions he wrote that the coded messages were "stupid," and that units on the island could have sent their messages by wire instead. When on nights, he had to make sure that the daily situation report was sent to headquarters in Sarajevo. As was the case when he was in the radio vehicles, he did not work alone. Now, there were even more radio staff. Some were attached to headquarters and operated either the transmitters or receivers, and other operators were at the company level working with units in the field throughout the island. The Nachrichten unit also included the phone and wire operators who had spread their communication lines throughout the island.

During nights in the early part of 1944, the radio traffic was pretty light, allowing him to read and write letters. But there were some nights that he wrote that he was busy, especially when the wire communication lines on the island were destroyed by Partisans, requiring what he called continuous transmission. On some nights there was nothing to do because of limited radio traffic. The down time was filled with cleaning and organizing the radio room, reading what newspapers were available, reading letters, and writing to loved ones. If it was not limited radio traffic, on other days the radio equipment was not working correctly, resulting in missed signals coming in or not being able to send updates to headquarters. He wrote of several reasons why the radios did not work. On some days, the radio, either the receiver or transmitter, was simply broken and they had to wait for a new one to come in from the mainland. Everything came by boat. Tubes also failed, which required him to go to the quartermaster to get new ones. If not the radios themselves, he also complained about atmospheric conditions that made radio reception difficult. And, in some cases, headquarters missed radio signals that he sent, but part of both the sending and receiving process also required maintaining an activity log. This saved him on more than one occasion when questioned about a missed signal.

To power the radios and charge batteries, they used electric generators. Gottfried referred to the generator as the "gg400" in his diary. The gg400 was the model number of the generator made by Auto Union, better known as Audi. It was the standard generator used by all German troops during the war and fitted in all types of vehicles, including the Tiger tank.[12] It had a crank start—as he wrote in his diary, "I crank for Germany." While a mainstay of the communications center, the gg400 gave him fits throughout his time on the island. If it was working at all, on some days it would fail because someone left the choke on. In other cases, there would be an issue with the carburetor, requiring him or someone else to dismantle the carb to get it going again. The generator was also thirsty, requiring Gottfried, or another radio operator, to lug gasoline in 20-liter gas cans to the communication center in the monastery, and later to the bunkers which were uphill and further away from the docks.

Being a radio operator connected him with the rest of the world. Gottfried would listen to the music from Radio Belgrade, the German armed forces radio station that transmitted music, news, and propaganda throughout Europe and the Mediterranean. The station was famous for transmitting the song "Lili Marlene" every night at 9:55pm that both sides eagerly listened to.[13] While Gottfried commented that the station had wonderful music, it appeared that it served another purpose. In one diary entry he wrote about listening to the music and talking with Raymund about the olden times—as much olden times as a 19-year-old could have. As part of another program on Radio Belgrade, soldiers could write in and request songs to be played for their loved ones, asking that their names be announced on the radio. He did this for his brother Georg's birthday and for Ilse, but he never heard their names announced. Gottfried assumed that the program never got his letters.

There were the daily military activities that he still had to perform. Close order drill was still required, even though he was technically part of the division headquarters and was a radio operator. Almost every day at 10am, with the exception of rain, being too busy, or working the night shift, there was inspection and drill in the square. Marching was also part of the routine. It was not looked upon favorably. On one day in February he wrote, "Close order drill as always—a method by superiors that the headquarters staff is not coddled [by the senior leaders]—but they can all kiss my ass." On some days, he had to fall out with all his equipment, including his helmet, bread bag, canteen, mess kit, and rifle along with "gas masks and similar jokes." In addition to his close order drill, many days involved weapons cleaning too. On some days these activities were dangerous. On February 28, a British aircraft strafed them while on drill. One person was wounded.

Already in February the enemy was reminding Weber that a war was on through repeated air attacks. The British, who he referred to as Tommies, and the Americans were hitting targets on the island, particularly the town itself, ships, and the docks at Korčula. Allied fighter aircraft from the 12th US Army Air Force and Balkan Air Force operating out of Bari, Italy, and the runway on the Island of Vis, were relentless in their raids. There were scout planes flying over, and strafing runs by enemy aircraft that often disrupted his lunch. On other days, the attacks were more intense and involved bombs. On March 2, the Tommies bombed the old rail yard near the bay and the exchange, where he watched his friend Corporal Bianna, the clothing man of the regiment, die from shrapnel wounds. The harbor, right near the center of town, was often the target. The number of aircraft raiding varied in number. On some days, it was one. On other days he wrote that there were six fighter bombers, or multiple raids occurring. The number of raids started to increase in March and April. If anything, the raids were unnerving. Multiple diary entries show he had to seek cover, and his quarters, first in the town and later his bunker, would shake considerably from the bombings. It also had to be frustrating. The only reprieve from these harassing raids were rainy days. The rains were good for another reason—heavy rains meant no close order drills.

They did fight back against the attacks. There were anti-aircraft batteries in close proximity to the town. Besides the 20mm quad anti-aircraft guns, there was occasional air support from the German Luftwaffe. Although the mention of air support in Gottfried's diary is limited, in January, Walter Raberson, a Messerschmitt ME-109 pilot out of Mostar, got his first ariel victory over Korčula by shooting down an American P-38.[14] On occasion, German fighters also patrolled the coastline, passing through the Korčula channel on low-level flights, shooting off flares to alert the skittish anti-aircraft batteries on the island not to fire. Ships in the harbor were also effective for air defense, if they were there.

There were also what he called the battle ferries that offered some defense. Actually named Siebel ferries, these watercraft were part of the Kriegsmarine. Prowling the channel between Korčula and the Adriatic coastline, they delivered supplies and troops to the islands. Originally designed to carry troops across the English Channel for Operation *Seelöwe*, the invasion of England, these craft were later repurposed and used as transports throughout the German zone of occupation. A catamaran-style design, the ferry was about 100 feet in length and had a 50-foot wide deck mounted on top of the two barge-like pontoons on each side of the craft. Manned by a crew of about 14, on the center deck of the ferry was the wheelhouse that mounted a 20mm anti-aircraft gun on the top of it. Depending upon design, these ferries also had the 88mm cannon mounted on the front. With flat hulls, and a shallow draft, these menacing craft were quite suitable for river patrols and coastal operations, especially performing transport and patrol operations in and around the islands in the Adriatic.[15]

Bob Bishop from No. 2 Commando remembers watching these Siebel ferries during one of his covert reconnaissance missions on Korčula. Bishop recalled that there were a total of four Siebels operating off of Korčula, patrolling and moving supplies from Orebić and other locales, including the port of Split. Bishop explained:

One of the Siebel ferries that patrolled the waters around Korčula. (Author's collection)

> The Siebel ferry is one thing you have to fear… well not fear, but you had to really be careful… You have to respect it and keep your distance. It's too slow to be an escort. It was an armored freighter—in the middle of some of them sits the notorious 88 millimeter. It would haul freight and troops. And of course fieldpieces could be rolled on and off the thing and lashed down there and brought over. It's an economical idea because it could dispense with escorts. It was clever.

The enemy bombing was becoming more intense in February to the point that Gottfried and his comrade, Suppan, had to build a slit trench close to their communications building and quarters to use during air attacks. It was a popular trench. One day he complained that a sergeant and cooks from the kitchen beat them to the trench during an air raid: "Those dogs! Here we slaved for two afternoons to provide our bomb safe dugouts, and in case of danger they want to feel safe in there…" Hustling down into the trenches was becoming a daily activity.

Other enemy aircraft in the skies above Korčula were more benign. Counting bombers became one of his pastimes early in the year. High in the sky the bombers from the US 15th Air Force from bases throughout Italy often passed over Korčula. No longer camouflaged to hide their presence in the sky, the aircraft created a bright aluminum overcast that reflected in the sun, a stark contrast to the peaceful blue sky. Flying in formation thousands of feet above to their targets, the unmistakable drone of their engines could be heard on the ground, piercing the breezy quiet sky. Their white contrails served as an ominous pointer of death and destruction that would soon be delivered somewhere in the greater Reich. Gottfried even wrote in his diary that it was a beautiful picture. Their presence had to be awesome, ominous, and frustrating to see, making him wonder where they were going. He was not ignorant on what the bombers were doing in Germany. In one of his diary entries, he expressed his concerns about bomb attacks back home, and Ilse's safety in Dresden. On March 14, he and Suppan were on top of one of the town's medieval towers counting bombers returning from their raids. He wrote, "Earlier they flew above us by the hundreds. And now they have wreaked their havoc in Germany, they are now returning in loose formation." Later, on March 19, he counted another 103 bombers on their way to destruction. On April 14, he counted 436 bombers flying in the direction of Hungary or Romania. These entries soon quit in his diary, perhaps because they were no longer a curiosity, but instead background noise in his daily life and a reminder that the war might be lost.

On some days the bombers dropped their ordnance much closer. The town of Orebić, located on the main Pelješac peninsula about three kilometers across the water, was a target for light and heavy bombers from the 12th and 15th Air Forces, and the Tommies from Bari and Vis. It was continuously targeted because it was a strategic location for the Germans, serving as a ferry stop and depot between the peninsula and the island. On March 21, he watched 12 bombers attack Orebić. This attack made him run for his trench. Throughout his time on the island, Orebić was targeted. He wrote that the muffled vibrations from the bombs could often be heard in his bunker.

* * *

If not Korčula itself, throughout 1944 other units of the 118th garrisoned on the nearby islands of Šolta, Brač, Hvar, and Mljet, were also targeted by the Allies operating from Vis.

The first large raid was on the island of Šolta on March 17, 1944. Šolta is positioned in the Adriatic between the port of Split on the Croatian mainland and the island of Vis. The purpose of the raid was to take the pressure off Vis from a potential invasion, and to neutralize the German positions on Šolta. The main mission was to capture the German garrison in the town of Grohote. This was a big raid by number. About 600 Allied troops made up of Partisans, No. 2 Commandos including Bob Bishop, and some from the American Group, including Group 4 that Mousalimas was in, were involved in the raid. Because of the number of troops, LCIs were used to transport the troops to the island. This raid used the same tactics as other raids conducted on Brač, Hvar, and Mljet: hit the islands fast and hard under the cover of darkness, take prisoners, and leave the island as fast as possible. According to Bob Bishop, "our modus operandi was to land during the night and throw a cordon around the town and pick the garrison off."[16]

New to combat, Mousalimas recalled the Šolta raid:

> We left on the evening on an LCI. Jesus… The LCIs are crowded… terrible, you are down below… you know, you can't stay on deck… you got all this equipment and you know some guys have got BARs, the others have the mortar, rifle, and then we got the ammunition and you're crowded in there… it's criminal. On gunboats we could be on deck as long as you don't smoke or anything you know… We weren't sure if the Germans knew we were coming or not. Fortunately, we landed and there was no opposition. The town that we were going to invade this time was Grahote.[17]

It was also his first time engaging the enemy:

> … and the first time we go into combat with the [No. 2 Commando], and we have never heard the German Spandau machine gun. It was the MG 42, I believe, and that son of a gun fired about three or four times as fast as our light machine gun. And it would go "buuuurp" and ours would go "tat tat tat tat"—it was beautiful… My group of 24 was right next to the British and we all fell on our backs right on the ground and there's Jack Churchill standing up, and he says "come on Yanks it's a long ways off." Well, they could tell by the sound. The darn thing was too far away from where we were because… you know experience…
>
> I could see this little village and we're firing our weapons and the next thing I know… I don't know who hit him… if I hit him or somebody else hit him, but I look down… and… something that didn't even bother me at the time, but I thought about it years later… I saw this pretty handsome German guy who's laying there dead… and first thing I'm looking for is a Luger… and no Luger, no nothing, so I look into his pocketbook and there's a photograph, I guess of him his wife and two kids, so I just threw it down… so this is how it is, I don't care at all… anyway we kept firing and then they told us to hold up, and I don't know… we could hear their machine guns firing at us, but so far there wasn't no problem and they told us to hold up. There was a platoon of Germans hiding out there… they would have annihilated whoever was there… even though it was our first combat, we didn't fire indiscriminately because I think our training came into play… a long time of training helped a lot… In the meantime we captured all those guys which never showed in the record book that it was a whole platoon. My squad was also sent out to clean out whatever was left over if you could find them, so we go into these barns and we found three Germans hiding out, so we brought them out and told them walk this way. They didn't have any weapons…[18]

Mousalimas also recalls the attack on Grohote:

> And all of a sudden these Kitty Hawks came in real low… you could even see the pilots, and they bombed the German village right in front of us. When the Kitty Hawks hit the communication center, which is a second floor building, it fell over—toppled over. So, as we're walking, we hear noises down below the dirt. To make a long story short, the communication guy was buried alive. He was very alive standing and we could hear him. What saved him was the air pockets underneath. We could hear him so we told the Germans to dig him out. We had these shovels, and the Germans were reluctant to do it. They thought it was Partisans. Well, as soon as they found out they were Germans, they started to dig like hell. So one of my guys said screw him, let's shoot the son of a bitch. I said, You can't do that man. You got the damn Germans… they want to take him out. I said, do you want to be like the Germans? … so it was my squad leader, I'm not going to deny it, it was my squad leader, and I argued with him. I told him that I think it's wrong, so we took the guy out and he was absolutely gray. Gray, from being there. We called in and said we had we had three Germans we captured and him, and we got some guys and took them back to our headquarters. I found that on the way to Vis he died—shock.[19]

The attack was not without Allied casualties. One American was killed and five others were wounded. One of Mousalimas' high school buddies that he joined with was among the wounded.

Bob Bishop from No. 2 Commando was also on the Šolta raid. In addition to the mortar rounds that they carried, Bishop carried his .45 pistol which was standard issue for the commandos, and a Thompson .45 submachine gun. Originally, they were issued drum magazines for the Thompsons, but these were so unreliable they threw them away with their pouches into the Adriatic. Instead, they found that two 20-round magazines welded end-to-end worked better. This configuration allowed for the easy reloading of the weapon. Bishop also recollects that:

> The Grahote expedition was March 19th. I remember that 'cause it was my birthday. It was "duck soup." We landed on the South side of Šolta, the island, and humped across during the night. We had to hump our 70 pound 3 inch mortars on our backs, and each bomb weighs 10 pounds; the base plate for the mortar weights another 55 pounds. Loads were very heavy. We were carrying about 70 or 80 pounds on the trail and more… and on dawn's early light, we formed a horseshoe around the town and morning came we went in and I think we only lost one…[20]

At the entrance to the horseshoe was Jack Churchill with a German-speaking person who ordered the garrison to surrender from the portable PA system that they carried with them. The garrison surrendered. The exercise went beautifully, said Bishop:

> We formed them up and called roll… we found the muster role and realized we got everyone and then we sent them away to pack their stuff up and come back. They did return and didn't want to venture out because of the rather bad manners and inhospitality of the Yugoslavs around the place. This is the reason that they behaved themselves because they thought they got a break being taken prisoner by us. We actually had quite a few problems with the Partisans over that, and we had to interfere with them—the handling of them [prisoners]. We marched them off and I believe some sung on the way back across the island. They helped us carry our gear and Jack Churchill played his bagpipes. We went back to Vis and everyone was happy.[21]

Both Bishop and Mousalimas participated in the Šolta raid. Clockwise: British commandos in battle; German prisoners in Grohote assembling under the supervision of American troops; blindfolded German prisoners at Vis island; injured being transported by German prisoners to landing craft. (War Department photos/Author's collection)

* * *

In April, knowledge of the Šolta raid had to exist on Korčula, especially with a radio operator who was connected to other units on other islands in the Adriatic. Combined with increased air attacks on Korčula, this gave rise to a general tension: Gottfried wrote in his diary that "something must be coming up." The town itself was getting attacked more by the British, and he wrote that he was concerned that they were going to lose the island—and his beautiful quarters. They were ready for retreat. If not the town, the harbor was a target where fighter bombers attacked the many boats that were ferrying troops and supplies to the island. In early April, he asked himself, "When is the offensive by the Tommy going to start? We are waiting for it. In our case we are sitting in a trap…" On Easter Sunday, he wrote that "the [headquarters] staff is supposed to leave tomorrow. Shit, it doesn't suit me at all. I would like to stay here, even though we would be in a difficult position on this island in case of an enemy invasion. The Tommy is trying to cut us off. That's why we packed in the afternoon. All of my belongings. My photo corner in my room is going to stay there for the moment. Only at the last moment will I take them down. As long as possible I will relax by looking at the picture of Ilse…" The following day, Suppan told him that their unit would not be leaving the island. They were staying, but their communications center and living quarters would now be in a bunker. Air attacks were getting too intense, and the risk of invasion was too great. The town itself could not be defended. It was time to move to the hills, into fortified positions. The tactical option was to build fortifications on the high ground outside of town that could be defended. The pressure was on.

Gottfried wrote that the bunkers were built on a high part of the island, not too far from the town. It was not one bunker, per se, but a series of them that included the communications bunker and machine-gun pits that provided for observation and a clear field of fire. Because the island was so rocky, the engineers blasted and cut the bunkers into the rock. In some cases, steps were cut into the Dolomite rock that led into the bunkers. The remains of the bunkers are still there, carved into the rock for eternity. Curious hikers can walk through the narrow entrances, many with crude steps, leading into the wider chambers that, in the case of Weber, served as the communications bunker that was large enough to house the radios, equipment, and a sleeping area with room for some cots.

While the actual details of the bunker system in his diaries are limited, Bob Bishop from No. 2 Commando described what they were like:

> What they did was they got the hell out of the towns, went to the nearest mountain of which there was no shortage of… These islands are extremely mountainous, very rough country—all of them, and then they [the Germans] pick a hilltop and mine all around it except one entrance to it, put barb wire entanglements around it, and leave it only to send strong fighting patrols out from it to get water or get food or other supplies… In other words, they fortified the hilltop. That made it very costly for us because they're very difficult places to attack. And barbwire. And then if you get through that you finally meet up with the angry man in gray with his usual complements of MG42s and God knows what on top of that when you get there…[22]

The bunker's roof was constructed of wood that Gottfried and his comrades salvaged from destroyed structures in the town and lugged up the hill. To camouflage the roof, they cut down pine branches and laid over the top of the boards. It was camouflaged well. In a photograph of his bunker that he took, the entrance is small and barely visible due to the amount of foliage they had on top of it. The bunker was also a continual work in progress during his stay on the island. To improve the living conditions inside, they built cots from scrap lumber. He and his comrades also had to repeatedly cut down fresh pine boughs to keep the bunker well-camouflaged. And, as late as June, he and Gossling, another radio operator, were collecting boards they had salvaged from a bombed-out hotel to build a wood floor in the bunker to make it a bit more comfortable.

While the bunker provided some protection against air raids, shelter against the elements was marginal at times. On those days that had hard rains, the water leaked through the roof. Multiple entries in the diary are dedicated to the leaky bunker ("dripping mightily," "it drips all night… shit…") making work and sleep unpleasant. On some occasions, the bunker was flooded from the rain. In June, Gottfried wrote that it took an hour and a half to bail the water out the bunker—about 350–400 liters they hauled out. Later in June, they had what he called another bunker catastrophe, the rain dripping all night on him, others, and the equipment. It was so wet at times that on sunny days they would dry out their wet items from the bunker outside in the sun. Later in the year, during the summer months, the hot temperatures and moisture in the bunker combined to make it unusually hot, humid, and uncomfortable. Mixed with the crowded conditions, it was more comfortable to sleep outside.

It wasn't just the change in their quarters. Now, they would receive a lot of their meals at the bunker instead of the mess hall. At first, the company was in charge of food, which Gottfried called slop. Then, they started picking up meals from the headquarters' kitchen whose staff he called the *Kartoffenstaffel* or "potato staff," picking up their rations in town and carrying them back to the bunker. Or, the

Weber's heavily camouflaged radio bunker on Korčula. In the entrance is another radio operator. The top of the bunker was covered with pine boughs to camouflage it from enemy attack. (Weber/Author's collection)

food would be brought to them. Oftentimes it was *Eintopf* or stew, whose quality depended upon its content and the motivation and skill levels of the kitchen staff. Besides Eintopf, they also received their cold rations—canned and packaged rations. Depending upon the situation, they received three-day rations, and because Gottfried was young, he also received extra youth rations, which were higher in calories and protein content. Although it was of mixed quality, sometimes there was no food brought up at all; he commented that "somebody should light a fire under the kitchen crew," the "stomach complains… it's comical that one should be able to live on air only," or, "we have to get used to living on air."

There were also constant skirmishes in the channel between Korčula and the Pelješac peninsula. British and Canadian MTBs and MGBs would patrol the area, targeting merchant shipping and German E- and S-boats patrolling off the shore of the peninsula. Of these, Canadian Tom Fuller, the commander of the eight boats in the 61st Motor Gun Boat flotilla, was perhaps the most well-known for his bravery and unorthodox tactics. Besides transporting operatives to the various islands, and sinking Axis shipping, on some occasions he would engage in piracy. Firing warning shots at the craft, followed by ordering the crew to surrender by using the boat's PA system, he would run his boat alongside the ship, where Partisans from his MGB (motor gun boat) would then board the craft and take control of the boat. The boat, crew, and contents bound for the German troops on the islands would then be towed back to Vis and the loot would be given to the Partisans.[23]

* * *

In April, hostilities on Korčula were increasing on the ground. One of Gottfried's officers, Captain Volland, and a sergeant were killed by a sniper on April 17. The captain's funeral was held on the 19th. Captain Herbert Volland was posthumously promoted to the rank of major. Born on July 26, 1914, he came from Leipzig, Germany. His grave, to date, is unknown. However, in 2015 during excavation for a new recreation center near a part of town called Ferijalni, workers discovered human remains. It was later determined that this was the location of a German military cemetery holding about 100 graves, that was destroyed after the war, eventually becoming local folklore over the decades. The German War Graves Commission in November 2015 began exhumation of the graves, where the remains were reinterred in the Mirogoj Cemetery in Zagreb.[24] Maybe Volland was one of those reinterred. However, the *Volksbund Deutsche Kriegsgräberfürsorge* website, the central repository for German war dead, states that Herbert Volland has not yet been transferred to a military cemetery set up by the Volksbund. Perhaps he is still buried somewhere on Korčula, or he remains one of the many nameless 2,000-plus soldiers buried in the communal plot in Mirogoj.[25]

On April 15, Gottfried also watched a supply boat burn from a fighter attack. To prevent it from sinking, it grounded itself on the shore. In some cases, the air attacks were close enough to have spent shells rain down on them. He also commented in his diary that "whenever a sail transport or supply boat enters the waters near Korčula—the aircraft show up." The town itself was also changing. Communist graffiti in the form of hammers and sickles, red stars, and slogans were painted on some walls, and some of the inhabitants were giving the troops what he called strange looks. Perhaps the residents knew that the German occupation was soon to be over.

Reconnaissance raids by OSS and Partisans were also occurring on the island. On April 15, eight Americans assigned to the OSS and 12 Partisans sailed from the island of Lastovo to Korčula to capture some Germans for intelligence purposes. Hiding in a cave the night of the 15th, the following day they hiked to the ambush site, one of the main roads on Korčula that was patrolled by the Germans. The mission did not go well. The group was surprised by a German motorcycle patrol, as was the patrol surprised by them. In a short firefight of about 15 minutes, the leader of the group, Lieutenant Benjamin Dobriski, was shot in the leg, and all five Germans were killed. To make sure that the Germans were dead, one of the OSS operatives then shot all five with his Thompson submachine gun. The Partisans then stripped the dead for their equipment and uniforms.[26] Sergeant L. J. Arsenault then took command of the group, and they carried the severely wounded Dobriski on a makeshift stretcher, evading German patrols, and hid in a cave until they could be rescued by sea. On the 18th, they took a small boat to the island of Lastovo, to

Partisan activity in 1944 became more aggressive and open on the islands. Here, Partisan slogans are painted on the walls of a building. (Author's collection)

the south of Korčula, where Dobriski was treated for his injuries. In retaliation for the attack, the Germans burned homes in a neighboring village, imposed a curfew, and took 20 locals hostage to be later shot.[27]

Until the end of April Gottfried also wrote about the shrapnel wound on his thigh that he picked up on the invasion. It just would not heal correctly, in his opinion. Into late April, he was having the staff doctor look at the infection in his thigh. To help speed up the healing, he was soaking it in hot water and laying in the warm sun. The wound also itched. To deal with this, he got some salve from a medic. He eventually stopped writing about the wound. It must have finally healed.

The First Major Attack

On April 22, the long-awaited attack on the island occurred. The day before, Gottfried wrote that they were in a high state of readiness, but he felt that their base was undermanned. It was a very large raid. From Vis the attack force of about 1,800 Partisans from the 12th and 1st Dalmatian Brigades of the 26th Division, along with British commandos, sailed for Korčula. The goal of the raid was to eliminate German forces on the west side of the island. They used coastal trading vessels called coasters to transport the troops and equipment. These large boats had shallow hulls, allowing them to access the shallow coves along the coast. Along with the coasters were the military landing craft assault (LCA) boats that each held approximately 30 troops. These barge-like craft were made of wood with steel plating, and had a large ramp on the bow, allowing for the easy unloading of troops and equipment. There was also a myriad of smaller boats that were used—whatever they could get their hands on.[28]

The forces landed under the cover of fog in various coves on the island in the early morning of the 22nd. One group attacked from the north side of the island, using coasters that towed eight boats full of troops and equipment. With them was a hospital ship. The southern attack group was made up of 10 coasters that towed 10 smaller boats behind, along with two British LCAs from the Special Boat Squadron (SBS) that contained supplies and 75mm howitzers.[29] In anticipation of rough seas, the LCAs had attached canvas "dodgers," or walls, to extend the height of the sides of the craft to prevent the heavy seas from washing in and swamping them.[30] Although the positions were heavily fortified with minefields and barbed wire, the Partisans readily took the harbor at Vela Luka and encircled the German strongpoint at Blato, which surrendered on April 23.[31] The raiders soon departed the island on the 26th, taking with them the majority of the citizens from Vela Luka and Blato back to Vis.[32]

Having afternoon duty on the radios on the first day of the invasion, Gottfried had the ultimate "spectator seat" to the fight. He wrote that "battle group Schmid was involved in a defensive battle… The enemy is using heavy mortars… Our forces fight to the last man, Blato was occupied by the enemy." Their partner station was also in distress, sending messages in clear text, and he wrote that the code key was in enemy hands. The following day he wrote that "the fate of our counterpart station is sealed." After a day-long fight, the station transmitted in clear text, "*Sieg Heil*" three times, and then destroyed the station. Closer to his own bunker, the main road near their radio tower was also attacked, and two soldiers were killed. But he wrote that German reinforcements were on the move. Optimistically he also wrote that "we are going to beat the enemy" and that "such little episodes he received though radio messages will probably never become known by others." In one of his entries that he placed in shorthand in the diary to conceal its contents, he wrote about how his colonel disagreed with the general on the radio about the battle: "He [the Colonel] states verbatim, my General, whoever tells me again to hold off to the last man, I will jump in his face. On the 24th, more troops were reinforcing the battle and Colonel F was personally leading the defenses…. Finally some Me's [Messerschmitts] show up." On the 25th, he wrote that the information from battle group Roedl "looks bad, but not hopeless!!!"

During the attack, his own location was hit by air by the Tommies, in his opinion because they were continuously being radio beamed, a method of using triangulation to identify where a radio signal was coming from. He could also see that other air attacks across on the peninsula caused large forest fires. The entire area was under attack, including the island of Mljet, that Partisan forces attacked as a diversion to keep the Germans wondering where or on what island the main attack would occur.

On the 26th he further wrote that "our battle groups are fighting to the last man." One of the groups was totally disintegrated. Only Lieutenant Hunter, who was wounded in the fighting, got away. All of the others were dead or taken prisoner to Bari (he assumed). More German forces were put into battle which lead to the tide turning. Now, he wrote that they were going from the defense to the offense. They also received orders that now they would be sleeping in the bunker at all times. On April 29, he wrote that the battle was over: "Did the Allies leave the island?" Characteristically the Allies would engage in hit-and-run tactics, leaving the island with their prisoners soon after the initial invasion.

The cost of the attack was high for the Germans. One source reported that approximately 756 Germans were captured or killed by the Partisans on this raid.[33] Another reported that 297 Germans were killed and another 439 were taken prisoner, along with the loss of equipment that included four 75mm howitzers, four anti-tank cannons, heavy machine guns, and mortars.[34] Another source reported that 459 Germans were captured and another 400 were killed, plus the loss of a large number of weapons and ammunition to the Partisans. The Partisans, meanwhile, had 184 wounded and 84 dead in the operation.[35] The Germans also managed to sink two of the coasters.[36] Regardless of which source is most accurate, German losses were high. The German prisoners were transported to a POW camp on the island of Biševo, near Vis,[37] and the captured spoils were put on display for a May

Day parade on Vis for Tito who was living on the island at the time.[38] No longer was the western part of the island in the control of the Germans. Now, the Allies and Partisans were even more of a threat to the island and Gottfried.[39]

* * *

In May, Gottfried was complaining in his diary about the planes, flies, and heat. To deal with the heat, he was issued a desert tropical uniform from the quartermaster that was located in the town's abbey. Unlike the field gray wool uniform that was suitable for the Dalmatian winters, the tropical uniform was made of khaki-colored cotton. The outfit itself included a long-sleeved tunic, long pants, shorts, and a tropical cap cut in the same fashion as his wool M-43 Gebirgs-style hat. He had to sew his own insignia on the tunic, which he did one night while on radio duty. The photo of him shows that his tropical tunic is German-made, perhaps surplus stock from their failed north African ventures that never made it across the Mediterranean. Not all people liked Gottfried wearing his shorts. He had a clash with one of his officers over wearing them while on duty one day. It appeared to be a terse conversation. In his diary he wrote, "I am not ducking and I give him sharp answers." He lost the debate and received two hours' close order drill the next day for his insubordination.

Others on the island were issued Italian surplus tropical uniforms. Rudy Wagner, who was in Artillerie-Regiment 668 that was based at Pupnat, told me that his

German troops were issued tropical uniforms to deal with the hot and humid summer weather on Korčula. Friends of Gottfried's pose near one of the entrances to Korčula town in their tropical uniforms. (Weber/Author's collection)

unit received surplus Italian tropical uniforms. These uniforms were only slightly different in color, cut, and style from the German ones. Rudy also said that they did not wear their tropicals when home on leave, because it would disclose their theater of operations. If granted leave, they were required to wear their field gray wool uniforms.[40] Some of Gottfried's pals also received Italian uniforms—a group photo that Gottfried snapped outside of the old town of Korčula shows soldiers dressed in Italian uniforms.

On a good note, in early May they now had permission to sleep below in their old quarters in the town during the day only, perhaps out of necessity. The bunker was getting more crowded with new faces, to the point that Lieutenant Mesitz ordered them to completely move out, but then reversed the order the next day. More room was still needed in the bunker, though. The following day, he and Haberscheck built another cot in the bunker to accommodate their new roommate by the name of Mang.

The insects, especially mosquitos, and the diseases they carried were also an issue. They slept with mosquito nets to protect themselves from bites and the danger of contracting malaria. It appears that Gottfried's net was important to him. He has multiple entries in the diary about washing it, and patching holes in it. One

Mosquitos were a problem on the island. One of Gottfried's prized possessions was his mosquito netting that he has wrapped around his hammock in this photograph to provide him some respite from the humid and cramped conditions of the radio bunker. (Author's collection)

photo of him under it on Korčula remains. Laying in a hammock suspended by a couple of trees, one can see Gottfried smiling under the net's protection. Even though he was careful, he contracted malaria in July. He described that his head hurt so much it was as if he was losing his scalp. For four days he had the shakes, a high temperature, and no appetite. To deal with the malaria, he wrapped himself up in blankets as a sweat cure. He wrote that he soaked through three blankets and felt as if he had a hangover when it was over. Raymund was at his side throughout the ordeal, except when he was covering Gottfried's night duty on the radio in the command bunker.

The enemy, without the knowledge of the Germans, were also on the island in May. In May, Bob Bishop was on the island on a reconnaissance mission observing the town of Korčula and the straits:

> [w]e sat on our butts there for about 13 days. The correct name, according to our war diary, was "officer reconnaissance." Jack decided to get rid of you for a couple of weeks… Couldn't spare valuable NCOs… On Korčula, I remember it was by MTB from Komiža harbor… about 11 miles to Korčula. I was just over 7 miles on the coast west of Korčula town, dumped there, and then we went to our RV [rendezvous] from there. Well, we were discreet… movements, equipment, shipping, coast watching, the patrols, the size of them that left Korčula town, vehicle presence… the whole gamut of things. I practically filled about 8 sheets of 8 and a half by 11 paper notes on the thing. I can't remember ever seeing a full count regarding the extent of a Garrison on the place, but they were never in excess of 200 that I observed at that particular point.[41]

British commandos were a common threat on Korčula. Here, Commandos pose with Partisans and civilians somewhere on the island. (National Army Museum)

Increased attacks were also going on in the neighboring islands too. From May 22–24, Mjlet was attacked by the American Group, Partisans, and No. 2 Commandos. In Operation *Farrier*, No. 2 Commandos, OSS forces, and Partisans were transported by LCIs from Vis and attacked the German garrison at Babino Polje. The mission did not go as planned. The forces got lost due to thick fog and the lack of Partisans to guide them. In fact, they were not even sure if they were at Babino Polje. Using their usual strategy of encirclement, followed by a request on a loudspeaker to surrender, it turned out that the Germans were not there. They had fled into the nearby forest and began shelling the invaders with mortars.[42] The OSS mission summary stated: "With imperfect intelligence and difficult terrain the enemy was engaged only at extreme range, and the evacuation schedule required withdrawal before actual contact was made."[43]

Mousalimas participated in this raid:

> The damn mountains… it was like ice cream cones, and I'm walking next to this British soldier. I'm just done and he's at least 26 or 27 and he's carrying the barrel of a 75 millimeter mortar they've dismantled. And as we were walking up this hill we're talking and I said: how long has it been since you been home? He said "I haven't been home since the war broke out in 1939." Now, five years when you're 19 years old, that's a lifetime. He said he was in India when the war broke out and he fought in Africa and Italy. I said you haven't been home, you haven't seen your mama and papa in five years?… "no young man, I haven't and we have to get this bloody war over with because my people are getting bombed every day and we have to finish this war." I said do you miss them? He said "yes I miss them, but we have to get this war over…" imagine five years especially… and I'm 19.[44]

He did not have nice things to say about his commander at Mljet:

> The commanding officer was a guy named Lovell. Lovell was a stockholder owner of Cannon Towel company and he brought two of his lieutenants with him, and they were members of our group. Here again, I was the runner… we're up on a hill and our guys are down below… the only one outside of the British and the Partisans was the 4th group—my group—they're down below… these are my buddies. I was up there for two days… two days and two nights… I didn't have one order. I wanted to go down and see what the hell is going down below. I wanna go down to see what the hell is going on and see if my buddies are doing OK, you know. I'm sitting there—that's hard. Once in a while, the British would come up and have their tea and leave again. They always had to have their tea. And Lovell's up there with his 2nd in command and they're talking about Mint Julips, swear to God, Mint Julips! And there's firing going on down there. I just sat there and didn't even talk to them. The British came up and I would ask them what was going on. And they would say not too bad… he says you know we're cleanin' it up—it won't be too bad.[45]

* * *

Once in a while there were aircraft crashes on the island. On May 31, Gottfried wrote that he watched a four-engine bomber crash on the island. He wrote that nine crewmen ejected with parachutes. The B-24H Liberator number 41-28685, named the *Leading Lady*, was from the 15th AAF, 765th Bomb Squadron, 461st Bomb Group, 49th Wing, operating out of Toretta, Italy.[46] It was piloted by 22-year-old Lieutenant Samuel Norris from Owensboro, Kentucky. The *Leading Lady* was on her way back from bombing the Concordia Vega oil refinery in Ploeşti, Romania, a regular target for the 15th, and was heavily damaged by flak over the target. Already losing altitude at the Romanian border, Norris and his crew tried to nurse the *Leading Lady* back to Italy. It was a futile effort. By the time they approached the Adriatic, there was no chance the *Leading Lady* was going to make it across. She was doomed to a watery grave in the Adriatic or a crumpled debris field of aluminum on the land. Lieutenant Norris ordered a bailout over Korčula. While Gottfried counted nine chutes, there were actually 10. Staff Sergeants Jefferson Farrell (left waist gunner) from Nashville, Arthur Bindrin (top gunner), Joseph Curtin (ball turret), Harry Ranieri (tail gunner) from Whitesburgh, Kentucky, Bufort Culler (nose turret), Tech Sergeant Glen DeSpain (right waist gunner), along with Second Lieutenant Everett Kamps (navigator), Second Lieutenant Edwin Baumann (co-pilot), who was wounded in the face from flak, and Lieautenant Edmund Stephenson (bombardier) all bailed out on Norris' orders. Norris was last to leave the dying *Lady*.[47]

They all made it out and landed on the island. All of the crew except Culler and Norris were immediately captured by the Germans, near Pupnat. Culler evaded German patrols on the island for two days until he was captured. Once on the Yugoslav mainland, Culler escaped again from his captors, but was soon re-captured. With the help of the local Partisans, Norris evaded capture, was transported to Vis and returned to Italy, serving as an intelligence officer for the rest of the war.[48] German Air Forces Command Southeast also recorded the capture of the flyers. Along with two other crewmen that were captured near Split from another B-24 that crashed on June 10, they were all given Red Cross food packages and then transported to Oberursel, near Frankfurt am Main. Oberursel was the Luftwaffe's main transit camp and interrogation center for captured Allied flyers. Here, the flyers were placed in solitary confinement to soften them up, were interrogated by Germans who spoke perfect English, and were then sent to their permanent POW camps. All of the crew from the *Leading Lady* were sent to Luft No. 4B POW camp in Germany.[49] Located about 30 miles north of Dresden in Sachsen, not too far from Gottfried's hometown, it was one of the largest POW camps in Germany during World War II, holding over 8,000 prisoners.[50]

* * *

There was also plenty of free time for Gottfried. In his free time, he would sit in the machine-gun pits near the bunker to soak up the sun, talk, and write letters to his friends—Hanni, Gerda, Kurt, Theo, his parents, and especially Ilse. He also wrote that he would "lay out under the trees, read, and dream of past times." After working the night shift, he and some of his comrades would still return to their old quarters in town to sleep during the day. It was much more comfortable, and perhaps the risk of an invasion was much less during the day, than evenings or dawn. Then, he would return to the bunker in the evening. For his 20th birthday in June, he celebrated by drinking wine and going on a walk with Raymund near the south bay.

Even though they were now basically living in the bunker, they could still go into the town on days when they had time off. The surrounding area was also explored. He still pursued his photography hobby, taking photos of the sights, and friends. One day, he and his friend Suppan got up on top of one of the town's ancient tower fortifications to visit the air raid lookouts. He wrote that it was an "overwhelming view, the island, the blue ocean, and far in the background the mainland. If it were peacetime how glorious it would be." He was correct. Visiting the area myself in the peace of the 21st century and standing on the same fortification, I found the views were stunning. The Germans had also constructed observation towers on the hills above the town to watch for enemy activities and the potential for an invasion of the island. Gottfried and his friends would also go on top of these to view the sights, watching ships slide by in the blue-green waters, and looking across the channel at the mountainous Pelješac peninsula with its green fertile coastline that abruptly shot up to form pale rugged and bald dull gray peaks.

Some areas were relatively safe enough to go to, especially the beaches that surrounded the town. One of the beaches that he referred to in his diary as the south bay was visited quite often for swimming, bathing, and laying out in the sun, either on the pebble-covered beach, or on the supply docks that were controlled by the Germans. There was also the regimental bay on the north side of Korčula town that he would occasionally go to, often with his friends, the entire commo section, or by himself. The beaches and swimming were a respite from work and perhaps the boredom and loneliness of military life. Already in April he wrote that he was getting homesick and of his excitement for his upcoming leave: "If all goes well and the Tommy doesn't catch up with us, it is my turn to go on furlough in October/ November." He already had planned out what he was going to do, including visiting Ilse, who now lived in Annaberg. On some evenings, they would also go down to the harbor to watch the E-boats leave on their missions. Walking around the south bay and in the local vineyards near Lumbarda was also a common activity. Tomatoes from the convent, and wine from the friendly locals were often sought. Figs were also purchased when in season. If not for sale, he simply stole them from the many trees that lined the paths and roads on the island.

In the town itself the military officials provided variety shows and movies for the troops, which he frequented. He also wrote that a lot of items were available at the PX, including lots of cigars, cigarettes to satiate his smoking habit, and rum. There was also many stops to see Paul the barber, who was somewhere in town. Even some shopping in private stores existed on the island in 1944. He wrote of buying stationery "and other stuff" from a photo store in town. These excursions, however, required that he be armed. In late June, he was reprimanded by the military police for not taking his rifle with him into town. Perhaps the MPs knew more than he did about the general security of the area. One had to be careful. It was still enemy territory.

There was also excitement over receiving newspapers that kept him in touch with world events and loved ones in Waldenburg. The receipt of mail from loved ones, or lack thereof, was often written about in his diary. In one instance, it took over eight weeks to receive a letter from his parents. The slow mail also made him worry about conditions back home. Besides newspapers and letters, he read books, such as *Waldwinter* by Paul Keller, a novel about living in rural Silesia, which he wrote was beautiful. Domestic chores included cleaning the bunker and his living quarters in town, and patching up his socks, uniforms, and swimming trunks.

He often wrote to his brother Georg. By this time his brother Georg was also in the Balkans theater of operations. Georg was a lieutenant in *117. Jäger-Division* and most likely had it much tougher than Gottfried, even though he was an officer. In June and July 1944, the 117th was on occupation duty in Greece. Like his brother's unit, the 117th was involved in a civil and guerilla war, trying to hold the cities and keep the roads and rail lines open throughout the country, while leaving a wake of atrocities in their path.[51] In a situation very similar to Yugoslavia, there were multiple warring parties in the civil war. There was the ELAS or National Popular Liberation Army, the EDES or National Republican Greek League, and the EKKE or Communist Party of Greece, all fighting one another and the Germans, vying for the future control of Greece once the war was over. In August, Hitler ordered

Image of Korčula. (Weber/Author's collection)

the slow retreat of Army Group E out of Greece and northward to Yugoslavia. On September 4, XXII Mountain Corps headquarters started burning its papers, and its commander, General Hubert Lanz, received new orders to begin the long bloody retreat out of Greece for the Germans.[52] Other units in Army Group E, including the 117. Jäger-Division that was operating in the southern part of Greece and committing its own atrocities against the Greeks, were soon on the retreat north too.[53] It would soon be over for Georg in Greece.

One of the benefits of living on the island was the wine—and lots of it. Not too far from the town of Korčula is the town of Lumbarda and its vast vineyards. Gottfried often wrote of he and his friends going to Lumbarda to pick up liters of "Kryk," a golden yellow wine made from the ancient *grk* grape. If not going to Lumbarda to purchase wine from the locals, the Potato Staff provided them wine as part of their rations. Some of this wine also came from the mainland. There were also some friendly locals where they got additional wine. When wine wasn't available, Raymund would sometimes make eggnog, using rum from the PX to give it some kick. There was more than one entry in Gottfried's diary where he wrote that they were imbibing and had become "tipsy," which was often followed by diary entries for the next day that included statements related to sleeping off a hangover at the south beach.

For the citizens of the island, life had to be tough. Already, the civilians had endured the Italian occupation that committed atrocities against the citizens of the island. A review of the Central Registry of War Criminals and Security Suspects (CROWCASS), that was established by the UN War Crimes Commission after the war, lists 10 Italian soldiers from the rank of carabiniere all the way up to General Attilio Amato of the Messina Division that were wanted by the Yugoslav government for murder during their occupation of Korčula.[54] If not the Italians, there were also Partisan reprisals against citizens before the German occupation.[55] And, of course, the Germans committed war crimes too.[56]

Gottfried also wrote that the destruction that the British caused from their bombings was extensive. Out of morbid curiosity, he and Raymund would sometimes walk by some of the bombed-out buildings. There were food shortages and hunger, and the political landscape was chaotic at best. The island was officially under the control of the Independent State of Croatia, but local leaders were subordinate to the German officials. All major civil decisions regarding the island and its inhabitants were made by NDH officials. However, officials in Zagreb could not send any relief to the local government officials on the island. In 1944, the NDH itself was in a great deal of turmoil and instability. Most likely the islands were not a priority, especially since the Germans, not the Croatians, had military and physical control of them. To add to the problem, Allied air attacks disrupted the shipping of civilian supplies to the island, while local Partisan attacks against local government officials made them weak and ineffective in governing the people.[57]

* * *

Throughout June, it was repeat of the earlier months. Gottfried wrote that the weather was glorious in June. There was also lots of free time that often involved bathing and swimming in the south bay, and exploring the area with Raymund. Perhaps the most significant date in June was the D-Day invasion on the 6th. In his diary he acknowledged the invasion, simply writing that "the long-expected invasion in the west begins…" with no other thoughts or comments related to the historical event that would lead to the downfall of the Third Reich. While Gottfried was dismissive of the invasion, perhaps the high command was not. He wrote two days later that all furloughs were canceled. The lazy days of summer may have also caught up with him personally. One day, he received a reprimand from a first lieutenant for not saluting properly.

It appears that Raymund was his closest friend on the island. Besides working and rooming together, they were companions off duty, exploring the old town and surrounding area, going to movies and shows, looking for girls to talk to, swimming in the south bay, laying out in the sun, and drinking large amounts of wine. Raymund was his confidant when Gottfried had his concerns about Ilse back home. Like all roommates, they had their occasional differences. Gottfried wrote that Raymund "broods or acts like a school child at times," and they would disagree about what Gottfried described as "unimportant nonsense." On one occasion, Raymund peeked in his diary and was upset about what Gottfried had been writing about him. After the incident, Gottfried wrote in his diary: "He did not want to hear the truth. He is too childish to realize how to handle life from the right angle. He was not properly brought up at home and is very spoiled. You can't take childish people seriously." If Raymund had a diary, most likely similar entries about Gottfried would be found in it.

Girls and romance was still part of young Gottfried's life on the island. Even though he had a sweetheart in Germany, Gottfried developed another love interest with a local girl in June. His diary was basically "silent" about this. What Gottfried did to conceal the relationship in the diary from any prying eyes was that he wrote about her in German shorthand, initially concealing it from my translations. However, wondering what the shorthand was about, a woman who worked at the Waldenburg City Hall, and knew Gottfried when he was alive, kindly translated the shorthand entries for me. The secret of 70-plus years was now out.

On their many wanderings, he and Raymund met some local women who lived near Lumbarda. There were three—Leni, Mila, and Wesela. He referred to them as "their darlings." He and Raymund would sometimes stop by Mila and Wesela's apartment, writing that they were very hospitable, giving them wine, figs, and apples: "Whoever doesn't like wine, women, and song remains a fool his whole life long," he wrote. Raymund was sweet on Mila, and Gottfried was smitten with Wesela. It appears that Wesela liked Gottfried too. In June, he wrote that he had the time of his life. "Wesela is quite a gal. Genuine southern temperament. She knows how to kiss. Will I reach my goal? It would be my fulfillment." If not going to their apartment,

Romance still existed for Gottfried. Left to right: Leni, Mila, and Wesela. Wesela was Gottfried's girlfriend while on Korčula. (Weber/Author's collection)

they would also meet at the beach, writing that his dark-haired sweetheart had "a wonderful soft, flexible body." Other shorthand entries tell of Gottfried going to her apartment with flowers, and how her kisses were "hot—dangerous—with abandon." They also walked around town together and Gottfried even took photos of them together. But Wesela also liked playing the field. One day Gottfried spied her walking out of the truck drivers' quarters in town, which upset him. "Unfaithful!" he wrote. And, he also started questioning her allegiance to Germany. In one entry he wrote about how the women were asking detailed questions about his unit, and what he did. He wrote that he gave diplomatic answers only: "They don't succeed in trapping us." By mid-August the romance was over. The woman that he described as giving him paradise was no longer part of his life. He attributed it to the Partisans who most likely turned her.

There was of course radio duty and increased air attacks by the Tommies, where he wrote that they were successful in sinking a ferry in the south bay, where some troops were wounded. The water works was also bombed on June 17, with little damage. Land attacks also continued. On June 16, 300 Partisans from Komiža harbor on Vis sailed to Blaca Rock, a small fishing village on the northwest side of the island, near Blato. As with the other raids, the 300 Partisans hit the island, took prisoners and equipment, and then promptly returned to Vis.[58] Beginning in June, there were now standing patrols on all the islands around Korčula that Tito and the new commander of No. 2, Major Edward Flynn, authorized. Flynn replaced Mad Jack after he was captured by the Germans during a raid on Brač in June, after being knocked out by a mortar round. Before being transported off the island on his way to being a POW, Mad Jack, using proper etiquette, left his captor, Captain Hans Thorner, a thank-you note "for the correct treatment during our stay with you."

He also commented that "the food was rather short and less than what we were used to, but that could not be helped under the circumstances. I hope that after the war we shall meet again," providing the captain his home address and inviting him to dine with him and his wife.[59] Being Jack, he ultimately escaped his captors and walked about 240 kilometers back to Verona, Italy, to get back in the fight. Mad Jack's claymore and bagpipes were still prisoner though. They were taken as war trophies by the Germans and put on display in Vienna.[60]

* * *

Life continued on as normal in July on the island. Manning the radio on days, afternoons, and nights, fighting with the radios and the gg400 generator to work properly, a crowded hot and humid command bunker, bad food, or no food at all on some days, close order drill in the hot sun, down to town to see Paul the barber for a haircut, writing letters, the excitement of receiving mail, drinking wine, the reprieve of swimming in the south bay, and sunburns was the tapestry of his life. But, there was one difference starting in July. No more letters to or from Ilse or any diary entries about her. Maybe it was because time and distance had finally let the relationship run its course. Whatever reason, Ilse just became past entries into his diary and fond memories of his youth on Korčula that perhaps put a smile on his face in his twilight years that others could not figure out. She was no more.

Air attacks by the British kept intensifying. Nowhere was safe. On one day British aircraft attacked the town when Gottfried and Raymund were in it. The first bombs dropped close, shattering windows and knocking roof tiles off. Rushing down into a basement, one of the persons with them, Sergeant Neuner, did not make it to cover in time. Caught just outside the entrance to the basement, shrapnel or debris plowed a fist-sized hole on the left side of his belly. Running outside in the debris and smoke, Neuner collapsed and was carried to the aid station by his comrades. He did not make it. Two days later he was buried in a military cemetery that the Germans had created on the island. Raymund made a wreath for his grave. Neuner's death appeared not to faze Gottfried too much. Later that day, he went swimming in the south bay.

The same air attack also killed three horses of the Kartoffenstaffel that were used to haul the mobile field kitchens that fed the troops in the field. Nicknamed the *Gulaschkanone* or "goulash cannon" by the troops, these square metal carriage-like field kitchens were mounted on a horse-drawn wagon that had wooden spoked wheels. Basically a mobile wood- or coal-fired stove on wagon wheels, it had a fire box that heated up the food. There was also a large tub or cauldron with a round lid for cooking stews, a flat stove plate for frying sausages and potatoes, some warming compartments, a large water reservoir for coffee—even with a tap—and other storage compartments. The round smoke stack poking out of the top of the stove made the contraption look like a cannon.[61]

The air raids were now basically a daily event on the island. One of the RAF pilots harassing the Germans on Korčula was 27-year-old Flight Lieutenant Arnold Walker, "Blondie," who was in the No. 6 Squadron of the Balkan Air Force. On July 18, he earned the notable honor of being inducted into the Goldfish Club, an unofficial award for pilots or aircrews that had to parachute into, or conduct a water landing. The club itself was the creation of Mr. C. A. Robertson, the chief draftsman at the PB Cow company that made rubber boats for the RAF. After having flyers stop by to thank him for the company's product in saving their lives, Robertson created the club. Upon a claim for admission into the Goldfish Club, the inductee was issued a laminated membership card, and was allowed to wear an unofficial and unauthorized cloth badge that consisted of a golden-colored fish sitting on top of blue waves. The cloth badge was worn under the left-hand pocket of the battle dress uniform.[62]

Flying his Hurricane with others from the squadron, Blondie and two other aircraft attacked a boat hidden in one of the many coves on the southeast side of the island. Attacking from the sea, right after firing his rockets mounted under the wings of his Hurricane, he heard two thumps, and his engine lost speed. Calling out a Mayday, he glided away from the island, about a half a mile off-shore, and prepared for his water landing, which he described as hitting concrete. Fortunately, the aircraft stayed afloat and he walked out on the wing, deploying his rubber dinghy. Protected by the German machine guns firing at him from the shore by some Spitfires that circled overhead, he was picked up a couple hours later by an American PBY flying boat, and flown to Bari. Once in Bari, he spent three days in hospital for the head wound he got when he hit the water. This crash did not slow him down. He was soon back in the fight and was shot down again in August 1944, after attacking two enemy schooners. This time, he floated around in the Adriatic for 12 hours and then was stranded on a rock outcrop for five days before being rescued.[63]

The same day that Blondie was shot down, troops from the No. 40 Royal Marine Commandos landed with some artillery on the north coast of Korčula to shell the coastal artillery positions at Orebić on the Pelješac peninsula. To conceal their positions on the island, they had disguised an LCI as a gunboat that was in the channel between Korčula and the peninsula, just out of the range of the German guns. Every time the commandos fired their artillery from the island, the LCI would send out puffs of smoke to make the Germans think the bombardment was coming from the "gunboat." The ruse worked. After harassing the Germans, the commandos boarded their craft and went back to Vis.[64]

July 20, 1944, was the famous assassination attempt on Hitler's life by Claus von Staffenburg and his ring of assassins that included many high-ranking and respected individuals in the German army. Gottfried completed his radio shift that day at 4pm, when the news was not yet out about the failed attempt on Hitler's life. About 8pm, the news service broadcasted the incident, but it appeared to have caused no concerns for Gottfried and others in his unit. He made no diary entries related to his thoughts concerning the failed attempt on the Führer's life. After the broadcast, at 9pm, he went to bed. The following day when he was on night duty, he listened to a speech by the Führer, Göring, and Dönitz. This was the only entry in his diary for the 21st.

On July 31, there was another known raid on the island as part of Operation *Decomposed II*. Here, a convoy of MGBs, ramped cargo lighters, and LCIs carrying 170 Partisans, nine field artillery pieces, and their crews, set sail from Komiža harbor on Vis for Korčula. Hiding in a cove at the island of Lastovo, a small island just south of Korčula, the raiding party landed on the south shore of Korčula, and then shelled locations on the island. The raiding party also shelled Orebić on the peninsula, which had to be very confusing for the German defenders, since the shells were coming from an island that they supposedly had control of. The following day, the raiding force, with no casualties, was picked up and taken back to Vis.[65] Later in August, the reverse was done by the Allies. In Operation *Grandfather I*, instead of landing on Korčula, forces now landed on the Pelješac peninsula near Loviste, shelling the Artillerie-Regiment 668 garrison at Pupnat, again leaving the next day for Vis. Reports show that this group was also unmolested by the Germans.[66]

* * *

The raids kept going in August and the routines of Gottfried continued on: fixing the stuttering gg400, that was wearing his patience thin, picking up documents in the burning heat of the sun to take back to the bunker, and dealing with terrible radio disturbances. In addition to the heat, humidity, and crowded conditions in the bunker, bedbugs also became an enemy, forcing him to sleep outside on the roof of the bunker to avoid their relentless biting. Close order drill still continued where they marched on the south road to the south bay to demonstrate their presence to the citizens on the island, and raise morale among the troops. As usual, the food was questionable at times; he and Raymund supplemented it with figs and grapes. He also collected blackberries near their radio tower. One day, he wrote that he had horse meatballs. On another day he stated: "Finally after a long time a very good dinner—noodles with goulash."

Their garrison and the entire region was basically under siege by land, air, and sea. On August 2 he wrote that at least 80 salvos from Allied ships hit Orebić, with the Germans firing back at the ships. Then, the attack shifted to their base: "Salvo after salvo is fired… it increases during the next two and a half hours to a steady bombardment—18 ships were supposedly involved. At 0900 hrs. there is a pause in the firing—or the destroyers simply left. On duty, it was a busy day… message after message. I spent all morning with Erwin at the radio for a total of 10 hours. I take care of division messages. Erwin has 30 messages for the battalion."

Partisan activities were also occurring more often on the island. On August 6, the wire landlines were interrupted to the extent that continuous radio reception for days was necessary…"I'm ready to throw up—still on permanent reception. Combined with this, the… transmitter is done for—requested a new one… radio traffic is now sent through Navy communications that breaks down because of overload. The last few days are wild. For two nights we haven't had time to sleep." Four days later, they got a new transmitter and generator, and were able to establish radio connections. On August 12, the Tommies built a loudspeaker system near Lumbarda, requesting them to surrender. They didn't. Gottfried started sleeping in his clothes because of the increased danger of invasion.

Some normalcy still continued. But the environment was definitely different, and their typical wanderings were getting smaller. Most of the time they went to the south beach to swim and bathe. Going into town from the bunker to see the movie *Tonelli* with Raymund, and walks around town still occurred. However, the Allies had caused massive destruction in the town. Even the monastery was damaged. One day when he and Raymund were loafing in a local vineyard, Berina, a local friend, warned them about Partisans in the area. One saving grace in August was that the incoming and outgoing mail system was still working.

Gottfried had to know that his time on the island was nearing its end. On the 13th, he walked Strasser, one of his comrades from his unit, down to the harbor to say his goodbyes. On the 15th, he went to the shoemaker to pick up a leather bag. He wrote that the man was a rascal, charging him 600 kuna for the bag. On the 18th, he wrote that replacements had arrived, and they would be leaving the

German troops from the 118th evacuating one of the islands in the Adriatic, retreating to the mainland. (Author's collection)

place soon. The following day, he purposely caught up on his writing in anticipation that they would be leaving soon, and that he would not be able to write for a while. Still he wrote, "Maybe I can leave on furlough soon—unimaginable."

On August 21, he had morning radio duty beginning at 7:30am. He wrote that there was strong enemy air activity. Later that day, it was over. He was told that headquarters staff was leaving the island, perhaps an ominous sign for the rest of the island garrison. Raymund was also ordered to leave. They would leave that night under the cover of darkness. One last-minute activity was going into town to say his goodbyes to Paul, his barber. At 7pm he also said goodbyes to his sergeant, and took his baggage down to the harbor. In his diary he wrote, "I stand on Korčula's soil for the last time. I think back to the beautiful time, even though at times it was very critical." A coastal sail boat took him and other troops back to Orebić where he was billeted for the night. He didn't know it yet, but now he would really be in the war.

CHAPTER 5

1944, The Mainland

In August 1944, the situation in Yugoslavia was rapidly deteriorating. The dominos were falling. King Michael I of Romania, with the support of members of the army and communist leaders, led a successful coup against the Axis-based Antonescu dictatorship. On August 23, a cease-fire was ordered with the Soviets, after which the Romanians declared war on Germany. Later, on September 12, Romania unconditionally surrendered to the USSR. The Romanians were now on the side of the Soviets.[1] Meanwhile, Bulgaria, another Tripartite ally of Germany, declared its neutrality in the face of the Soviet onslaught and began seeking peace in August with the British and the United States. On September 5, the Soviet Union declared war on Bulgaria. About the same time, there was a successful coup against the pro-fascist government by Bulgarian army units and communist forces that moved into cities and towns, seizing power, and overthrowing the existing pro-fascist Bulgarian government. On September 8, Soviet forces entered Bulgaria. On about September 12, Bulgarian forces were merged into the forces of the Soviet Ukrainian front.[2] Virtually overnight, the Germans were facing 450,000 enemy Bulgarian troops marching into eastern Yugoslavia.

On the other side of Yugoslavia, the whole Dalmatian coast was becoming more unstable. The Germans had decided to withdraw from the coast as it could no longer be held. To cover their retreat from the islands, the Germans engaged in Operation *Seidlitz*. Using commandos from the Brandenburg Division, on September 3, forces landed on Brač to engage the Partisans as a diversion to cover the German retreat in other areas. Then, on September 6 and 7, the Brandenburgers also attacked the island of Hvar from Split, where 1,800 Partisan forces from the 1st Dalmatian Brigade on Vis engaged the Germans.[3] Later, on September 11, the Germans started to evacuate Brač under Operation *Eisbär* (*Polar Bear*).[4] On September 18, the last of the Germans on Brač surrendered to the Partisan 1st Dalmatian Brigade, after their transport left them literally at the beaches because the rescuers were afraid of air attacks.[5] On September 12 and 13, Korčula and Mljet were done. Under Operation *Zirkus* (*Circus*) the last of the 750th and 668th were pulled off the islands and the western part of the Pelješac peninsula.[6] Rudy Wagner in the 668th claims that his guns were the last ones on the peninsula to fire on the Partisans. Because they did not have enough transport available to the mainland, they had to shoot their mules to prevent them from falling into Partisan hands.[7]

As the Germans withdrew, the Partisans rapidly grabbed up the terrain, while starting a new offensive in central and south Dalmatia, further destabilizing Dalmatia and weakening the loyalties of the German allies. On September 18, more than two companies of Croatian troops from the 370th Croatian Infantry Regiment, who were defending Janjina on the Pelješac peninsula, killed their German officers and joined up with the Partisans. Those that stayed were disarmed by the Germans out of concern that more desertions and more fratricidal killings would occur.[8] Even some of the more radical pro-fascist Ustaša were deserting to the Partisans. It was estimated that 65 percent of the VI Ustaša Brigade were lost, due to fighting and desertions to the Partisans, because the troops did not want to leave their homes. Last-minute Ustaša atrocities against those who did not support them, including Muslims, and even Catholics, also occurred in some areas.[9] This is what Gottfried was experiencing.

* * *

The mainland was already a hotbed of Partisan activities before Gottfried's arrival. In February 1944, Rudy Hansinger had completed his basic training in the Banat with the Prinz Eugen division. The fresh recruits were loaded into boxcars and shipped south, down to the Mostar area, where he said they were received with gunfire all around them. Once he was in the field, he was given an MG-42 and became part of the machine-gun team of four to five men, and assigned to *2. Kompanie/Regiment 13* of the Prinz Eugen division. He said: "the MG 42 ate ammunition like nothing. It was too fast. Too much. What we had to do was just give short bursts and then stop." He also explained it was very effective. He started crying when telling me about its killing abilities. Operating the MG-42 would be his primary role throughout the war. His education in German and Serbian from his time in Belgrade was also useful because he was sometimes used as a translator.[10]

In some cases, Rudy also had heavier weapons to use against the enemy. He said: "They also trained us in the PAK 37 (a 37mm anti-tank cannon). Then, you would get a mule to carry the gun that came apart in pieces. Their backs would always get sore if you did not have enough blankets and the mules' backs would fester. So, we lost a weapon through the loss of a mule, not the weapon."[11] And sometimes the paths they took were very narrow and steep. He explained that if you load a mule up with a cannon and other equipment, and you walk on stones and rocks, it is slow going uphill. And, when going downhill, the weight of the equipment is pulling the mule down, which makes it walk faster. To control mules going downhill, they had to put ropes on them, someone in the back pulling on the saddle or equipment to slow them down, and others pulling from the sides. If there was not enough room to control the mules, in some cases, they lost them in the steep mountain terrain. Then, they became the mules.[12]

They would walk the hills and mountains in assigned areas. The enemy was everywhere, he said:

> You can't march there without being watched. Most of the time you were on your own as a group. We were in squads. With heavy weapons, you have 4–5 guys, but our battalion commander would sometimes assign our group to a unit if they asked for a MG. We had small units out and then get a kampfgruppe [a larger fighting group] together if they were available. If you did not have a good sergeant with the maps, it was a problem. Most of the troops were farmers and did not know how to read a map. They were never soldiers—they were soldiers when they had to be… And, they did not have a radio to communicate with other groups or their command. They just wandered a certain area looking for the enemy.

He also said:

> Every time you make a move, it was a battle. Once you had contact with the enemy, you had to stay with them. If you let them go, they would disappear and become a civilian or a farmer… That's why you had to try to keep them together. They always had a plan to get together someplace else. They were always doing surprise attacks in small groups. We would try to surround the enemy and try to get another company and make a big circus out of things. They [the enemy] did not want to get banged up unless they wanted to win… The problem for us was always to get to the high ground.[13]

The fighting of course did lead to the death of Germans. Rudy said, "We had to carry our dead to a town to bury them. There were no cars. We had to clear the mines [in the roads] first to get there." It was always the Partisans that he fought. On one occasion, they met up with some Chetniks in a village. Nothing happened between them. He said Chetniks were easy to identify because they had beards; Partisans did not.

Hansinger and his company were also involved in Operation *Rösselsprung* that began on May 25, 1944. The mission was to attack Drvar, a town northwest of Sarajevo, to destroy the British military mission there, capture their representatives, and destroy supplies and supply bases. Most of all, they wanted to capture Tito whose headquarters was in the area. The mission was supposed to be a secret, but Rudy said that they knew the plan in advance. Using SS paratroopers and gliders that landed at Drvar, along with ground forces that advanced in all directions toward the city, it was a well-designed plan. During the operation, Regiment 13 advanced west or on the left flank toward Drvar to force the 12,000-strong enemy to the west, seizing towns and the rail line along the way. Encountering strong enemy resistance along the way with attacks from Allied aircraft, it was a long and hard fight, lasting until the first week of June. While the operation was declared a victory by the Germans, Tito was not captured and fled to Italy after being rescued by Allied aircraft. But they did capture his dress uniform that they found in his headquarters in a cave just outside of Drvar. About 1,400 Partisans were killed, and the Germans temporarily gained some ground in northwest Bosnia.[14]

For his work in *Rösselsprung*, Rudy was promoted to the rank of *Unterscharführer* or sergeant. He was also awarded the Iron Cross Second Class, and the black wound badge. He said he was not sure why he got the Iron Cross. The wound medal was easy to explain. He told me that he was wounded multiple times throughout the war. When I asked him why he did not receive higher grades of the wound badge, such as silver for three or more wounds, his response was simple and to the point: "Nobody keeps track of their wounds in battle. The main goal was to stay alive."[15]

From there, Regiment 13 wound its way through Bosnia and beyond. Rudy said that he never really made it to the Adriatic coast. During his time in Bosnia, he was in Mostar two or three times. He recalled that in Mostar there was a copper mine: "I remember crossing the bridge. It was fascinating." They were also south in the Neretva river valley in Metković, and then they went south to Kotor in Montenegro, where his father served in World War I. From there, they made their way north into Montenegro, stopping for a day in Nikšić, and then moving and fighting their way to the Eastern Front to meet the Bulgarians and Soviets.[16]

* * *

While Rudy Hansinger was in Bosnia, Gottfried was basically in the lead of other units and troops who were leaving the islands and the Dalmatian coastline. On August 22, Gottfried was awake at 7am, and by 4pm, he was leaving Orebić in a mule caravan over to Trepanj, a port on the north coast of the Peljesac Peninsula that served as a ferry stop across to the German held port of Ploče, which was near the mouth of the Neretva River. He wrote that it was a difficult march from Orebić. It was an uphill and downhill trek. From Orebić, there is only one road between the two towns that follows the contour of the mountains, rising up about 500 meters in some locations. His trip was most likely under the enemy's eyes. In the 21st century, the trip is about 30 minutes by car. But in 1944, it was a different situation.

Winding up to the top of the peninsula, he wrote that got his last look at Korčula. By 8:30pm he was in Trpanj, and waiting to cross over to Ploče. That night, he and the other troops had to sleep in the streets; he commented in his diary that "I think of my soft bed at home—ouch." On the morning of the 23rd, he went swimming in the harbor at Trpanj, drinking wine in the evening, and waited to cross over. This would be his last swim in the Adriatic. At 9pm, their boat arrived to take them over to Ploče, which is on the Croatian mainland. However, they could not immediately leave because of English MTBs or MGBs patrolling the waters in the area. He and others spent the night on the boat, "sitting on my hocks half asleep," waiting until it was safe enough to make the 17-kilometer crossing to the mainland. Finally, at 4:15am, the boat left for Ploče.

Once in Ploče, he met a few more comrades from his company where they prepared for their train ride east to Metković. Located in Croatia, close to the border of Bosnia and Herzegovina, Metković is about 25 kilometers east of Ploče, over the mountains, and about 50 kilometers south of Mostar. Just a short distance inland from the Adriatic, its location on the Neretva river in the Neretva river valley served as a gateway to the entire valley and the town of Mostar itself. It was also part of the important rail line for the movement of troops, supplies, and bauxite that was desperately needed for aluminum production in the Reich.[17] And the rail line went all the way to Sarajevo, serving as a vital connection in that part of Bosnia. Metković was a strategic location that needed to be held against the Partisans.

The trip to Metković was also delayed because of the Partisans. The train before them was blown up and was blocking the rail line. To pass the time until the tracks could be cleared, he, Raymund, and another soldier in his unit named Franz looked for grapes and figs in the area. At 5pm, the train left Ploče, snaking up the west side of the Neretva river the whole way, arriving in Metković at 9pm. At Metković, he then went by rail to Čapljina to get to his final destination, which was Ljubuški, about 25 kilometers northwest of Čapljina. Contacting his company, he was told that there was no transport to pick them up. Again, he would have to sleep that night on the ground at the rail station which was "very hard, uncomfortable, and dirty." The following morning they wandered through the town, waiting for transport. Finally at 6pm, a truck arrived and took them to Ljubuški. Arriving at 9pm, they reported

The war was brutal. Dead Partisan fighters who appear to have been executed, lie on a road as Chetnik and German troops look on. (Author's collection)

to the master sergeant, and Gottfried got to sleep in the company quarters. The next day, he got up at 6am, and dragged his baggage to command station Kroell on the mountain. He reported to his chief at midday, and in the afternoon took care of his equipment. At 8pm, he went for a walk in the town with Herbert Delling and then went to sleep at 10pm. The following day, he got up at 7am and reported to Sergeant Maggauer for duty.

He didn't know it yet, but Ljubuški would be a temporary home for him from September 1 to October 22. Located in western Herzegovina, a few miles southwest of Mostar, and near the Trebižat river, this town, along with others in the area, was occupied to defend Mostar from attack.[18] Like Korčula, if there was not a war, the area around Ljubuški would have been a beautiful place to be in 1944. The entire area has unique geological travertine formations, including the Kravica waterfalls where the Trebižat river tumbles over 100-foot limestone cliffs to a large pool below. Other geological formations, forests, and gorges make the area a hiker's paradise. There is also the medieval fortress of Herzog Stjepan that sits high on one of the local peaks that overlook the city of Ljubuški.

Ljubuški, as well as other nearby cities, formed the new defensive line away from the Dalmatian coastline and near the cities and towns of Rijeka, Senj, Velebit, Knin, Mostar, Nevesinje, and Gacko.[19] This new front line for the Germans would use the mountainous terrain as a defensive barrier to protect them to some degree from the Partisans that were encroaching on them from all directions. The line needed to be held. By now, the evacuation of Greece was in effect and the center of Yugoslavia became an escape corridor between the Soviets and their allies from the east and the Partisans from the west. It had to be maintained to ensure that troops coming from the south could make it home to the Reich. Moreover, Sarajevo, the main transit point for German troops in the Balkans, was only 130 kilometers from Mostar.

This part of the Neretva river valley had already experienced the war and a had dark past—and future. Beginning in the summer of 1941, after the fall of Yugoslavia, Ustaša forces rounded up Serb families from villages in the area, transporting them to various execution sites, using the same rail line that Gottfried rode on. The sites they chose were the natural limestone cave formations that formed deep pits in the area. One of the largest execution sites was the Golubinka pit located near the town of Prebilovci, about 25 kilometers southeast of Ljubuški. Here it was estimated that 1,500 Serbs, entire families from the area, were thrown into the 300-foot-deep pit alive, to die a slow death.[20] But it was just not the Ustaša committing atrocities. From May to September 1942, the Chetniks, in their quest to have a larger and homogenous greater Serbia, killed over 2,000 Croatians and Bosniaks on the left side of the Neretva river, forcing many others to flee the area.[21] In a letter sent to Mihailović in early September, Petar Baćović, a Chetnik commander in the area, wrote that his troops had destroyed 17 villages from Ljubuški to Vrgorac, killing all males 15 years or older, while skinning alive three Catholic priests.[22] The same report also stated that the east side of the Neretva was free of Croats.[23] Because of the atrocities, Muslims sometimes formed their own militias, called Green Cadres, to defend themselves; the NDH was not protecting them from Chetnik violence. All of these actions occurred under the watchful eye of the Italian occupiers that considered the Chetniks their allies.[24] The Partisans also extracted their vengeance on collaborators in the area in 1945 when they finally seized the Neretva river valley. In 2010 and 2011, the skeletal remains of 60 persons in and around Ljubuški were exhumed; some of the older citizens recalled that they were executed by the Partisans.[25] No side had clean hands or a clean conscience in this war.

From September 28–30, Gottfried's days followed a similar routine: guard duty at 7am, digging ditches for the defense of the area, close order drill, and radio duty at 3pm. There was very little radio traffic these days. He wrote that he was bored stiff. To assist them in securing the area, the IX Ustaša Brigade was created from garrisons in Herzegovina and southern Dalmatia to protect the Neretva valley south to the Adriatic. Beginning in September and into October, the IX Brigade suffered heavy losses from the Partisans in the area.[26] Croatian troops were originally there too. But, because of what happened with Croatian forces deserting on the coast, and killing German officers, they were ordered out of Ljubuški.[27]

While Gottfried's diary is silent on what he did in Ljubuški in October, the area was nevertheless alive with enemy activity. To the north of Ljubuški, Livno fell to the Partisans on October 10. Later, on the 17th, the Germans started to evacuate Dubrovnik on the coast.[28] Partisan forces soon entered Dubrovnik on the 18th, followed by mass executions. Some of those executed were prominent intellectuals who were taken to the nearby island of Daksa and sentenced to death by firing squad by the Partisan Court of the Military Command for the South Dalmatian Region. They were buried in mass graves. In 2009, forensic anthropologists discovered two mass graves that held 53 victims.[29] During Gottfried's stay in Ljubuški, there was also one report of Partisans exchanging captured Germans for Partisan prisoners. The exchange took place on a bridge over the Trebizat river, just outside of Ljubuški.[30]

The Air War

The air war over Yugoslavia was intense in the second half of 1944. Bombers from the 15th Air Force flew over Yugoslavia to targets in Romania, Austria, Germany, and Poland, almost on a daily basis. Cities and strategic locations throughout Yugoslavia were also targets. One B-24 crewman, a tail gunner, who flew over Yugoslavia on many missions was Fred Lashinsky. Born in New York, Lashinsky was drafted into the Army Air Corps in 1943. By early 1944, Lashinsky was receiving his basic training in Miami Beach, living in a hotel and training in the streets and parks in the area. He then went to aerial gunnery training in Panama City at Tyndall Field, and from there went to Lincoln, Nebraska, for crew make up, and then to Pueblo Colorado for crew training.[31]

The crew picked up their brand new B-24 in Topeka, Kansas. Being the original crew of the aircraft, they had the privilege of naming it. They named it *General Delivery*. Each of the crew also chipped in some money to have its name and the Disney image of José Carioca professionally painted on the nose of the aircraft. From Topeka, they flew to New Hampshire. From there, they stopped at Gander, Newfoundland, loading up on Kings Cigarettes for 50 cents a carton because they heard that they were good for bartering overseas. From Gander, they landed at Santa Maria Island in the Azores, and then flew onto Marrakesh, Morocco, and finally to Tunis, where the plane crash landed due to a faulty landing strut. Tunis was the final resting place of the *General Delivery*. It never saw combat. Lashinsky and the rest of the crew had to wait for two weeks until a Women's Airforce Service Pilot (WASP) unit could get them to their new home in San Giovanni, Italy with the 740th Bomb Squadron, 455th Bomb Group, and 304th Bomb Wing of the 15th Army Air Corps.

Little did Fred know that this would be one of four crashes that he would experience in his service as the tail gunner in a B-24. His second crash landing happened on February 21, 1944, when they were the lead plane on their bombing raid to the marshalling yards in Vienna. Just as they dropped their bombs, a dud flak round tore through the underbelly of the aircraft, just behind the co-pilot's seat, exiting the top of the aircraft, near the top turret. The plane made it back, but was scrapped due to its extensive damage.

His third crash occurred on October 14, 1944, after Lashinsky's B-24 successfully bombed the Odertal oil refinery in Germany. On the way there, one of the aircraft's engines had supercharger problems, resulting in the aircraft barely keeping up with the group. He recalled:

> When you go on a bomb run, they go to full military power, and they just pulled away from us and we're all by ourselves and we went over the target, dropped the bombs, and we turned to go back now and there was no one else around us... We were developing more trouble and using more gasoline than necessary and losing altitude because of the engine not operating correctly... What we started to do is we jettisoned all of our ammunition... we stripped our guns and everything that we could throw overboard. We threw everything overboard that was not absolutely necessary to keep on flying, and we finally got in a undercast and we're heading back to our base but then it became apparent that we were too low to cross some of the mountain ranges in Yugoslavia... and besides it was questionable about the amount of gas. In the rec room [back at the base] they had a map... a full wall size map of Europe and it showed the area that we are involved with in Europe, our bombing area, and it showed fields of fire and other anti-aircraft guns in all the different places they knew... also Yugoslavia was color coded depending on your probability of being picked up by Partisans or Chetniks. And, so we picked an area that would have a 90% chance of being picked up by one of the groups, the Chetniks or the Partisans, and we bailed out over there... and since I was the youngest, they made me go out first because they weren't too sure that if they left me on board that I would jump out, but anyway...

When I jumped out, I wanted to make sure that the parachute would open, so I pulled the rip cord pretty soon, but nothing happened. Well, I was surprised how pretty calm I was, scared but calm, and I thought maybe the pins that hold the chute closed might have been bent and maybe I didn't pull hard enough. So then I ripped the D-ring with two hands and the chute did open. As I got close to the ground it looked like I was going to come down on the mountainside that was covered with fir trees… and so I covered my face and crossed my legs, so I wouldn't get a branch up there. And when I hit the ground, I hit very hard and it turns out I wasn't on a mountainside. There were a lot of sinkholes in this one area in Yugoslavia, and I came down into one of those, the bottom of one of those, and it wasn't fir trees—it was giant ferns. I think it might have been like 4, 5, 6 feet high. When I took off my helmet, I could hear voices on the top of the sinkhole and I gathered my parachute together and hid it in the ferns and loosened up my 45 in case I needed it… I didn't take it out, I just took the strap off and so it's, you know readily available, and I started crawling up the side of the sink hole. And, when I did as soon as I got the surface, I looked and I saw a group of women and children, and they saw me the same time and stopped dead in their tracks.[32]

Soon after, some men with rifles showed up. Lashinsky pulled out what was known as a blood chit to show to the crowd that he was an American, while also saying "Amerikanski" to them. A piece of fabric about the size of a standard sheet of paper, these rescue patches had the image of the American flag on it, along with a statement in about eight different languages for the area the crews were in, stating that he was a downed American flyer, and needed help. And for their help, they would receive a reward. After verifying that he was an American, one of the men reached out and started shaking his hand, followed by everyone else. One of the Partisans could speak a little English, warning him that Germans were in the area and that they may have seen him come down; they needed to leave. After toasting each other with some rakija that one of the women brought with her to the site, they were on their way. Lashinsky said that:

> … then they quickly took me to a barn and Cray King, one of our waist gunners was in that barn. They told us to take off our flying clothing you know, and in the meantime they made up a two wheeled oxcart with hay on the back of it… and I put our flying clothing underneath the hay and they had us sit down on the back [like a tailgate] and a patrol of Partisans went down the road and got to the first curve on the road, and they also sent another patrol up on the hill on the high ground running on top, and with hand signals they would signal that it was clear. We started traveling toward Sanski Most, and it took three days to get there. During that time we stopped overnight in two places. One was kind of like a Partisan headquarters at a crossroads on the first night, and a private cottage house with three floors I slept in the second night… We had passed German tanks and German trucks along the way that had been destroyed.[33]

Sanski Most was located in the northern part of Bosnia, which was part of the Croatian NDH during the war. Even though it was enemy territory, Lashinsky said it was really controlled by the Partisans:

> We could walk around freely. They had a high opinion of us. As we walked around the streets everybody would salute, you know you have to return the salute… they even had a hospital for their wounded in there… They assigned us to a house with a mother and her two daughters as the housekeepers. They prepared the meals and there wasn't much else they did. We were

on the 2nd floor. We slept on straw and they always had a sentry in that room with us... we found out later on that his purpose was to get us out of there and move us further up into the mountains in case there was a German attack, because that happened one time.[34]

The Partisans had the equivalent of a United Service Organization (USO) in the town, and they held dances in the town square in the evenings. Lashinsky and the other flyers would dance with some of the younger women who he said were dressed in old German uniforms, without insignia, and had grenades dangling off their belts. The women, he said, were anxious to dance with Americans. The band even played American songs. On one night during a dance in the town square the Partisans all started shooting their guns in the air to celebrate. Belgrade had been liberated.

About three days after the whole crew reassembled in town, they all walked out to a meadow outside of town to be picked up and flown back to Italy. It was pitch black and a big contingent of Partisans came with them, lining themselves about 10 yards apart in two rows, about the width of a runway. The radio man got on the radio when they heard engines overhead. He identified the plane as friendly. The Partisans had wooden torches that they lit up, and the plane landed in between them. The Partisans served as human landing lights. They extinguished their torches right when the plane passed their positions. In the pitch black, they loaded the injured and wounded first, and then loaded up the others, based on the length of time that the flyers were there. Since Lashinsky's crew were the last ones in, they had to wait for the next pickup, about three weeks later. When the plane was loaded up, the Partisan commander shouted and the Partisans again lit up their torches and the plane took off for Italy.

Lashinsky said that it was not too unsettling not to be flown back to Italy that night. He felt very safe to the point that he had already given away his .45 pistol to a Partisan; he felt that the Partisan needed it more and could make better use of it than he would. To pass the time waiting for the next plane, they walked around and looked at things around the city. He said that there was a Turkish coffee shop that they went to. One time, he went to church. He was the only American there and the parishioners sat and stared at him in awe. To pay for things, each flyer had an emergency escape kit issued to them with $50 worth of gold coins in it. He and his crewmates used their escape money to buy food. They would go out in the surrounding area to buy eggs, chickens, and turkeys to supplement the black bread that their housekeeper usually served them. There was even a vendor in town who had a food cart. It was the first time he ever had some pita bread, or the equivalent of it, that was served with some meat (probably goat) that was simmered with gravy and onions.

About three weeks later, they were ready to be picked up.

They took us out to the meadow in the afternoon, and I was quite surprised. There was a quiet kind of easy about it. What happened was a squadron of P-51s appeared with the C-47. They patrolled the area overhead, while the C-47 came in and landed and picked us up... It was much safer for the C-47. It could come in and land during the daytime because it was quite a risky landing in one of those meadows at night time and taking off in it. I'm pretty sure, you know, they learned a little bit more, and that's why I think they took us out in the daytime with the P-51s.[35]

When they got back to Bari, they were taken right to the hospital. They were crawling with lice, which was also one of their diversions while waiting to be picked up, hunting lice on one another's uniform and killing them. The hospital staff had them strip off their clothing, which he assumed was then burned; they showered, and were then powdered head to toe with DDT. They were then given pajamas and sent to their beds. A few days later, he was determined fit for duty and back flying over Yugoslavia in another B-24. On another mission in 1945 he would be using his parachute again.[36]

The Eastern Front

Another unit on the Eastern Front in Serbia fighting the Russians was *Sturmgeschütz Brigade 191*. As part of Army Group V that was destroyed in Sevastopol in December 1943, Sturmgeschütz Brigade 191 was evacuated by sea from the Crimea (Krim) in Ukraine, and unloaded at Costanza in Romania, in 1944. The brigade then refitted in occupied Poland, was redesignated *Sturmartillerie 191*, and was sent to the Niš area of southeastern Serbia.[37] Hilmar vonCampe was assigned to this unit.

vonCampe's story starts in 1943, when he was drafted into the Wehrmacht. He explained that he was an older draftee. Instead of being drafted in 1942, when he was 17, he was drafted at the age of 18, because a knee injury from a ski accident in Switzerland initially exempted him from military service. And he never served in the RAD because of the injury. But in late 1943, his injury no longer prevented him from military service. The Reich needed every soldier it could find. He was originally a member of the elite *Grossdeutschland Division* that fought and was eventually decimated on the Eastern Front in 1945. He had wanted to be a pilot, but his colorblindness prohibited him from volunteering for the Luftwaffe.

In his home in Alabama, vonCampe showed me his memorabilia from the war, along with some other items that his mother had managed to take with her from their home in the Sudetenland, when she and his sister retreated from advancing Soviet troops in 1945. Among these items were his Soldbuch, or military identification book, his Iron Cross Second Class medal awarded for bravery in combat, a Tank Badge for being in armored assaults, and his Grossdeutschland cuff title. He also showed me some photos of young vonCampe on guard duty, proudly wearing the cuff title. Looking back, Hilmar commented that:

> [N]ot being drafted in 1942 saved me a year and maybe my life… We were never indoctrinated to be a Nazi. If they had tried to make us Nazis, I would not have volunteered anymore. I went and fought on my own convictions… Hitler had the generals in his pocket, he didn't need us

to be Nazis. He needed us to defeat the enemy… I had always been afraid that I would be too late before we won the war to get into the army. I was quite excited to be in.[38]

He said that training in Grossdeutschland was rigorous and long. After about a year of training, he graduated and received the coveted Grossdeutschland cuff title, that was worn on the lower left sleeve cuff of his uniform. Fortunately, he was never sent to the east to fight with the rest of the division. Instead, vonCampe was transferred to the *Sturmartillerie Battalion 191*, which was a mechanized assault artillery unit that used the *Sturmgeschütz III*, or *Stug III*, a heavily armored assault vehicle that closely resembled a tank. vonCampe had no idea of tanks. In fact, he was never in one before he received his orders to transfer to the unit. Considered to be the workhorses of the German army in World War II, these tracked vehicles were used as mobile artillery support for the infantry. Because of their big 75mm gun and low silhouette, they could be used as tank hunters too.[39]

vonCampe explained that the Stug III was not a typical "tank" by design. Instead of a having a rotating turret, it had a low profile and a 75mm gun that would only shoot straight, serving as a field artillery gun that could travel with the infantry. The vehicle had a crew of four—a driver, commander, loader, and gunner. He was trained as a gunner; his responsibility was to aim and shoot the 75mm gun. He sat on the left side of the gun, directly behind the driver, and in front of the commander. It was a tight fit for the three. Unlike the commander that was often exposed while directing the fire and giving vonCampe the target and its range, vonCampe was safer in the hull of the crowded tank. On the right side was the loader's position. There was also a machine gun mounted outside the tank on the top right side that the loader operated. This machine gun, however, was often dangerous to use even though it had a shield or mantle on the front. Using the gun often exposed the loader to enemy fire.

After training in Germany, his unit was sent by train to Yugoslavia, the assault guns on flatcars, and the soldiers in "40 and 8" boxcars. He recalls that it was in July, around July 20, because he heard news about the plot to kill Hitler when they were in Serbia. The unit was originally sent to the southern part of Serbia, near Niš, south of Belgrade, to shore up a defensive line in anticipation of the impending Soviet onslaught. Niš was the location of one of the few road and rail systems that were needed to move troops from Army Group E who were retreating from Greece and Macedonia. He said that his unit moved around a lot. In some cases, they were close to Romania, and he recalls one day they actually went into Romania.

In October, he was sent north to fight in the battle for Belgrade. Belgrade, the capital of Yugoslavia, was an important transit and communications center for Germany. In October, Belgrade was under attack and occupied in part by Tito's Partisans from southwest Serbia and Soviet forces from the east. vonCampe's unit was in the fray. For two or three days he described his combat as a "war from houses," where the enemy was shooting down at them from rooftops, windows, and doors, something that he was not used to from his usual support of the infantry in the field where they were never in a close combat situation. Now, instead of a large area to maneuver to support the infantry, they were in narrow streets—not a good place for an armored vehicle that had a gun that did not traverse, and a vulnerable rear end and sides whose thin armor could be penetrated by anti-tank weapons, and an enemy that could approach and mount the tank at any moment. Unlike their typical field experiences, now they had to close their top hatches, and the tank commander, instead of being on top and outside of the tank directing fire, had to sit inside and peek out through the slits in the cupola or use the periscope to identify and call the range of the target to vonCampe. The targets were much closer than their usual artillery targets in the field. And, in a lot of situations, their targets consisted of knocking down buildings occupied by the enemy. The sound of small arms pinging off the tank's armor was very unsettling, vonCampe said. He recalls: "We would get attacked from the back. The Russian army was shooting at us. They ran into their deaths. It was pure stupidity. The commanders did not care to send them to get harmed. Anybody was a good target... They were targets."

After Belgrade, vonCampe's unit moved further north to defend the province of Syrmia, in the same area where Gottfried was. He was glad to be out of urban combat and back in the countryside. In his time in Yugoslavia they exclusively fought the Soviets and Partisans. He said:

> ... I have never touched one though. They were barbaric. There was not one soldier who didn't know what was expected when captured by the Soviets. We did not expect anything good from them... I can't remember what river it was, but on the other side were two women battalions of the Soviets. They had a reputation of being very cruel. So, we made quite sure that we would not fall into prisonership.

Throughout 1944 Hilmer said that "we were in retreat... It was always retreat. We went with our unit and we always had enough gas." Hilmar also commented on living conditions and equipment:

> We lived with our [Volksdeutsche] hosts. We ate with our hosts. The food was mixed up [they shared]. We shared our chocolate and cigarettes... with them. There were no German newspapers and not much to eat... I did not really suffer. We sat in our warm houses for up to a week while the infantry was in the cold. They had to stay outside. We had very good equipment. And enough. I do not remember any time that we did not have enough equipment. I do not remember anytime that we ran out. It could be up to a week at time before we went into battle. The people we lived with... they stayed. I don't know what they did. But I doubt that they could get out. I really don't know. Their fate would not have been very good. They were Volksdeutsche. I saw them [the Soviets] shoot others.[40]

* * *

In the later part of the year, the Prinz Eugen division was part of Army Group F, and on the Eastern Front near Niš and Lekovic. Transferred to the East in fall, 1944, the majority of the Prinz Eugen division was also defending the area around Niš against the Soviets and Bulgarians. Rudy Hansinger recalls, "When it got close to September, we knew the Russian attack was coming. They all switched sides. In 1944 that was the last harvest—August, Sept, October—that's when all of the soldiers I was with were thinking of their fields. There was no such thing as a leave."[41]

In October, the fighting around the Niš area was heavy. Prinz Eugen and other units were getting pounded and destroyed, trying to protect and hold one of the escape routes for Army Group E coming out of the southern Balkans. Hansinger explained what his unit had to do: "We were supposed to keep the roads clear. Every time they blocked the roads, they rang the bell and Prinz Eugen had to come. Those guys were sitting and waiting to get home. Our farms, our families, have been murdered at the same time, and we're supposed to… that was a crime. If they just grabbed a couple guns they could have opened the roads themselves. We could not do anything about our villages. More than a hundred were burned."

Finally, the Bulgarians were breaking through the lines around Niš, and they could no longer be held. Hansinger said that one day, "All of the trucks were burning in the road. Bulgarians came down the road and shot them all up. Partisans all over—all the hills were taken. It was the end of the retreat of the soldiers out of Greece."

On October 9, the division received permission to retreat. On the 14th, Niš was lost to the Soviets. Getting caught by the Bulgarians and Partisans, most of Prinz Eugen's vehicles were destroyed, and the survivors had a five-day retreat on foot through the mountains.[42] Adalbert Lallier from Prinz Eugen also recalls the retreat:

> In three days of fighting we lost 90 percent of everything. We lost 90 percent of our trucks. My truck was the only one to have survived the massacre because I was skillful enough—I was the driver—I was skillful enough to hide it behind a church, and I was lucky enough to have escaped being directly shot at—I had to cross a bridge, and right at the bridge there were dozens of German vehicles destroyed by anti-tank fire, and I was next in line to be shot at. And I had my five guys in the truck, and I was driving like a madman, trying not to hit the bridge, but before I made a sharp turn, I decided to stop just for a brief moment. I don't know what made me stop. And at that moment I stopped, the shot from the anti-tank weapon buzzed by the front of the windshield of the car. And then I just so… noticed that, they needed about 17 seconds for a second shot, and I accelerated and got away. I was the only funkwagen who was saved from the whole division. The division had 37 wireless communication trucks.[43]

The loss of Niš and the surrounding area resulted in one of Army Group E's main road and rail routes for its evacuation being eliminated. The 250–300,000 troops and 10,000 vehicles that stretched in a column more than 1,000 kilometers in length, slowly moving north out of Greece and Macedonia, were now forced to move up through Kosovo, and then up through the Drina valley and then Sarajevo to make their escape.[44] In December, the majority of a battered and war-weary Army Group E did make it to the Syrmian front, after losing an estimated 35,000 troops in October and November along the way.[45]

The Prinz Eugen troops worked their way north from the Niš area, moving up towards Belgrade, that had recently been lost, and beyond. In Kraljevo, a city south of Belgrade, Rudy's cousin, also serving in the Prinz Eugen, was killed. In December, Hansinger also found himself close to home in the Banat on the Syrmian front after making it out of the Niš area:

> I came through Brod. That was just before Christmas, and there were many Catholics. There was a settlement nearby, so they had priests. A family invited me to come to eat with them, but they were Muslims. That was the first time I was in one of those houses. The whole side of the wall was beds. For me, it was nice. They were friendly, nice. The same thing you found with a Serbian family. They probably think, what is going to happen to us now? They had to be nice.[46]

The Syrmian Front

On October 22, Gottfried was on the move again, this time to the Eastern Front. Already, other battalions from the 750th had been sent east, fighting in the battle for Belgrade in October. By the end of the battle for Belgrade, which was lost, the strength of the two battalions was estimated only at 180 men.[47] From Ljubuški, they went back to the rail station at Čapljina, and took the train to Mostar. From Mostar, he went by rail to Sarajevo and then north to Slavonski Brod, on the Sava river, on the Croatian and Bosnian border. From Slavonski Brod, they marched about 100 kilometers in an easterly direction to Vinkovci, and then another 30 kilometers southeast to the town of Tovarnik, not too far from the Serbian border. Unlike the hills and mountains of Bosnia, this area was a flat river plain. The division was now part of Army Group F, whose forces were tasked with defending Syrmia, an area that makes up a narrow wedge-shaped region between the Danube and Sava rivers and is in both Serbia and Croatia. If Syrmia was lost, the essential roads and rail lines from Sarajevo to Slavonski Brod would be lost too. These routes were the means of escape for the retreating troops from Army Group E that were fighting their way north from Greece and Macedonia and other areas south.[48]

To defend Syrmia, the Germans built a series of fortifications to protect it from the Soviets of the 3rd Ukrainian Front that were advancing north toward Hungary. Tito's Partisans who had recently helped to liberate Belgrade on October 20 were now also advancing north into the Vojvodina and the Banat where Syrmia is located.[49] Using the Danube river on one side, along with heavily forested areas, and the Sava river to the south as natural defenses, the Germans constructed seven defensive lines that they could fall back on, if needed. Reminiscent of a World War I battlefield, the lines were heavily fortified with trench systems, barbwire, mines, machine guns, and supported by artillery that were effective in slowing the Soviets, Partisans, and Bulgarians who were sent to the front.[50]

For the next couple months Gottfried was assigned to various locations and battle groups along the various lines of the Syrmian front. He also had another new activity as a radio operator. When not posted to the radio, he and others would now be outside, defending their posts, and watching for a possible attack from the Partisans that were occurring on a daily basis. Even with the fortifications in place, local Partisans were still a threat. And, there was also a new threat that he was not used to: the deadly artillery that was raining down on them from the Bolsheviks. Along with the artillery were the *Katyusha* rockets that were fired from launching racks mounted on the back of trucks. While not as accurate as artillery, the screaming waves of these rockets overhead and their subsequent explosions were unnerving.

For a couple days he was a radio man in the central station. On November 1, he was sent to the lines to be a radio operator with battle group Lindenblatt in Martinci, a couple kilometers east of Kuzmin. This was the location of the "Red Line," that was defending the major rail line in the area. He wrote that this was also the HKL—the *Haupkampflinie*—or the main line of resistance. The Germans had the practice of using the names of commanders, and not the specific unit, as an identifier. In this case, the line was commanded by Major Herbert Lindenblatt of Jäger-Regiment 750. Later, on May 3, 1945, Lindenblatt would be awarded the Knight's Cross.[51] After staying there for a few days, on November 7, Gottfried went west to Kuzmin, a short distance from the front, where he had a reprieve from the deadly Russian artillery, writing that he had "a glorious and fat time as a farm manager," working and living on a Volksdeutsche farm for the time being.

Gottfried spent a lot of his time zig-zagging the roads and towns in the area. But they were getting pushed back. On December 5, he was on his way west to Šid, a large city in the area that was southeast of Tovarnik, about five kilometers northwest of Kuzmin. Šid was located at the intersection of two major rail lines and on the Nibelungen Line, the next line west of the Red Line. Writing about the heavy artillery and mortar fire in the area, the next day, on December 6, he was on his way northwest to Tovarnik, a large rail center that was also located on the Nibelungen Line. On the 7th, he wrote that Partisan forces attacked the outskirts of the city. The Partisans were defeated, but the Germans were still forced to retreat. The same day artillery fire hit their communications truck while they were driving, destroying their personal baggage that was in the back. The artillery was so intense that day that they had to retreat west out of Tovarnik. The 8th was no better. He wrote it was pure chaos to the point that they almost had to blow up their radio equipment because they feared getting captured by the Partisans. To escape, they followed the rail line west to Orolik in the morning under "continuous enemy bombardment," then traveling back east about noon on the main road back to Ilača, about 5 kilometers east from Orolik. The same day he received his orders that they were to retreat at 5pm from Ilača. In response to the heavy artillery that day, the Germans also fought back with their own artillery.

About 5pm on December 8, Gottfried's partner radio communications center was already on the move, along with the infantry who were leaving their positions at Ilača and retreating back to Orolik. Gottfried wrote, "We cannot keep this position for radio communications… a mad drive across the plank road." They did get some relief from their artillery, making the retreat a little more organized under the artillery's protective shield. During their retreat on the 8th, they loaded the communications truck with seriously wounded men; he and one of his comrades named Ernst rode on the running boards to allow more room for the wounded in the truck. He did this all the way to Orolik. Under the cover of darkness that most likely offered some protection from the Bolshevik artillery, they dropped off the wounded and then drove west to Slakovci. But they were not out of harm's way. About 5am, they were attacked by local Partisans who fired their machine pistols into their vehicles. The Partisans were fought back, but Gottfried's truck was filled full of bullet holes that he saw when he got out of the vehicle. Not knowing it, most likely because of adrenaline and the confusion of the battle, he was hit in the arm with bullet fragments, writing that it was a "damned mess." Scrubbing out the wounds with iodine from the first aid kit that all German vehicles were equipped with, he removed some of the fragments with tweezers during his radio shift, writing that he had "terrible pains." After his shift, he went to the staff doctor who removed another piece of shrapnel from his arm. Instead of being evacuated for this minor wound, he wrote that he stayed with his unit. While the town of Orolik that he retreated from the day before was now safe, he wrote that Slakovci was now bearing the brunt of the Bolshevik artillery. They simply couldn't get away from the creeping onslaught of the artillery.

Slakovci would be his new post from December 10 until December 26. After his friend Sepp found them new quarters, they were tasked with building a new radio command center in a basement in one of the buildings in town, while under heavy bombardment. He wrote that a lot of things were going on and he was very busy working in the command radio bunker. There were no walks to explore the area because of Russian artillery, and the fact they were basically on the front lines. Incoming mail was very slow, in comparison to his time on Korčula. Letters from home were sporadic and very late; the mail system could not keep up with his movements. Now, his life was also subterranean. His day consisted of emerging from his sleeping quarters in a crude bunker, making a run for it to the command post to man the radios, and eating limited food rations. He wrote that the air was always filled with metal fragments, and dust and dirt. On some days, it was so bad that metal fragments pinged off his helmet that was now constantly worn.

Most likely some of the artillery support was coming from Rudy Wagner's unit. Wagner and Artillerie-Regiment 668 were now also on the Eastern Front in Syrmia. In December his unit went by rail to Mostar from their positions near the Adriatic. From Mostar, they had to march the remainder of the way to Sarajevo because the Partisans had blown a bridge near Jablanac, and the pioneers had not yet repaired it for vehicle traffic. Making it to Sarajevo, they then went to Brod by train. Rudy wrote that they felt really good. They had new mules, and the Goulash Cannon was under full steam. They were getting good food. Making it to Slavonski Brod, they were then positioned on the line near Vukovar to stop the Soviets who he recognized as having arms superiority, in comparison to the Partisans that they were used to fighting on the islands and on the peninsula.[52]

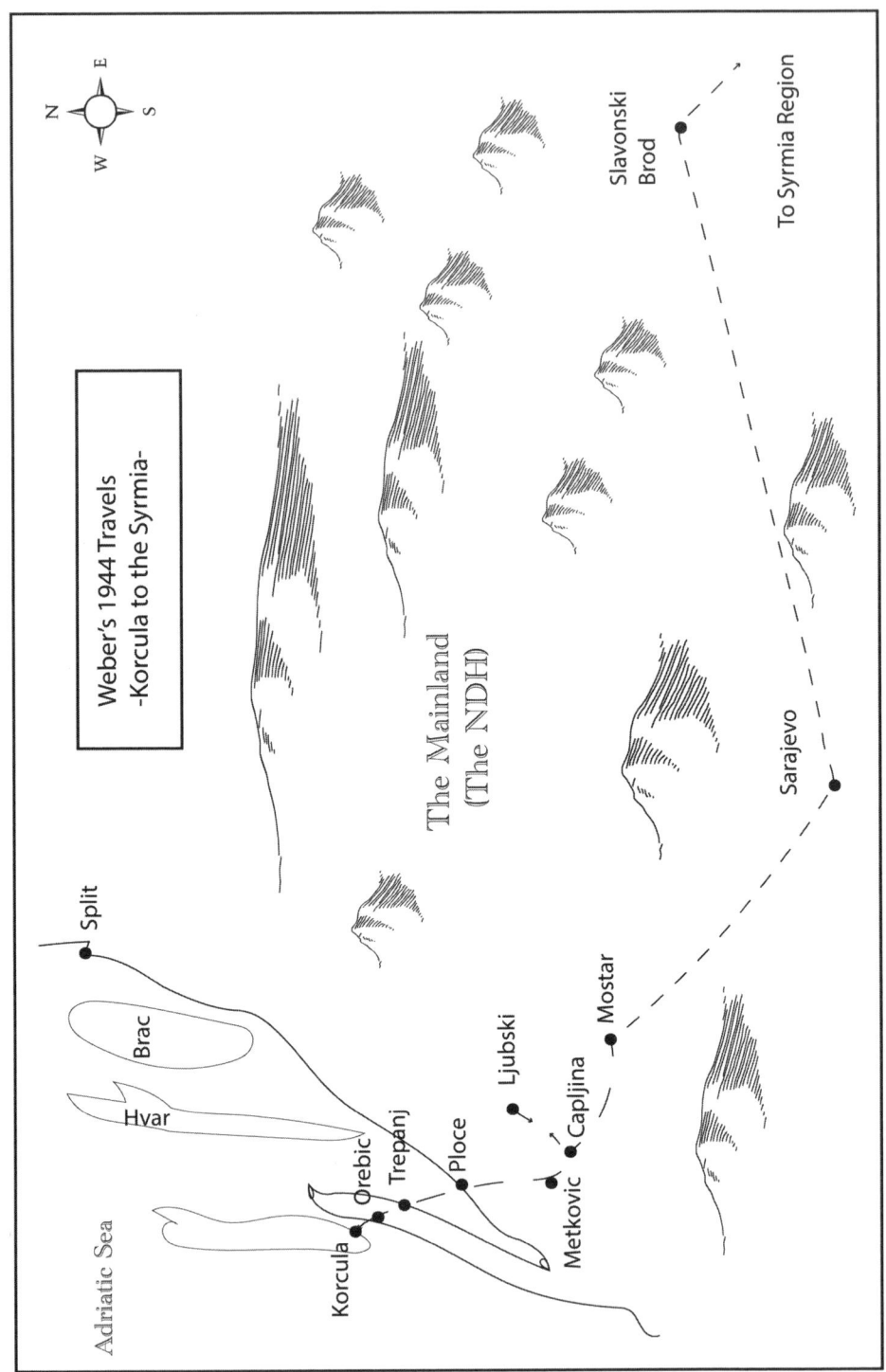

Weber's 1944 Travels
-Korcula to the Syrmia-

The Mainland
(The NDH)

Adriatic Sea

Split
Brac
Hvar
Korcula
Orebic
Trepanj
Ploce
Ljubski
Metkovic
Capljina
Mostar
Sarajevo
Slavonski
Brod
To Syrmia Region

N E S W

On December 20, Gottfried was recognized for his bravery in the battle. In his diary he did not explain why or how he was recognized for valor in combat. He was awarded the Iron Cross 2nd Class. Dating back to 1813, the Iron Cross is an integral part of German military history. In the shape of a Maltese cross, it is constructed of a silver frame that denotes the valor of battle, and it has a black iron core that symbolizes the drudgery and horrors of war. To display his award, he could wear the 1.25-inch-wide ribbon through the second button hole of his uniform. Wrapped and sewn through the button hole angling down at about a 45-degree angle toward the button flap of his tunic, it could be readily seen on the uniform. The ribbon was trimmed in black and white on each edge with a wider red center. The red denoted the national color of the Third Reich, while the black and white colors tied the medal back to its imperial origins before Germany was a unified nation, signifying the black and white national colors of the state of Prussia, where the medal had its origins. Along with the medal came a paper award certificate that was signed by the commanding officer of his unit. In some cases, the award document was signed by the commanding general. An official record of the award would also be entered into his Soldbuch and Wehrpass. It was a common practice to mail the medal and award certificate home.[53] There was no need for them at the front. In 1944, there were no longer any victory parades where soldiers could wear their dress uniforms, proudly displaying their medals. If anything, now his parents could show off the medal at their home, along with a framed photo of Gottfried alongside it, reassuring them that their son was honorable, brave, and fighting hard for the Führer and Fatherland.

The Chetniks

The Chetniks were also losing ground to the Partisans. Beginning in late 1943, after the capitulation of Italy, they were already on the run. In 1944 it continued. They no longer had the protection of the Italians and they never recovered from their defeats in 1943. Even though the Chetniks loaded up on weapons and supplies abandoned from Italian garrisons in their former zone of control, the Partisans did too. And the Partisans had more weapons, and supplies, thanks to the British. More people were shifting their allegiance, due to Chetnik violence against Muslims and Croats that pushed them to seek the protection of the Partisans. Combined with increased Partisan victories, especially when Serbia itself was invaded by Tito's forces and the Soviets in 1944, even more Chetniks defected en masse to the Partisans. Ustaše even joined the Partisan ranks.[54] The writing was on the wall.

In 1944, the British changed their strategy in Yugoslavia. Since 1942, the British had been sending Mihailović's and Tito's forces supplies from air and sea to help in their fight against the occupiers. The Allies also sent British SOE and American personnel to both groups to determine their needs, and to report back on their fighting capabilities. Based on the information from the missions, and intercepted secret messages from the Germans, the British concluded that Chetnik units were collaborating with the Germans. Combined with more evidence that the Chetniks were collaborating with Italians and Germans against the Partisans in Operations *Weiss* and *Schwarz* in 1943, Churchill determined that the Partisans were the people to support, even though they were communists. The communist issue could be dealt with later, after the war. The Chetniks, while still allies, and supporting King Peter, were simply unreliable. Their commitment to fighting the Germans was too questionable.[55]

Mihailović's "wait and see" strategy failed. Politics finally destroyed the Chetniks. On June 1, 1944, a new Yugoslav government in exile was created, and Mihailović was not included as the commander of military forces in Yugoslavia. Simply too many reports were coming into the SOE that the Chetniks were collaborating with the Germans to defeat the Partisans. Now, the majority of Allied support would be directed toward the Partisans. One of the greatest stabs was on September 12 when King Peter announced on the radio that all Chetnik forces should place themselves under the command of Tito's People Liberation Army.[56]

Mike Kristovic' said that the decision hit them hard. He felt betrayed, saying that "Churchill is the one I do not like much." What really offended him was that they were still helping out the Allies, saving Allied airmen who had parachuted into those areas that they controlled.[57]

In 1944, Mike said the supply runs from the Allies dried up. The shortage of basic supplies caused a lot of hardship for himself, the troops, and the Ravna Gora movement. Now, they had to rely even more upon the citizens to support them, who were also struggling after four years of war. Weapons and ammunition were really not an issue, he said. They were doing little fighting anyway. They still had weapons and ordnance from the British, and what they stole or received from the Germans and took from the Partisans were adequate. What was lacking, however, was food, and medical supplies. Now, their patrols included foraging for food and supplies more than looking for the enemy. On one of their foraging patrols, they found a B-24 bomber that had crash landed. Sifting through the crashed aircraft, they managed to retrieve a couple of the .50 caliber machine guns and ammunition. They also siphoned out some of the fuel from one of the wing tanks that they used to barter for supplies in a local town.

Clothing was another issue. The part-time soldiers wore what they had brought with them from home. Those that were Yugoslav soldiers still had parts of their uniforms, supplemented with British stores. Many of the full-time troops were now wearing German field gray tunics that were stripped of their insignia. They also wore German pants, boots, hats, and helmets. On one occasion, Mike said that he almost shot one of the men in his group. The fighter returned late to their assembly point after a mission, and in the darkness Mike said he saw what he thought was a German soldier coming into the light of their fire, wearing the tell-tale German coal-scuttle helmet and field gray uniform. He said that the only defining feature of many Chetniks' uniforms was the *Šajkača*, a military-style cap that was made of black or gray wool. Attached to the front of the hat was an enamel white, blue, and red Serbian cockade or some other metal badge that usually consisted of the double-headed eagle with a crown. If not wool, the cap was sometimes made of fur. Their Partisan enemy also wore similar hats, but theirs had the classic red enamel communist star pinned on the front of them.

For Mike, his clothing was a little more military in appearance than others he fought with. He showed me an artist's rendition of what he looked like in 1944. The picture shows a young Kristović with long flowing brown hair, and a quasi-military uniform that was a British battle dress tunic and pants. In 1944, his original military-issued shirt was beyond repair. As a replacement, a local woman had made him a shirt out of a white parachute that was retrieved from an earlier supply drop from the Allies. He said that lice had a hard time attaching to the silk, making his life a little more bearable. The women, he said, also liked to use the white silk for wedding dresses. He was also fortunate because he had acquired a pair of British boots when they were still receiving supplies. In 1944, boots were very scarce. Many other Chetniks had to make their shoes from tires. The rubber treads served as the soles, while the tops were made of leather straps that gave them a sandal-like appearance. When the leather uppers on the boots were still serviceable, they would also use the tires to re-sole their boots.[58]

Alfred Roehler

The Reich still needed new troops for Yugoslavia and beyond in 1944. Alfred Roehler was one of those new recruits in 1944. Roehler was from Schwäbisch Hall in Southern Germany. Like most recruits, he served six months in the RAD in Germany, near Eisenbach, constructing water storage facilities for fire departments in the area to ensure that they had enough water to fight fires caused by the incessant Allied bombing raids. Roehler finally got his marching orders in April 1944, where he was sent to the Italian province of Udine, on the border of Austria, where he was trained as a Gebirgsjäger or mountain trooper. Roehler recalls that:

> The base itself was nice—an old Italian barracks near Gorizia. There were marble floors and beautiful buildings—you know solid, like Italians build… really nice and vineyards surrounding it. It was a nice place except we didn't get enough to eat. Terrible dry cabbage soup and that's about it, and a slice or two of bread a day, one cigarette, and all the water you want! It was so bad… they had a storage facility there and they would unload trucks and trucks of German baked bread—army bread, and we had to unload these and stack it in there. One of my friends next to me let a loaf disappear under his jacket, and they caught him. It was so embarrassing the guy killed himself right next to me when cleaning rifles. It was bad. It was really bad.[59]

He also recalled that:

> The officers would organize a raid on the surrounding farms and whatever because they say there's guerillas there, but it was just to get some meat in the officer's club, you know. They would snatch the chickens and the bicycle and the pig and whatever else, and drag it home. And we all thought "oh man we gonna have food now..." They took it all away from us. Put it in the officer's club. They ate it, we got nothing. That's when the lights started coming on. You know. Somethin' ain't right here...[60]

Besides the food, equipment and training in 1944 were not good:

> The uniforms we got were too big, too sloppy, too old... hand me downs. Terrible. Good thing I brought my own shoes—that would have been a big trouble. We didn't have any boots. They had these regular working shoes issued to us, you know, and they wouldn't fit... these guys just throw it at you... here that fits... get outta here... Your shirt sleeves were hanging down over your hands by six inches, you know... roll, roll them up.... well it was terrible. I was very disappointed... the supplies we had were lousy and the weapons probably on the bottom of the totem pole as far as weapons... That's when I lost all my enthusiasm.
>
> The training was very disappointing... just a regular basic training like in any army... Got yelled at, run around, do calisthenics, go in the field, shooting, and that was about it. They had a Russian T-34 tank that they ran up and down the field, and we had to lay in front of it and roll out of the tank's way in about the last three meters and then jump on the back of it and put a magnetic explosive charge on it. That was about the worst of the training at all... It's a lot of marching... we had mock battles, you know, transition, throw grenades, barb wire, and all this good stuff. I remember I was in the hole with my Sergeant and he says, now throw the grenade. I pull the string... we had these wooden handle jobs... and I took the cap off and pulled the string and the string wouldn't come out, and I hold it up, "The string won't come out..." He yelled at me, throw the damn thing away! I barely got it over the hill, over the hump, and off it went. I thought the string had to come out, you know...
>
> We were treated well. Well, I must say they weren't mean or anything. We were treated decent. They expected you to behave. You know, be honest, don't steal and don't lie. As long as you march the line, you were OK. They screamed at us a lot, you know, but it's harmless, it's like water off a duck. Never got a day off, never got paid either. I don't know if that money disappeared somewhere else... And, I remember that during the day, we couldn't do much because we always had air raids. All these formations flying over high, you know. They chased us out in the vineyards to lay between the rows of grapes so to be out of the building, I don't know what that would accomplish. They were way up high... traveling from one end of the world to the other.
>
> I didn't believe that we would ever lose the war as a kid, you know. My first thoughts came when I was in boot camp and my Sergeant went on furlough home. He was from Cologne, and he came back after two weeks and said, "Boys the Americans are across the Rhine." And, I told myself why did that idiot come back? You know, I mean disappear... Come on! The war is over, but he was so... you know... determined to serve his country or whatever you want to call it, and he came back to us and he went with us all the way. I don't know what happened to him later—got separated after we got shipped South, I guess. He was a nice guy, but foolish.[61]

Nearing the end of 1944, he was finishing his basic training and his unit was supposedly ready for battle. He said: "After basic they took our battalion and split it in half and said: this is North and this is east or South rather, and the South was us and we went down to Yugoslavia and the North wound up to Norway and most

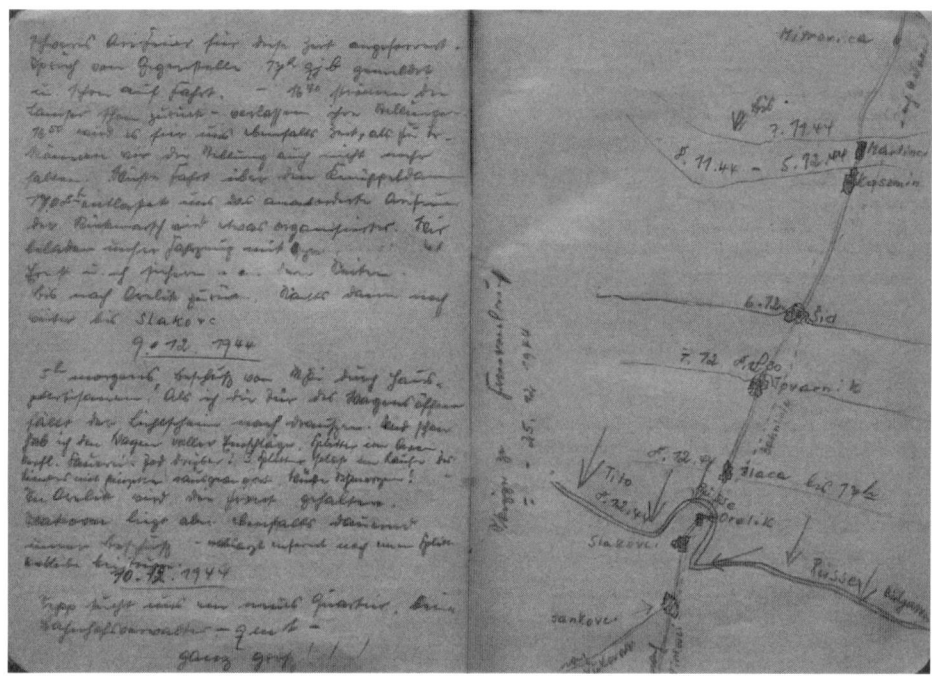

Hand-drawn maps from Weber's diaries of his movements in Syrmia in late 1944. (Weber/Author's collection)

of them never came home. We knew we were gonna go South." In 1945, he would be on his way to Bosnia.[62]

* * *

On December 27, Gottfried wrote that his latest wounds were healing nicely, even though he had problems with pus oozing from them. The company was also back on the move. A new command group was replacing them, and they were moving to Mirkovci. They started loading up in the afternoon at 4pm for the large rail center on the north side of Vinkovci to an unknown fate. By rail, they were on their way northwest to Zagreb on the 29th, 30th and 31st. He wrote:

> [E]verything moves slowly. On 31 December we ended up on a lonesome stretch of rail 83 km from Agram [Zagreb]. Rail lines were interrupted by Partisans in 50 places. A number of mines are being dismantled. Goebbels speaks at 2100hrs. This was a very quiet evening—no food or drink. In my thoughts I am at home with my loved ones. Such passed the year 1944.

CHAPTER 6

1945, The Twilight of the Gods

The *Götterdämmerung* or collapse of the Third Reich was fast approaching in 1945. Hitler's favorite composer, Richard Wagner, wrote about the mythological end of the world in his opera, *The Ring,* where the Rhine river was flooded by the gods, ending the known world. Now, Wagner's final act of the *Götterdämmerung* was playing for the Third Reich: the Allied gods were consuming the Reich in vengeance and fire, flooding the former occupied areas and Germany itself with Allied troops and destruction. Wagner's beautiful maiden Valkyries with their shrieking cries, flying over the battlefields, and carrying their chosen dead German warriors back to the hall of Valhalla, are fatigued. Well over a million German troops have already entered Valhalla, away from the pain of the battlefield and to an afterlife filled with drinking mead. Many more were still waiting for their ride to Valhalla.

The Reich was not giving up without a fight. On the Western Front the successful surprise attack in the Ardennes in Luxembourg and Belgium in December 1944 gave hope to the Germans, but it was starting to stall in favor of the Allies. On the Eastern Front, the situation was grim. The Soviets were at Warsaw, about to begin their new offensive in southern Poland and against Army Group Center in Czechoslovakia. In Hungry, Soviet forces, now including their Bulgarian and Romanian allies, plowed through the countryside with their sights set on Vienna. They earned every bit of ground through blood; the Soviet forces took huge losses as commanders and political commissars pushed their peasant armies into the juggernaut of death.[1] The commanders did not care. Victory for Mother Russia and Stalin easily trumped the death of a few million peasant soldiers. In Yugoslavia, Army Group E was still moving through the kingdom, trying to get home. A lot of Yugoslavia, especially the center of Bosnia, and the NDH or Croatia, were still mostly in the hands of the Axis powers, while the Partisans had become very powerful, thanks to the Allies supplying them, along with the flood of individuals joining the people's cause.

* * *

January 1, 1945, found Gottfried stuck on a rail line somewhere near Zagreb, listening to the Führer's New Year's speech to the Wehrmacht, assuring the troops that they would succeed in parrying the enemy's offensive operations and finally breaking them through counterblows.[2] He also passed away the boredom by writing letters, and complaining in his diary that his most recent wounds were oozing pus. Cleared at 5pm to move, they made it to Zagreb the next morning. From Zagreb, the train progressed northeast into Hungary, moving east through the city of Nagykanizsa about 10 kilometers, and finally unloading in Komarvaros on the 2nd. It was a relatively fast trip to the new front. From there, Gottfried went by vehicle north toward the village of Balatonszentgyörgy, located about a kilometer south and near the western end of Lake Balaton. In his diary he commented that they had to get used to the Hungarian language, and that Balatonszentgyörgy was a lonesome village. The food came from division staff, and he had enough time to take care of his wounds. Two days later, he was straight to work in Sávoly, about five kilometers south of Balatonszentgyörgy, and about 8–10 kilometers behind the front.

The train station in Nagykanizsa that Gottfried stopped at is still there. Its lobby is restored to its pre-war looks, in stark contrast to its plain exterior. The large steel girder canopy that once protected the rail cars and passengers from the elements was

Weber near Zagreb in January 1945. No longer wearing his tropical uniform, he is now wearing his heavy wool overcoat that is needed for the cold Eastern Front in Hungary. (Weber/Author's collection)

destroyed by Allied bombings during the war. It was never rebuilt. Much smaller in size and run-down in appearance, the Komarvaros train station is also still there, and very close to the only road that goes in the direction of Lake Balaton and through the villages that he stopped at along the way. With some imagination, it is easy to visualize the area filled with troops and equipment; the young fresh baby-faced recruits from the homeland in their clean uniforms, and the old veterans, like Gottfried, preparing for the next leg of their journey to the front. The well-kept villages that he stopped at along the way often do not have any name signs. Without a map, the only way to determine their names at times was to find the train station, if one was present, that always had a name on it, or look for a concrete culvert with the name of the village stenciled on it. When retracing Gottfried's journey, it also seemed that every village I entered in the Lake Balaton area had its own monument to the fallen of World War I that somehow survived the battles in World War II. The long list of names made one wonder how these communities, that were simply decimated of young men from 1914 to 1918, managed to survive.

Gottfried was now on the Margit Line in Hungary. Created in September 1944, the line was designed to protect the western side of Hungary from the advancing Soviet forces. The line ran across Hungary, from Budapest down to Lake Balaton, and then south to the Croatian border on the Drava river. Already, in the fall of 1944, the Soviets had penetrated deep into Hungary, one of Germany's last allies in the war. On November 1, the Soviets started their attack on Budapest. By Christmas, the city of a million inhabitants was surrounded. On January 12, Pest, on the east side of the Danube, was taken. Later, on February 14, the battle for Buda ended with remnants of the German defenders retreating west.[3]

From January 7 to March 5, Gottfried was in Sávoly, about 8–10 kilometers from the front. He wrote that Sávoly was a large village, having over 1,000 residents. For the Germans, it was a strategically important area. A road network ran northeast to Lake Balaton and southwest to Nagykanizsa, a major city in the area. A rail line and railroad station also ran in the same area, while the water canal east of the village was an ideal defensive asset. Based on his diary entries, things were not too bad for him in Sávoly, especially when considering that he was now fighting on the Eastern Front, and it was 1945.

Going through Sávoly in the 21st century, probably not a lot has changed in the village since 1945. Unlike other villages in the area where Gottried was that still have unpaved dirt roads, the main road is paved and lined on each side with a mix of aged pastel-colored stucco-painted homes, with weathered wood windows and shutters shedding their paint. Many of these had to exist in 1945. At the "T" intersection in the town is a yellow-colored Catholic church with its onion-shaped dome that Wehrmacht and later Soviet soldiers trudged by during the war. Next to the church is a monument to the fallen of WWI. Dated 1914, at the top of the monument sits the stone remains of a human figure holding a fallen soldier. The head and shoulders of the figure have long since been shot off—most likely from the fighting in the area when Gottfried and his unit were there—or maybe due to target practice by Soviet or German forces. What remains is the jagged outline of a human being, making it unclear to an observer if it was originally a man or woman holding the limp, fallen Hungarian soldier draped over the statue's knees. The old rail station is still there too. On the exterior walls pock marks from artillery and small-arms fire can still be seen and felt. Even though cosmetic attempts using paint to conceal the ugly scars of war have occurred over the years, some of the damage is simply too deep to hide to make the station appear normal again. No makeup can fully cover the lesions of war and the extent of the the heavy fighting that occurred in this area in 1945.

Gottfried was quartered in a Hungarian family's home. He commented that he spent the first evening in the host's kitchen, drinking wine. Because of language barriers, the conversation was hard to keep going. The weeks went by. Throughout his time there, he wrote it was cold and snowy, and mixed with thaws, making the area muddy. There were also the "Stalin organs," the nickname given to the Katyusha rockets used by the Soviets that were used to attack the German positions. The first few days he was on permanent reception until cables were laid and the phone communication system was established. After permanent reception duties, he was moved around to do signal work for various units who had set up radio communications in the village. Initially assigned to the command center, he was then moved to a mountain unit to dictate code, and then to the Luftwaffe command center on the 14th. The Luftwaffe assignment was new to him, and he received some training from an officer on how to directly communicate with aircraft. This also required a new radio that he picked up from the command the following day. Besides his radio shifts, there was close order drill, digging trenches, guard duty, and training new radio operators that were arriving at the company. Picking up supplies, food, and gas for the generators were also required, as well as something new that he never previously wrote about in his diary: political training that was most likely directed towards the benefits of National Socialism—in an effort to raise the morale of the troops. The second week of the month, he was also issued a new rifle for his additional role as a trooper in the command center; being so close to the front, when not working the radios or performing other duties, he also had to defend the command center from potential attack. As it was winter, fuel for the stoves was needed too. In comparison to his time in Bosnia and Dalmatia in areas that were heavily wooded, he wrote that firewood was sometimes hard to find.

He still had some free time. There were the mundane chores of mending clothes, laundry, organizing his knapsack, and cleaning his rifle and living quarters. He even helped his host family pick corn one day. That he wrote, was unusual, giving him blisters on his hands. There was also a cinema that was set up in the Catholic school in town, where he went to see movies including *Sophienlund, Immensee, The*

Girl of My Dreams, and *The Golden Spider*. Besides movies, the company had also set up other forms of entertainment for the troops. There was singing, unicycle riders performed one night, and on another night, there was a lecture on "Kohlberg and the old Nettlebeck" where troops learned about how a citizen's militia led by *Burgermeister* (mayor) Joachim Nettlebeck successfully defended the fortress city of Kohlberg on the Baltic coast from the French who laid siege to it in 1807.[4] On February 19, a general even stopped by the company to give a pep talk: "We can, we must, and we will be victorious," was the topic. Gottfried's contact with the outside world—mail—was still coming in, but it was slow. On January 13, he received the last of his Christmas packages from home. Other mail was more sobering, reminding him that the war was impacting his loved ones back home. In early March, he received a letter from his family that Waldenburg had been bombed on the 13th and 14th of February. This news was shocking to him. He wrote, "hit by bombs… the terror attack upon my quiet beautiful hometown… I'm still very glad my loved ones are healthy." Card playing and drinking with his friends, including Raymund who was still alive, sometimes led to him writing that they became "zigzagged," a slang term used by soldiers, meaning that they got drunk and were unable to walk a straight line. By the end of his time in Sávoly, his Hungarian improved to the point that one night in late February, he was able to have a conversation with Annuschka and Margit, a couple of local girls, on a bench in front of his host family's home. Not all his memories of Sávoly were fond. Bobby, the mascot dog for the radio unit, became sick with a bad cough that did not improve. He wrote that he was really attached to Bobby. The dog even slept with him at times. It was his job to shoot Bobby to end his suffering.

Spring Awakening

In March, Gottfried was in one of the last large-scale offensive operations of the war, named Operation *Frühlingserwachen* or *Spring Awakening*. Forces that were previously deployed on the Western Front in the Battle of the Bulge were refitted and secretly sent to Hungary to fight the Soviets. The operation would consist of a three-pronged attack on the advancing Soviets. First, forces in northern Hungary would advance toward and secure the region on the west side of the Danube river. South of Lake Balaton, where Gottfried was, the *Eisbrecher* or "Icebreaker" prong of the operation would involve the 2nd Panzer Army that would lead the assault to push the Soviets eastward. Further south, under *Waldteufel* or "Forest Devil," forces from Croatia would attack north from the Drava river. It was anticipated that this three-pronged assault would push the Soviet advance back, and encircle some of its armies, just like the Germans did in their invasion of the Soviet Union in 1941. More importantly, this victory would secure the oil fields around Nagykanizsa and southern Hungary that were so desperately needed. With the loss of the Romanian oil fields in 1944, Hungary was now one of the last large reserves of oil that the Germans had.[5]

Not knowing that he was involved in such a large-scale offensive, on March 4 Gottfried wrote that his departure from Sávoly was set. As early as February 28 he wrote that there were rumors that they would be going to battle near Lake Balaton. This rumor was reinforced by several other radio units packing up on March 1, where Gottfried and Ernst went from unit to unit, saying their goodbyes to them. On the 4th at 3pm, Gottfried's unit loaded up their trucks and were ready to move on, which he described as a "heart rending departure." However, they had a surprise reprieve: they were ordered to go back to their quarters for the night. They used their last day accordingly. They had an impromptu party at their command station, where some of his comrades, Borucki, Fleck, and Gresch, played dance music that attracted young dancers from the village. Soon, the room was full of young girls. Everyone was in a good mood. Besides dance music with what real musical instruments existed among them, they also had what he called their "regular concert," using combs and cigarette paper as instruments. He concluded his diary entry for that day writing, "it could have been so beautiful here." But they were moving on.

At 8am the next day, they left Sávoly in a snowstorm, heading east in a convoy of 17 vehicles into what he described as a sad and desolate countryside. Having driven the same route, I agree. The area is flat and rural, very different from the hills of Bosnia and the Dalmatian coastline. In the winter months, the cold, mud, and carnage of a war littered with emplacements, trenches, and destruction would further amplify the drab setting he was in. Three hours later, they were at their new assignment at the village of Szenyér, just to the south and east of Sávoly by a few kilometers where a new defensive line was established. The village was already busy with the artillery units setting up for the offensive. Living conditions here were much worse for Gottfried's unit than when billeted in Sávoly. Besides being "lousy cold" weather, he had to sleep in what he described as a hut. He wrote that at least it was warm.

The offensive began on March 6. Assigned to various locations along the line, his unit was responsible for securing the left flank of the attack, up to the south shore of Lake Balaton. He wrote that even though the Stalin organs were flying, their losses were light on the 6th. Made up of a collection of units that he identified as Commando group Steyr, by his account they created a 20-km-wide breech in the Soviet lines, on the 6th. That night it snowed heavily, and he felt as though he was getting a cold. It was miserable. The Soviets were not giving up easily. The following day, the Soviets broke through unsuccessfully, trying to storm a local forest. It was again lousy cold, and snowing. His feet were cold, and he was still fighting a cold in the damp bunker in the trench system. While on radio duty, he wrote that attacks on each side of the lake were being mentioned in the army reports. So far, they were victorious. On the 9th they also changed positions again, moving 10 kilometers to

Sávoly, Hungary, in the 21st century. Most likely not much has changed since Weber's unit occupied it in the spring of 1945. (Author's collection)

the southeast, some of which were cross country and not by road. At least he had new quarters off the front line that he wrote were small, clean, and cozy. On guard duty that night, he wrote, "One hardly lays down and we get disturbed."

On the 10th he was south of Szenyér. His days were much busier than when on Korčula. He was now in battle. He had guard duty from 2:30 to 6am to protect his comrades, while they established the radio connections. Finally, at 6am, he got some sleep in a trench, but in the afternoon, he now had to start a new task—digging anti-tank ditches. After spending a few hours digging ditches, he then had to build radio antennas with Ernst. Then, in the evening, he and a fellow comrade by the name of Spiegel were sent out to patrol along one of the local country roads to find Sergeant Sager, another person in his unit (who was late or lost) whose vehicles would take them to Böhönye. Finding the vehicles, they then had what he described as a terrible drive over soft and muddy fields.

In Böhönye, Gottfried was able to get settled in for a few days. He and some others were assigned living quarters with a Hungarian family and the host lady fed them well. He was also able to enjoy some free time, reading *Tristan and Isolde*, catching up on writing letters back home, and drinking wine. When not on radio duty, he was building plank roads, cutting wood, and performing guard duty. He

The Szenyér Line today. Gottfried's unit had to contend with the muddy fields in spring, 1945. In the background across the fields were the advancing Soviet forces. (Author's collection)

also had to construct a latrine for his chief. He also managed to get his first haircut in months. He wrote that his hair looked like a wig. On the 16th, their offensive was stalled. The Soviets had begun their counteroffensive. Within three days, the Soviets had recaptured all the territory they lost in the initial German offensive.[6] Little did he know that this would most likely be the last reprieve he had in the war. Now, the Germans would continually be on the retreat.

By the 19th, they were back on the move to assist the II./750th on the line. The roads, if they could be called roads, were so muddy that the radio truck got stuck around midnight in a narrow pass. All attempts to get it moving again were in vain, so they were forced to leave the truck and carry the essential radio components on a horse-drawn cart they found, without a horse. Making it to the front line and their bunker on the 20th about 4am, they moved forward into the trenches, establishing radio connections under heavy MG and mortar fire. The following morning at 10:30am, the unit counterattacked the Soviet lines and was successful in taking the railroad signalman house. After a short battle, the Soviets were forced to retreat. The Soviets didn't give up easily, however. That night, Gottfried was under heavy artillery fire as he tried to doze in their trench.

On the 21st, he was on the move again, writing that bullets whistled around their ears as they went to regimental headquarters that was a bunker in the woods. For their new assignment, they loaded up some mules with radio equipment and moved further away from the front. Using the cover of darkness, they made it to their new assignment on the 22nd, establishing their radio center in the basement of a building. One of the men with them went missing. Muli was nowhere to be found. Even though they looked for him, Gottfried and his comrades concluded that he defected to the Soviets. That night, he had some dry bread to eat and he actually got to sleep on an old sofa instead of in a corner of a noisy bunker on a dirt floor. He wrote that he was "sooooo tired."

At 7am on the 23rd the German guns were trying to fend off another Soviet counterattack. Running about 200 meters from his position to a field kitchen, he wrote that "the air is full of metal—a lot of action—the Russian answers with mortars and rockets." On the 23rd and 24th they stayed in this position, but by the 25th they were on the run again. He and Ernst had to carry the radio receiver on their backs, cross country, in conditions that he described as "under a glowing sun where sweat ran in streams." Walking on foot about five kilometers, they made it to a country road. In the process of leaving a wooded area, they had almost walked into one of their own minefields. He did, however, have time to reflect on one good thing that happened during the day. On their hike he saw a good-looking Roma girl: in his words "the first clean gypsy I have seen." Hoping that they could catch a ride to Böhönye, they waited on the side of the road. But there were only medical vehicles heading away from the front, and they had no room for them. They were forced to walk another 16 kilometers on foot.

They made it to company headquarters near Vése about 2:30pm that day. He got his first shower in a month, got deloused, and received some new underwear, writing that it was a "wonderful feeling." There was even mail available, but nothing for him—again. He finally got some good food too, instead of the typical Wehrmacht rations. His meal included a 300-gram tin of meat and about 150 grams of bread, along with whatever goods were obtained from the occupied countries, such as chocolate and wine. After their two-hour break, they picked up a horse from the rolling stock, loaded it up with equipment, and marched another 10 kilometers to staff headquarters. Dead tired when they got there, they fell on some cots for a quick nap. The next day (the 26th), it was back to walking to their new assignment. Up at 7am, he wrote that he had a good breakfast, and they were ready to walk back to the Böhönye area. His knees felt like rubber, he wrote. While pushed back by the Soviets, he was still optimistic: "The comrades up front are waiting for us—kilometer after kilometer—the sun beats down… we have some pauses now and then—the good wine refreshes us." On the way he saw some rabbits that he shot at, missing all three. At 2pm, they were at their new location. Sepp, who he referred to as the "old organizer," and the person who kept them healthy, was already there. He had found them quarters and food.

From the 26th to the 29th they were still in the Böhönye area. As usual, they needed food and supplies. With Sepp, Gottfried went on an "organizing tour," bartering with the remaining locals for eggs and ham. Later, with Ernst, they scrounged for telephone cables. The weather was still cold and rainy, while the Soviets provided their own form of weather: a rain of steel shrapnel that Gottfried and his comrades had to escape from during their organizing tour. On the 28th, they were ordered to move again. The Soviets had penetrated deep to the north and south of them, and they faced the threat of being encircled.

On the 29th everything was set for their departure. They started their retreat about 11am, moving north out of Böhönye. In the afternoon their column was attacked by Soviet aircraft. The first cannon rounds hit about 10 meters from Gottfried, followed by bomb explosions that hit about 75 meters away from the column. Nobody was injured in this attack, but a lot of their equipment was destroyed. The air attacks were continuous all day. About 8pm, Gottfried came across a severely wounded soldier who had accidentally stepped on one of their own mines. His left foot was only hanging by tendons. There was not much that could be done. Carrying their injured comrade to their vehicle, he and Ernst cut off his foot with a bayonet, and wrapped up the stump the best they could. To try to save the soldier, they left their vehicle column and drove to a military hospital in Kiskomarom, arriving there about 10:15pm. The "poor devil," he wrote: "He is going into surgery immediately to be amputated again—we receive high praise for our quick help from Dr. Lob—we might have saved the comrade's life—he is fully conscious—he thanks us, and we take leave. I look like a butcher, covered with blood top to bottom—that can be cleaned up…" They continued on with their trip to Kisrécse, just to the northeast of Nagykanizsa. That day, he estimated that they retreated 40 kilometers, which he wrote was necessary.

Today, like the rest of the area, there is not much to Böhönye. Two old dirt roads wind through the small village. Many of the homes date to the time that Gottfried was there; a plaque on one home is dated 1919, most likely housing German troops during the war. Many show their age. The only outstanding feature of the area is the large Böhönye Kriegs cemetery located at the junction of the two roads just to the south of Böhönye for soldiers that were killed in Somogy County. It was originally a cemetery for troops from the 1st Mountain Division, but from 1990 to 1993, other fallen German troops were reinterred from field graves in the area to create the new Kriegs cemetery.[7] In the center of the cemetery is a large crucifix of Christ, giving visitors to the cemetery hope that these young soldiers have found everlasting peace. A somber stroll through the cemetery shows that in 1944 and 1945 the cost was high for the Germans. Under the cold gray granite headstones that resemble an iron cross, the names of Gottfried's comrades are a testament to the long lost battles. Many of the headstones list "Jäger" under the name of the soldier. And most are young. A couple of his fellow Jägers include Robert Schrobenhauser, an 18-year-old from Traunstein who according to official records died at Drau u. Plattensee on the first day of the German counter offense, and Harald Steigmayer, another Jäger and 18-year-old from Graz who fell by Böhönye, west of Kaposvár.[8]

The 2,000-plus soldiers in the cemetery do not lie alone in their graves. Paired, or even tripled up in their graves, they lie together for eternity in perfect formation. Rank no longer matters here. Captain Hans-Joachim Pusch lies with *Gefreiter* (corporal)

Steffan and *Stadbsgefreiter* (administrative corporal) Steinbruck in a triple grave. Many others have no name, and are simply listed as *"ein unbekannter Deutscher soldat"* (an unknown German soldier), known only to God. They have not been forgotten by their comrades that made it home. A commemorative plaque at the cemetery from *1. Gebirgs-Division* states that "Those who die in war work for peace for all in freedom and justice." Another plaque from *11. Kompanie* of *Grenadier-Regiment 98* gives thanks for their fallen comrades. Personal notes and even photos lean against some gravestones. Willi Frishmann from the *71. Jäger-Division, Grenadier-Regiment 221, 14. Panzer-Jäger-Kompanie*, stopped by to pay his respects, propping a paper note against the gravestone of one of his comrades, thanking him for his own survival in the war, and in memory of his fallen comrade. Another gravestone has a photocopy of an image of a young Soldat with his wife, who was the unfortunate recipient of a letter from the soldier's commander, that most likely described his bravery to the end, and his sacrifice for the glory of the Fatherland.

The last couple days in March, Gottfried was back on the radios and on a westerly retreat. He wrote he was dead tired, and "[d]epressed—I'm pessimistic—how will this mess be solved?" While the enemy had been stopped, "my faith is starting to shake even though it always held up until now." The 30th found him to the west of Nagykanisza in a temporary radio quarters with their only means of retreat on the main road blocked. The roads west were jammed with destroyed equipment, dead horses, and retreating troops, with Soviet aircraft and artillery further sowing a path of destruction. The smell of death, and the sounds of battle, had to be overwhelming. The narrow black sooty smoke trails rising from the burning buildings, vehicles, and

Böhönye, Hungary. Many of Gottfried's comrades that fell in the early months of spring 1945 defending the Szenyér Line are buried here. (Author's collection)

equipment served to identify where the fighting was going on behind him. To the west were clear skies devoid of death, and clear signs of the hope of survival. On a good note, on March 31 he received one letter that was eight weeks old.

Lashinsky

While Gottfried was on the ground dodging Soviet artillery and Katyusha rocket fire, Fred Lashinsky was back in the air, hitting targets throughout the Reich, and crashing planes. On March 12, on his 25th mission, he was in one of the lead planes sent to bomb the Floridsdorf oil refinery in Vienna, Austria. The 747 B-24s and B-17s sent on the raid dropped over 1,600 tons of bombs on the refinery and other targets that day.[9] While the mission report showed that the raid was a success, for Fred and his crew, it was not. They were shot down again. Without knowing it at the time, Fred and his crewmates literally fell right into the Waldteufel prong of Operation *Frühlingserwachen*, not too far from where Gottfried's unit was located.[10]

As lead plane, it was critical to pinpoint the target because all of the other aircraft in the formation would drop (or "toggle") their bombs based on the actions of the lead bombers. To ensure that they could bomb the target in any type of weather condition, Fred's B-24 also had a radar set and operator on board. Just around the time they dropped their bombs, their radar set got hit by flak, wiping it out. Then, they received another flak fragment in their number one, which is the outer engine on the left wing. The propeller ran away, revving up to a very dangerous level. The whole plane was vibrating so badly that it seemed like the engine might tear itself off of the wing. The plane had to pull out of formation.[11]

The number one engine finally froze up. And when it did, the now dead propeller caused a lot of drag, and the Liberator started to lose altitude. To keep it aloft, they jettisoned everything on board that they could and headed for Pécs, Hungary, having been briefed before the mission that the Soviets had just secured an emergency air base there. With no navigation because the radar set was dead, and the sextant useless because of cloud cover that they needed to stay in for protection from enemy fighters, the pilot dead reckoned it for Pécs. Once they got close to what they thought was Pécs, the pilot started his spiral descent, breaking through the clouds to find the emergency runway. When they hit about 4,000 feet, they spotted two rivers and realized that they were not over Pécs. The two rivers were the Danube and Drava, about 30 miles south of Pécs. At the same time, Fred saw three German fighters appear at 7 o'clock low. To scare them away, he turned his rear gun turret in their direction, even though he no longer had any guns or ammunition to fight them off. His bluff worked. However, they also started receiving large caliber anti-aircraft fire from the ground, from both the Soviets and the Germans. Fred recalled:

… both sides are firing at us, and we got a lot of hits right away. The back end of the plane had some smoke in it and the pilot ordered a bail out. I think there were five or six men in back, and by the time I turned around to get out of my turret, everyone except one of them were out of the plane. Colt was the only one for some reason in there; he was gonna wait for me to come round the other side of the escape hatch. I waved to him to go out, and when he did, I don't know what happened, but the escape hatch came down, and when I got there, I saw a boot stuck in between the frame and the escape hatch. And I thought, what do I do? … I thought I would have been strong enough to hold it with one hand, you know, and open the hatch with the other. But when I did that, I saw he had just fallen right out of his boot. When I jumped out, I saw some big anti-aircraft bursts right underneath the wing and the number two landing gear came down and some person jumped out of the front section. When I opened the chute, the next thing I heard was the sound of bullets going past me because I was being fired on from the ground. And, so I pulled my shroud lines to spill air out of the chute so I would fall a little faster and also oscillate to make myself a harder target. As I came down, I saw that I was coming into… right in front of barbed wire and trenches.

… when I landed, a head appeared above the trench without any helmet or anything on, and he beckoned me with his finger to come that way. And I thought, well since he didn't take a shot at me that's the way to go, so I quickly unfastened my harness and jumped in the trench. The next thing I noticed was about 10 or 12 field gray German uniforms with the eagle and a Swastika over their right breast, and they had bayonets on their rifles. The guy that stuck his head above the trench put out his hand said "pistol"… It was amazing. Growing up, you watch these movies on World War I with the trench warfare, and that's what it looked like. I was in the midst of that kind of stuff, like I didn't know that there was that kind of stuff being done during World War II… and they took me to a dugout where a German officer was sitting on the floor with a metal desk, and they set me down in one corner there, and he and I were alone for several hours. I still had my flight boots on when I landed, and while going back with the guard that took me back to this dugout, my ankle started to hurt a lot. There were German troops coming up the road, heading towards the front, and they were eyeing my shoes that I tied to my harness. I thought if I don't get those on my feet, someone's gonna take them away, so I just sat down on the ground and put the boots on. I didn't take them off for several weeks because my ankle swelled so much I was afraid that if I took it off, I would never get it back on again. The soldier that brought me to the dugout was maybe three or four years younger than me, and he could speak a little English. He said to me: "if you manage to live for two months, you'll be a free man."[12]

Fred was eventually taken to Gordisha in Croatia, to a large building in the center of town that appeared to be their headquarters. He recalled that there were desks all around the place and there were runners coming in and out. There was a German officer reclining on a sofa, maybe taking a nap or something. He was taken to one soldier that could speak English. He was ordered to take off all of his clothes, so he stripped down from head to foot, and then they started to question him:

I just answered back with my name, rank, and serial number, and when the interpreter repeated it, you know, to the officer, he kept on getting more and more agitated. I guess he was cursing at me, but I don't know what he's saying, and there was also a big potbelly stove nearby. I could just think about visions of torture. Anyway, they questioned me about whether we had been in Dresden, killing woman and children. And, they were going through my clothing. I carried a little prayer book with me, and the interpreter looked at that and said, "you carry one of these and you kill women and children?" and he hit me in the face with it. I kept on giving my name, rank, and serial number, and he said, "what are you gonna say when we say we're gonna execute you?" And I thought a little while… I thought, well it doesn't make much difference anyway, so I gave my name, rank, and serial number again. And, after a few more questions they told me to get dressed and they took me downstairs and we headed straight for a brick wall… All the movies you ever saw flashed through your mind and we headed over there, and I thought, well this is the end, and they'll never know whatever happened to me because nobody would know where we were because we were so far from the regular area. But they just walked over to it, and made a turn and went down a street and into a house. When I got into the house, the other five crew members who had been taken prisoner were in there. I was the last one to be brought in. We were all happy to see each other and we started comparing what happened to one another.[13]

From there, he and his crewmates became part of the retreating German army. All of the others in the aircraft drifted over to the Soviet side, and were repatriated at the end of the war. Along with the Wehrmacht troops were some SS that he felt wanted him and the others dead. Fred said that he had the feeling that the only reason that he was kept alive was because that during the trip it became obvious that their German escorts wanted to surrender to the Americans, and he and his crewmates might serve as a safe conduct pass. For five or six days they retreated on foot. They were close enough to the front to be able to hear the shells exploding, the scream of the Katyusha rockets, and other sounds of the fighting. He got practically nothing to eat; he recalls that he got four rye crackers the whole time.[14]

Then, they were put on a German troop train in a divided "40 and 8" boxcar—a railcar designed to hold 40 men or eight horses. Leaving in the late afternoon, within two hours they were attacked by three fighters that strafed the train. For the rest of the trip, the train traveled by night. Before daylight, he said that the engine was disconnected and hidden close by, while the rail cars would be left on a siding. The boxcar was crowded on their side. On one side were the prisoners; the other side were the guards. Stuffed in the boxcar were the six from Fred's plane, plus 10 additional Americans, along with 13 Bulgarian officers, and a Russian officer. It was so crowded that they had to lay on their sides when sleeping. Sleeping on the hard wooden floor, they had their heads facing the outside wall and their feet in the center of the car. It was so tight, he said, that in order to roll over, everyone else would have to turn over too, in the same direction. Occasionally, the guards would let them out of the cars to stretch, relieve themselves, and find water from a local ditch or stream. Food was also limited. They would have nothing to eat for days on end. One time when they were near Zagreb, some local farmers learned about them being there and brought them milk and cornbread, which Fred said was delicious. Reflecting on this, Fred said that it was amazing the nice things that people will do in the worst case situations. He lost a lot of weight.[15]

The train continued on its slow journey north to Germany. The air attacks were not over. They got bombed in Maribor, Slovenia, and also got bombed out in Regensburg while they were left locked in a boxcar. He recalls that it was right around April 14 because the Germans were talking about Roosevelt's death. The bombing at Regensburg was so intense they had to break their way out of the rail car to seek shelter. Some other foreign prisoners who broke out from another rail car came up with the idea to kill the guards and make it to the American lines. Fred and his crew thought it was too risky to take that chance. They were better off for the time being with their German guards who treated them well, given the situation. The plot never materialized. From Regensburg, they were then marched south to their POW camp in Moosburg, sleeping in barns along the way. On April 26 they finally made it to Stalag VII-A at Moosburg in Bavaria. Three days later, on the 29th, Patton's Third Army liberated the camp.[16]

Bosnia 1945

While Gottfried was in Hungary in January 1945, Alfred Roehler was on his way to Yugoslavia. He said:

> We knew we were gonna go south. They told us already. We went by train to Vienna to get the winter equipment like white snow sheets and this baloney stuff you know, and then by train back to Klagenfurt… I remember that it was a rainy night. We only went through there by night, we didn't stay long. There was a whole bunch of British prisoners of war working on the tracks and I remember that they were singing and carrying on. From Klagenfurt, we went through the tunnel into Slovenia. And, as we came out of the tunnel there were P-38's from Italy and they blew the hell out of the engine. Everybody was out on the field you know… there was snow on the ground. I was smart enough to come out on the other side, and I hid behind the stone building, the railroad control building. You know, one of them small crossing things that they have down there. That's what saved my machine-gun group, and I jumped around the house playing peek a boo with the guy in the cockpit.[17]

After the attack, his unit waited for a few days in the local village until they could get a new locomotive. They had very little food to the point that Roehler and some others traded their newly issued camouflage winter clothing to some other troops for food. From there, the unit traveled south to Zagreb in open rail cars, covering themselves in blankets to keep warm. The whole time he had not seen a German airplane. From Zagreb, they switched over to the narrow gauge rail line in Bosnia and made their way to Sarajevo. There was no sightseeing in Sarajevo. They were immediately assigned to units and sent on foot to the hills. Because he was trained on the MG-34 machine gun in basic, he was assigned to an MG-42 machine-gun crew.

> When we got into Yugoslavia, we were issued the MG42. The gun was terrific. Terrific… just couldn't carry enough ammo 'cause it would eat it up like crazy. Then, besides we got ammunition from Germany, it was sabotaged, and the cartridges would rip off and get stuck in the barrel, and stuff like that. It was terrible. Terrible. We had a crew of three. You have the gunner and the number 2, and the number 3. Number 2 assisted the gunner, feeding the ammo into the gun… and you know get it [the ammo] out of the box and whatever, and the 3 was just a gopher, so to speak… We changed over, took turns carrying the big machine gun.[18]

Alfred could not recall any of the villages by name that they went through while in Bosnia. He said that it was all hills and they had to carry everything on their backs. He also said that in some cases, they had mules to carry mortars and other heavy equipment. Under fire, he said that once in a while a mule would decide to stop walking: "I still remember this like yesterday. The guys would carry a tin can, an old tin can with charcoal and a lid, you know, smoking like a Catholic priest in the church... They would stick it under the mule's rear end—man did they take off. I will never forget that. I will never forget that."[19]

His group spent most of their time defending a certain area, or simply wandering. In most cases, command would tell him to put their machine gun in a certain area to defend it and stay put until another unit came to get them:

> Our people would say: you get up here and hold his line. And sure enough, after a while you would get the first feelings of the enemy feeling along the line, and then the shooting would start. Then, they would try to penetrate our lines if we would let them. That's how it went all the time until the pressure got so bad we had to retreat... It was towards the end you know, and it's never fun retreating. A lot of us got sick, cold, cold weather... it's snowing and what have you—it wasn't fun at all. The food was lousy...[20]

He really didn't have any idea what units he was with. He said that it was just a company of troops that used the young troops as cannon fodder. He felt used.

> We were walking down the road and my Sergeant turned around and said "Roehler, you get up in the hill and check the sides"... you know, and I would be all by myself strutting through these bushes, up and down all by myself, waiting to be shot at. You know, it really ticked me off. I thought this guy is using me, he's trying to get rid of me. Yeah, one of the old timers, you know...[21]

They never stayed in barracks. Most of the time they slept in the field. In some cases, they slept in homes. He said:

> The Bosnians hated us. They hated us because we would stay overnight in their houses sometimes... They had these funny toilets and this stuff, and you know we don't take our shoes off, and you know Muslims. We kids didn't realize what we were doing there... walking around in the houses with the shoes on... we look out the window and down on the courtyard where all their shoes lined up like that, and we were laughing about it—it was funny to us at that time.[22]

The enemy was also hard to find. There was really never a concentration of them. Instead, they were scattered throughout the woods and hills, "They would hit and run, you could never nail him down you know." In one of his first enemy encounters, the attack was at night where the Germans went up the backside of a hill and down the other side where the Partisans were located:

> ... and we let him have it with whatever we had and they disappeared... kind of hit them pretty hard... and we went down the hill the next morning and collected the leftover ammunition. I remember that distinctly 'cause they had this good shiny brass ammo. We had all of this grey garbage that wouldn't work anymore... We could never find the Partisans. [23]

In another battle he said that the Partisans had some artillery pieces that were deadly:

> … and then we saw them running around here, and then we tried to take a shot at them and my buddy in the foxhole next to me kept yelling over to us—you guys, I can't see nothing, I can't see anybody… The next morning, I was getting ready to split out of there and yelled: "time to go"… No answer. So I crawled over there, and he was still looking out of the foxhole with a bullet hole between his eyes—eyes still open—so they got him overnight…[24]

April 1945

On April 1, 1945, Easter Sunday, Gottfried and his crew loaded in their radio truck and made it to Rigyác, which is located just west of Nagykanizsa. Getting there about 1am, he went straight to work on the radios. By 10am, the Soviets started their air attacks again: "Can't sleep any longer—damned shit—and that's supposed to be Easter," he wrote. That night, they moved on through burning villages that were hit by the Soviet aircraft, rockets, and artillery. On both sides of the road were burning and destroyed vehicles, along with carts, dead animals, and dead German soldiers who were torn up by shrapnel. Early in the morning on the 2nd, they were out of Hungary, crossing the Mur Bridge into Croatia to get to their new position in Muracsany (now Goričan). Column after column of troops and vehicles, in what he described as walking tempo, were behind Gottfried's vehicle, all waiting to cross into Croatia. The pioneers had already prepared the bridge to be blown, using leftover Luftwaffe bombs that would be electronically detonated. Gottfried wrote that "we are more than happy to have the bridge behind us…"

However, on the 3rd he was back in Hungary, trying to hold the last bridgehead. It was sheer confusion. There was heavy rocket and artillery fire with rounds detonating between the different radio centers that were located in houses. The Soviet fire was so heavy that he didn't know which way to go. To escape it, Gottfried ran into a meadow and crouched behind a heavy tree that was knocked down from the fire. Still optimistic, he wrote: "even that we'll overcome." Even though there were no losses, he wrote that the battles and subsequent retreats were causing "serious effects on our psychological and moral conditions." That day, they had to give up the bridgehead.

On April 5 they were assigned to Battle Group Lindenblatt. This would be Gottfried's second time serving with Lindenblatt, and his second retreat under his command. They were the third radio station with this battle group in the last three days. The other two radio units had to blow up their equipment and flee because they were overrun by enemy tanks. The regiment took over the Mur River defensive line and slowly retreated in an organized manner. Still in Hungary, on the 6th he was about 20 kilometers from the Slovene border, according to his estimates. The 6th was the first day that he did not have any enemy bombardment as they headed west. He wrote: "But what does my homeland look like? I would have never believed that I would return this way—it makes you want to cry."

For the next two days Gottfried was out of the front lines and the incessant danger of the Soviet artillery, aircraft, and Stalin organs. Now, the residents spoke German which had to be a comfort to him, being in an area where he could hear his native language. Even though the area was filled full of retreating German troops, with the help of Sepp who was stationed next to them assisting the artillery, they were able to find some quarters in the town. Radio traffic was also light, and he even had time to polish his boots—something that he had not done in months.

April 9–12 found him just west of the Mur River, where the borders of Slovenia, Hungary, and Croatia meet. Here, he had time to do his chores, including his laundry; he found a girl to do it in exchange for some coal that he took from a freight train. After going without good food to eat for months, they finally had some, including potato salad, from their host parents. Sepp and Ernst had also gone into the countryside to barter with the locals for some eggs. He had to know that the end was near. In his diary on the 11th he wrote:

> … today it occurs to me for the first time the sad recognition in my conscience how much my loved ones must worry about me—because they will hardly receive any mail from me. But no, I will try to fight my way through. Someday, this will all be over—going on for 16 months… my heart is unspeakably sad. I pretend to be happy toward my comrades…

Little did he know the next day that his family in Waldenburg would be experiencing the war firsthand.

Waldenburg

Waldenburg had changed since Gottfried left it in 1942. There were now two Wehrmacht hospitals, one in the left wing of the castle, and the other in a school. So far, Waldenburg itself was relatively spared from large-scale air attacks that were targeting industrial centers and large cities throughout the Reich. Beginning in 1944, however, there were some low-level fighter air attacks from Allied aircraft. One of the places that was damaged by aircraft included the castle greenhouses. The air attacks also forced the residents to use the *Luftschutz* or air defense bunkers that were constructed around town. The district party headquarters had its own air raid bunker. Even though new non-essential construction was halted in the Reich during the war, in 1943, the district party headquarters justified the building of a 30-meter shelter in the garden next to their building. It was not classified as a shelter. Instead, it was their new "command post."[25]

The Americans were well on their way to Waldenburg in April 1945. The Allied plan was for Patton's Third Army to drive east to Chemnitz, near Waldenburg, and then turn southeast into Austria. At the same time, other forces would be moving into Bavaria to prevent any last-ditch efforts by the Germans to establish a stronghold in southern Germany.[26]

On April 13, the city was in jeopardy. Already, a flood of German vehicles had been passing through the town the previous days, fleeing the rapidly advancing American Third Army and the 4th Armored Division that was using the autobahn to travel from town to town in Sachsen. Otto Kastner from the Waldenburg newspaper described it as a great mass of uninterrupted vehicles speeding through the city to safety that was further to the east and even south into Czechoslovakia. Allied aircraft attacking targets in front of their advancing armored columns forced the residents of Waldenburg to move into the air raid shelters.[27]

The town was to be defended by the local *Volkssturm* forces that consisted of those too young or too old to be drafted into the army. Wearing their normal civilian clothes, with a "Deutsche Volkssturm" armband on their left arm to identify themselves as combatants, they were issued rifles from the last war, and disposable anti-tank *Panzerfausts* (meaning "fist tanks"), simple weapons that consisted of a steel tube and a hollow charge head that was fired from the shoulder. To supplement the last-ditch Volkssturm force, reserve troops, and wounded soldiers from the hospitals in the town who were still able to fight, were also sent to the town's defensive lines.[28]

They were no match for the Americans who had already been tested against seasoned German troops in the Battle of the Bulge in 1944, and their many fights on the way to Waldenburg. The German defenders were nevertheless brave. Using the symbolically important NSDAP Party headquarters in town as their strongpoint, they waited with their *Panzerschreks*, the German equivalent of bazookas, Panzerfaust anti-tank weapons, and MGs, positioning themselves in defensive posts around the perimeter of the upper town. One of the staff from the local newspaper wrote that the defense of the town was complete madness, given the limited means of defense available. Everything available was too little to face the advancing Sherman tanks.[29]

If some of the residents of Waldenburg were not aware of, or were deniers of what was happening to the Jews during the reign of the Third Reich, it could be no longer be hidden. On the 13th, a truck convoy pulled into the Waldenburg Marktplatz. Packed in the back of the trucks were 1,100 Jewish slave laborers from the Hugo Schneider AG (HASAG) company, an ammunition manufacturer and the sole manufacturer of Panzerfausts and Panzerschreks for the Reich.[30] During the war HASAG rented concentration camp inmates from Buchenwald. Housing them on company property in barracks next to the factories, they were worked to death. It is estimated that HASAG was the third largest user of forced labor in World War II.[31]

Most likely the inmates came from Leipzig where one of the HASAG plants was located.[32] And, the majority were certainly female. Surviving HASAG records show that there were over 5,000 females and just a couple hundred men working at the Leipzig location. Females were cheaper than males to rent from the SS.[33] Still dressed in their gray and white striped clothing and hats, about 5pm these gaunt, dirty, and starving inmates were marched by their SS guards south, out of town to an unknown destination and fate. With the Americans fast approaching, the guards soon fled on bicycles, leaving the prisoners on their own. One of the trucks from the convoy that remained in the square was filled full of food. The hungry locals looted it before it could be secured by the German troops in the area.[34]

The rats were also leaving the ship on the 13th and covering their tracks. The Nazi leadership of Waldenburg including Dr. Welcker the district leader, the propaganda leader, and the party cashier who took 10,000 Reichsmarks with him, allegedly to pay party members in advance, fled the town. They left the city in the morning in a BMW car, heading in the direction of Glauchau. After realizing that the Americans were already close to Glauchau, they then fled south towards the Czech border. Later that day, the Volkssturm leader, Robert Lott, and the city's five police officers also fled on their bicycles to the south. The only civil government person left in town was Paul Meinhold, the town inspector, who was the former mayor of Waldenburg before the Nazis came into power. Back at party headquarters other staff members were busily destroying documents. Files were thrown out the back windows of the party headquarters, landing on the back slope of the property that faced the Mulde river. Someone defending Waldenburg obviously didn't like the Nazis. A bazooka round was fired into the building, killing one of the party members inside.[35]

On the tails of those fleeing were the forward elements of the 4th Armored Division. Coming from the west, two tank columns and supporting troops used the autobahn to seize towns and bridges over the Zwickauer-Mulde on their way to Chemnitz, with Waldenburg in their path. Using speed to their advantage, elements of the 4th Armored plowed ahead, while other units moved through the secondary roads and towns, mopping up any resistance that existed. Avoiding Glauchau, the Americans approached Waldenburg from the north side of the town. Soon, the woods surrounding the town were in flames, serving as an ominous signal to the townsfolk of what was coming their way. Encountering increased machine-gun and anti-tank fire as they advanced into town, at about 7:30pm the tanks started fighting their way down the Altenburger Strasse that led into the town square, running into a hail of MG and anti-tank fire, and shooting up homes as they went. Making it into the town square, the fight continued with the Germans firing their Panzerfausts at the American tanks. At the time, Paul Meinhold was hiding in the basement of the town hall. He was eventually allowed to leave about 9:30pm, where he recalled that the square was full of American tanks. Nearby, the castle palace and its gardens could be easily seen in the glow of the many fires that were burning throughout the town.[36]

The battle was a moving fight. Once the town square was cleared, the next stop was party headquarters. Advancing through the Königsplatz and right past Gottfried's old watering hole, the Gewerbehaus, tanks and troops then took party headquarters.

Then, some of the German defenders also holed up nearby at a house called the Alte Farbe, that eventually went up in flames from the American guns. Other German defenders that were assigned to the side streets fled to the Hellmannsgrund, a heavily wooded area south of town, and across the Mulde River before the fighting broke out. The bridge at Waldenburg was taken intact at 9:45pm. The unit records for the 4th reported that "considerable sniper fire was received as they pushed across the bridge, establishing a bridgehead in the vicinity of Oberwinkel."[37]

In that day alone, Patton's 4th Armored Division covered 112 kilometers. Enemy losses inflicted during the day included 160 killed, 103 wounded, and 2,601 taken prisoner. A total 16 German defenders were killed in the battle in Waldenburg. A monument listing their names exists to this day in the town. The Americans on the total drive for the day had 10 enlisted killed, and 29 wounded. Three officers were also wounded in the day's fighting.[38] There were no deaths of US troops in Waldenburg. The old town where Gottfried's home was, and where his parents lived, was spared during the battle.

The following day, the 14th, machine-gun fire could still be heard in the vicinity of Waldenburg. After the fighting, troops searched houses and cellars for Wehrmacht soldiers, captured some deserters, and interrogated Waldenburgers. Many of the unguarded concentration camp prisoners had returned to the town the night before, squatting in apartments that were empty from the residents moving into the air raid shelters. Some Waldenburgers who lived along the Altenburger Strasse had to give up their homes to the American troops who needed temporary living quarters. Other residents were also homeless from the fighting. Even the post office became troops' quarters, while the church square became a parking area for vehicles. The American presence attracted curious onlookers who came out to gawk at their new occupiers. One of them recalled that the public was amazed that the Americans were fully mobilized with jeeps, trucks, and tanks as they rolled through the town toward Chemnitz.[39] The German army still relied heavily on horse-drawn equipment in 1945.

The Americans were fast to set up the civil affairs of Waldenburg. At 9:30am on the 14th, the American commander met with Prince Gunther von Schönburg-Waldenburg, whose family owned the castle, and Dr. Sterkel, the senior physician at the hospital in the castle. The commander appointed Meinhold to be the mayor of Waldenburg, who now had to work with the Americans to create some semblance of order for the citizens of Waldenburg.[40] Perhaps that was the curse of being the remaining town employee that could be found.

The following days Meinhold had a chaotic situation to address. The population of Waldenburg had virtually doubled. The prisoners from HASAG, refugees from the east fleeing the Soviet advance, and foreign workers freed from their servitude from surrounding farms, demanded food and shelter. Looting and theft were occurring, some of this by the residents of Waldenburg. To keep the peace, American troops patrolled the city in their armored cars. To assist the HASAG prisoners, a commercial building, the old party headquarters building, and the Grünfeld Inn were converted into refugee housing. By the 19th and 20th most of the US troops had withdrawn. Now on their way to Bavaria, only a handful were left in town.[41] April 20, Hitler's birthday, was obviously not publicly celebrated in Waldenburg in 1945.

* * *

For Alfred Roehler, the situation was not good. Roehler and his unit were on the retreat somewhere in Bosnia or the NDH. He really didn't know where he was. Toward the end, in April, the three of them were separated from their unit. Luckily a Luftwaffe anti-aircraft group came by and the commander told them to jump in. He recalls:

> You know we're just kids… my goodness, I was 17 years old, and we jumped on with this anti-aircraft gun group and they hauled us off until they stopped and got into the next position. Where that was I have no idea. I was just going north, just get north. We spent three days with them. The commander of the battalion knew my uncle who was in the anti-aircraft; he was an officer in the anti-aircraft somewhere else in Germany, or whatever. He said, I know your uncle or whatever, so you can stay with us, but then you better mosey because if the feldgendarmes [field police] come, we are all gonna be in trouble. At that time you could see guys hanging off the telephone poles with signs around the neck "I deserted my comrades," or whatever. They were awfully rough on us, so you were scared to death to get caught with no orders or no reason to be there, or whatever.[42]

They eventually caught up with their unit. By then, Alfred was done.

> So we head over there. They were laying down in the shade, sleeping under the trees, and we went up to our sergeant and dropped the machine gun at his feet and said here, take that shit, you can have it, and we split. By then, the word was out that Hitler was dead, and the war was over… the whole thing fell upon everyone to try to get home as fast as possible. Then, towards the end, we got a new Lieutenant just out of Germany, and he thought he could have hammered discipline into us because we wouldn't carry out the dead anymore. He made us carry the dead because you can't let the enemy know how many losses you have… You try to carry a dead guy over the hills without food, you are exhausted in no time. It was either throw the weapons away or drop the dead guy. We left our dead. Yeah, that was a bad time… it's never fun retreating.

The weather and food were also lousy, he said. During the retreat he remembers coming upon some Germans trying to destroy a supply warehouse, so the enemy would not get the contents. They were very hungry, standing there with their tongues hanging out as they watched a *Panzerspähwagen* (armored car) rolling over tons of supplies. Right when they were destroying the warehouse, an enemy fighter, that might have been a Soviet Yak, started strafing them. They could only get a few bars of chocolate before the place was on fire and they had to flee.[43]

They were not the only ones retreating. Along with them were fellow Germans, some Hungarians, and even Cossacks. He described the Cossacks as "nuts—I mean crazy… With their sabers and fur caps sittin' on top and runnin' around like crazy, yelling and screaming… putting on a show. Their uniforms were ragtag… not really uniforms that I can remember… They would cut a Partisan's head off just for fun. They were mean. I mean running around on their little horses. Unbelievable. Screaming and yelling."

They also encountered Chetniks on the way. Roehler recalls that the Chetniks would be moving around the woods next to them at times:

> You never knew whether he's gonna shoot you or gonna help you. I look over at them and they would look at us. You never know whether they were gonna be friendly or not. They changed their mind every three days. They looked like tough… tough tough people… tough. We were their first enemy… We weren't mad at them. We just didn't trust them.[44]

* * *

In January 1945, Rudy Hansinger was more fortunate than Roehler. He was selected for anti-tank training in Czechoslovakia because of his experience in using a PAK in the field. He was told to report on January 10 to the SS Panzergrenadier school Beneschau in Prosetschnitz, Czechoslovakia, about 40 kilometers southeast of Prague. He recalled that it was a small town with a castle (the Konopiště Castle) that had many rooms. At this school, he was also trained in using the Panzerfaust and Panzerschreck, explaining that some of the training required him to sit in a foxhole, while a tank ground over them. There were others from Prinz Eugen at the school too.[45]

Completing this school, he was then sent to the 12th Company that was now fighting the Soviets in Hungary, not too far from the Banat. He didn't spend a lot of time on the Eastern Front in 1945, which probably led to him surviving the war. He was soon sent to officer training school that was located in Bad Tölz, about 30 minutes south of Munich. When asked why he was selected, he said:

> My company commander probably suggested leave for that school. I think I was selected for school because I remember with one group they sent me to, and I don't even know what unit, it was a motorized unit with *Schwimmwagens*, and I was with a group on the hill. It was a clear view for us, but it was all rock—you had to hide behind rocks. I was the Untersharfuhrer with 12 guys—most squads were half that size. One of our commanders was shot. He was about as young as I was. There was a steep area to the road, and I took the guy to a *Sanitar* [medic] down at the bottom of the road. They had so many wounded people, many dead Partisans laying in front of us, and there were even some women laying there, you could hear them scream. I took that guy down to the road and then went back up to the hill.[46]

Hansinger said that school was until April 1945. He was never promoted to lieutenant—it was the end of promotions. The command at Bad Tölz had to make up its mind whether to keep them there or send them back to the front to stop the Soviets. They would fortunately stay in Bad Tölz, or at least in the safety of Germany and Austria, to hold out. Others, however, went to fight. The school put together a group of mountain soldiers and gave them mules with supplies, along with weapons, and sent them up into the mountains in Austria. They took Rudy's group as far as possible with a truck, fixed up a mule, and sent them into the mountains. Up there, the group found a seasonal chalet above a road coming from Innsbruck to Schwaz and then onto Kufstein. From the chalet, he said that the town of Kufstein could be seen. The owner of the chalet was obviously a black marketeer who used the mountain retreat to hide his illegal stash. A locked storage shed was filled full of food and other provisions that they enjoyed. The war was not over yet, but everyone knew it was over, he said. It was a good place to sit out the end of the war and to figure out what to do. He had some peace of mind about his family. They had fled Belgrade on October 4, and were now living in a displaced persons camp near Munich.[47]

The Chetniks

In 1945, it was over for the Chetniks and Kristović. The Chetnik movement fell apart. Mike said: "[Forty-five] it was a rough time… We were chased by the communists… We were in the mountains of Montenegro, going higher and higher… We never went down in the valleys… it was too dangerous." They needed higher elevations to watch for the enemy, and the rugged mountain terrain provided them some safety, while also allowing them concealment, and a means to control the trails and passes that led to their camps. Supplies were even slimmer than in 1944, and the numbers of persons in his unit were dwindling. Some of the farmers who joined went home. Others deserted to the much stronger Partisan forces. He said that he really couldn't blame them. There was no shooting anyways, Mike said.[48]

Many units fought on in some manner in other areas. Supplied by the Germans, some units were still fighting the Partisans and protecting areas in Serbia to help with the escape of German troops retreating from Greece. Another 5,000 Chetniks opted to be sent by train to Austria and Germany and were assigned to Organization Todt labor battalions.[49] Mihailović and some of his followers chose to remain to fight and would eventually be defeated by Tito's forces in Serbia after the war ended.[50]

For others, the decision to retreat was made. Under the command of Chetnik leader General Miodrag Damjanović, with the approval of Mihailović, some Chetnik forces moved north into Slovenia where there was still a strong Chetnik presence. Eventually, they made it to the Isonzo river near Udine, close to where Alfred Roehler received his basic training, and to the safety of the British.[51] Some other units made it into Austria and were later returned to Yugoslavia by the British after the armistice, to face the vengeance of the Partisans. This was contrary to Churchill's recommendation in late April 1945, that anti-communist fighters, including the Chetniks, be disarmed and sent to refugee camps.[52]

Already in fall 1944, Mike's group had received orders to retreat. Montenegro could no longer be held. The Germans were abandoning Montenegro, and without their presence, the Chetniks would be rapidly defeated by the Partisans. While some Chetnik units went north into Serbia, Mike's orders were to escape to the Adriatic coast and make it to Italy. It was believed that Italy was the place where forces loyal to King Peter would be protected, and maybe they could then regroup, return to the kingdom, and take it back from Tito's forces. To get to Italy, the plan was to go through Dalmatia and make it to Fiume (now Rijeka). From there, they would cross over into Slovenia, and then cross the Italian border near Trieste, and reach the safety of the British lines. The total distance of the retreat would be about 800 kilometers.[53]

They first moved down to the coast of Montenegro, ending up near Podrica, near the Adriatic, where they had to pass through German control points. From there, they worked their way north up the coastline. Mike said that there were thousands of Chetnik troops and families trying to make it to the safety of Italy. Along the way, more Serb civilians still living in the area also joined their column to escape the Partisans. The young and old, along with their possessions, sometimes carried on their backs or in oxcarts, slowed their progress. They would often spend days in one area, trying to find food and other supplies, and letting the civilians rest. As they moved north, more refugees kept joining them.[54]

Mike said that now his primary job, in his mind, was to protect the innocent Serbs and get them to Italy. Most of the time, they were left alone while retreating. Many Partisan units had already left the coastal area to fight the Germans who had moved further inland. The influx of more Chetniks into the area, along with the existing Chetnik troops from the Dinaric division in Dalmatia, and more in the Istrian peninsula and those in Slovenia, actually made them numerically more powerful than the Partisans in some areas.[55] But the Partisans were still a threat; they still had their firefights, and his unit's role was to provide a protective screen from Partisan attacks. In the case of the Germans, there was no fighting between them. They both had the same goal of getting out of Yugoslavia.[56]

Near the end of the war in April, they made it to the Trieste area. He said he walked for weeks; he never took off his boots and described his socks as being glued to his feet. He remembers that they passed by Rijeka (or Fiume) and from there, they made it to the Italian border. For days, refugee columns passed by them as they provided rearguard protection.[57]

To control the influx of refugees, the British were blocking the way into Italy, allowing access to civilians first, and then soldiers. Colonel Anthony Barne of the British army was at one checkpoint observing the retreating Chetniks. He wrote:

> … long columns of weary, scruffy, long-haired, leather-faced, dark men of the mountains straggling along the road. They are laden with Bren guns, Sten guns, German revolvers, and knives. A few wild-looking women travel with them and old wagons pulled by tired thin ponies. It's a scene straight from the last war…[58]

Ustaše and Germans were also at the border, trying to make it to the safety of the British lines. Mike said that they did not fight one another. In his mind, and most likely theirs, the war was over and all they wanted now was to be in the safe hands of the British. Before crossing into Italy, the British sorted them out by their affiliation. The Axis forces were disarmed right away when they crossed and were sent to a holding area to be processed. The Chetniks were also disarmed, but they were able to freely move about and be with their families. Soon, Mike and the others would be sent to refugee camps in southern Italy, near Naples.[59]

Götterdämmerung

While Waldenburg was being overrun by American troops, Gottfried was in eastern Slovenia in the village of Ormož, which he described as pretty. From there, they moved to Luttenberg on the 16th, quartering in a hotel in the middle of the town. It was a great hotel. So far, it was untouched by the war, and everything was on hand for them, including a bath and a bedroom. The comforts were short lasting. He was back in Hungry on the 17th again, writing that they were the last German troops in the country. Digging in their truck to protect it from the heavy shelling, they were there just for the day, returning to Schützendorf (or Stročja Vas) and then back to Luttenberg and then to Urschendorf (or Noršinci) on the 18th and 19th. On the way he was met by Ernst who handed him 26 letters. "Unbelievable," he wrote. While the letters were old, they were nevertheless something that connected him with friends and family back home. On April 20, they were warned by some Soviet prisoners that an attack was coming. They were correct. That night in heavy rain they were slammed with Soviet artillery. Working and sleeping in their vehicle, they were assigned to Group Deutz. On April 22, the weather broke and he had some free time, building a child's waterwheel in a local creek in the morning, and then driving that evening to their new post. On the radio he was monitoring what was going on at the other fronts. He knew that battles were taking place in Berlin and on the Eastern Front, and that most likely the situation for Germany and his unit was dire.

Rudy Wagner's artillery unit was less than five kilometers to the south of Gottfried after retreating from Lake Balaton in the same area where Gottfried was fighting. In April, Wagner was fighting around the hills and vineyards of Jeruzalem, near the eastern border of Slovenia. It was a slugfest between their artillery and the Soviets, who were on the other side of some adjacent hills.[60] Retracing his escape route many years later, I stopped at Jeruzalem to look at the terrain. With rolling hills and acres of well-manicured vineyards soaking up the afternoon sun, it was much different from the flat marshy terrain of western Hungary. One of the locals who was old enough to remember the war fondly recalled how nice the German troops were; they gave him and other local children candies. He also provided an overview of the battle, pointing to the east at Kog where the Soviets were, and literally pointing down the back slope of the ridge that we were on to explain that the German gun emplacements were below. Walking down into this wooded area, we found that remnants of the battle are still there. It was easy to see the many artillery craters on the pocked forest floor. The vineyards themselves show no history. What craters and shell fragments once existed are now filled in, replaced with grapevines. Only the old people remember, while some small signs in surrounding towns explain the battle to curious tourists and the young. Soon, like Gottfried, Wagner and his comrades would be in a full-on retreat, leaving their guns behind and moving on foot with the remaining units of the 118th.

In May, they were still on the retreat, heading west. The Soviets were relentlessly pounding them with their artillery and Stalin organs. It was not just the Soviets that were a threat. Partisan forces, disregarding the original Yugoslav frontier, were moving north from Slovenia and into the Austrian provinces of Styria and Carinthia, creating a situation where the German forces moving west from Hungary could be encircled, dashing any hope of the relative safety of surrendering to the British but instead, falling into Soviet captivity. But they always had enough supplies, food, and even fuel for their radio truck. There were even items available at the PXs along the way of their retreat. But he knew that the end was near. In his diary, he wrote some ideas on some possible escape routes they could take, even going as far north to Prague to make it home. News on the radio was increasingly bad.

A scene from Jeruzalem where Rudy Wagner's unit was positioned. Weber's unit was just to the south and then to the north of the area in April 1945. (Author's collection)

Gottfried was also knowledgeable on what was happening on a larger scale. On May 1, he heard over the radio that Hitler was dead, writing: "the greatest statesman of all time, we bow to this man that we swear by." Questions also arose: "What will Admiral Dönitz do now that he takes over leadership and the supreme command of the once so proud armed forces? All only wish in their hearts to see our beautiful homeland, to see our loved ones soon and again. Peace is at the door." On the 2nd, more radio signals were received about army groups surrendering without a fight. Some were close by in Austria, including the Steirmark area and the city of Salzburg. But other cities such as Prague were still holding out. Later, on May 5, while on radio duty, he heard about the surrender of German forces in Holland, western Germany, and Denmark, making him write "…and we?… anything happening…?" For the day, they were not on the move, allowing him time to sleep in a garden in the sun and later pick up 10 liters of wine from the town of Seibuttendorf to celebrate Sepp's birthday: "…long live Sepp—the wonderful past and all else—we drink to everything—the result—we get drunk… our desperation must be rinsed down…"

On the 6th, they continued their retreat west. Gottfried wrote that the divisional commander wanted to get the unit to the Western Allies, which, in his opinion was "a reasonable thought." The retreat westerly began about 4pm that day, but the road was barred by rolling stock. By midnight, they had nevertheless made it to Labuttendorf on the east side of the Mur river, an area that was experiencing heavy fighting. The enemy was everywhere. A grenade thrown by a Partisan landed in his direction; grenade fragments struck him in the left hand and thigh, causing him to lose a lot of blood. Even though he was wounded, they set up a radio post in a wine cellar close to the marketplace. The only medicine for his pain, he wrote, was drinking Labuttendorf wine that they found in the cellar. It was soon too dangerous for them to stay. They were among the last troops to leave the town. As they left, a farm near the rail station was on fire, and there was enemy fire throughout the area.

The next day, on May 7, General Alfred Jodl signed the surrender documents at Supreme Headquarters, Allied Expeditionary Force (SHAEF) in Reims, France. Under the terms of the unconditional surrender, all German forces in the east and west were to surrender before 11:01pm on May 8.[61] The terms of the surrender stated:

> The German High Command will at once issue orders to all German military, naval and air authorities and to all forces under German control to cease active operations at 23.01 hours Central European time on 8 May 1945, to remain in all positions occupied at that time and to disarm completely, handing over their weapons and equipment to the local Allied commanders or officers designated by Representatives of the Allied Supreme Commands. No ship, vessel, or aircraft is to be scuttled, or any damage done to their hull, machinery or equipment, and also to machines of all kinds, armament, apparatus, and all the technical means of prosecution of war in general.[62]

Gottfried heard about the surrender after he and Ernst returned from a bartering mission with the friendly locals, finding 20 liters of wine and a kilogram of pork. He wrote:

> [W]e returned to the radio position and Sepp gives us the latest message—peace is here—the message still unconfirmed—we cannot believe it that the moment has come that we look forward to for 6 years—especially for the last 4 years when we were involved ourselves—general Field Marshal Jodl is reported to have signed the unconditional surrender and we are now at the mercy of the victors—in Reims—we listen to the whole world on the air waves—messages are coming in feverishly.

While there may have been a surrender, and the terms stated that German forces cease active operations and remain in their positions, Gottfried's unit was still on the run. That night, they drove another 30 kilometers to St. Georgian, allowing some other companies to pass them on the road. On the 8th, the surrender was confirmed. Gottfried wrote: "Declared a day of victory in Europe. Churchill and King George address the world." But they were still on the run. At 1pm they left St. Georgian by way of Kirchberg to get to Leonhard, getting lost on the way. Luckily, they met up with a fuel truck and took on 60 liters. Driving in the rain, they eventually made it to the regimental headquarters in Leonhard. After the rain cleared up, some girls came out to his radio truck to listen to music, bringing him some coffee and cake. One of them gave him a spray of red flowers for his hat. "Let the flowers speak—a regular declaration of love," he wrote in his diary. That afternoon, they drove on. Even though the war was officially over, it was not over for him and many of the soldiers escaping out of Yugoslavia and trying to make it back to the former Reich frontier. The entire unit kept heading west to an unknown destination.

Following his escape route in the 21st century, as one moves into Austria the terrain becomes more mountainous. Small villages tucked into steep wooded valleys are connected by narrow and oftentimes steep roads that wind along the edge of the hills. These ancient trade routes are often single-lane roads that connected the villages and were not meant for a modern military force. They would have slowed the retreat of the refugees.

For most of the others in this book, on May 8 their futures were unknown to them. Hansinger was in the relative security of Austria, hiding in the mountains and living off the black-market goods in the chalet with some other SS troops from Bad Tölz.[63] Roehler was somewhere in the former Kingdom of Yugoslavia, trying to work his way north to Austria with thousands of other troops and refugees fleeing the Partisans.[64] Wagner basically followed the same escape route through Austria as Gottfried, heading west as fast as he could to escape Soviet captivity, which he said he knew would probably lead to a slow starvation and death. If not captured by the Soviets, falling into the hands of the Partisans would most likely lead to a swift roadside execution.[65] The only safe one of the bunch was Fred Lashinsky. On May

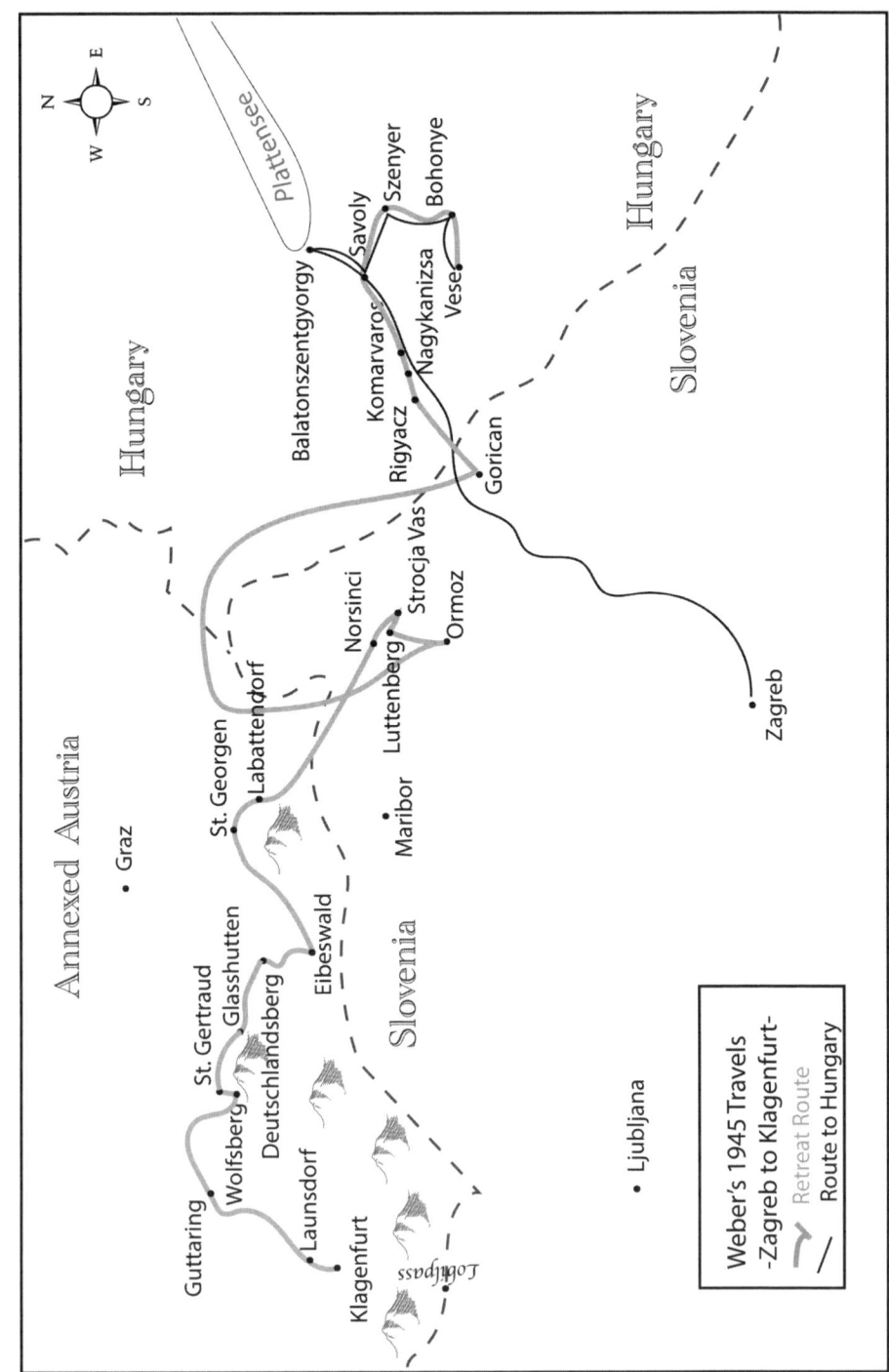

8, he was at Camp Lucky Strike in France, a tent city of over 50,000 GIs, all waiting to get home. Fred and his crewmates on the 8th were getting medically checked out after their time as POWs, getting some much-needed rest and relaxation, and preparing to go back to the States. Fred traveled home by ship this time.[66]

CHAPTER 7

Peace

It's over. The once-mighty troops of the Wehrmacht, Luftwaffe, Kriegsmarine, and SS are coming to the stark realization that they have been beaten. Even though May 8 was the official armistice, some of the die-hard units facing the Soviets did not give up. As late as May 11, troops from Army Group Center around Prague were still fighting their way to the American lines to avoid the Russian gulags and, most likely, a slow miserable death not worthy of a proud German soldier.[1] If not already in a POW camp somewhere in Europe, other troops are sailing back to port, or assembling for departure from the far reaches of the former Third Reich, such as Norway. Both the troops and families back home are commiserating about the fate of their loved ones. Going home for many will be traumatic. Most of the major cities throughout Europe, and especially Germany, are simply rubble. Families are displaced and many are dead from the bombings and the Allies plowing through the country. Now, the long process of reconciliation, de-Nazification, and peace, whatever that means, will be the mission of the survivors of the Thousand-Year Reich that missed the mark by 988 years.

* * *

Dreams became ashes, but at least Germany still existed on the world map—somewhat. In February, 1945, the Big Three—Churchill, the failing Roosevelt, and Stalin—met at the Black Sea resort city of Yalta and decided that Germany would be divided into four zones of occupation, with the USSR, the United States, Britain, and France controlling their respective areas. Austria would also be divided up among the Allies. The USSR would also have its sphere of influence in Eastern Europe. At Yalta, it was also agreed that a new Yugoslav government be created, based on the Tito-Šubašić agreement that included Tito's Anti-Fascist Assembly of the National Liberation (AVNOJ) and former members of the last Yugoslav government that did not compromise themselves by collaborating with the enemy.[2]

German civilians also bore the brunt of the war. Even before the war was over, the brutal expulsion of ethnic Germans from the East and Yugoslavia was occurring. The occupiers, Soviet forces, those governments that existed, and citizens, now sought revenge for years of tyrannical occupation. If not revenge, others probably needed to prove their allegiance and seek amends to their new masters for their collaborative activities during the war, targeting the ethnic German civilians that were once their neighbors—for centuries in some cases. After the war was over, others were enslaved by the Soviets under the guise of "reparations in kind"; the Yalta agreement allowed for the victors the use of German labor, that Stalin greedily used.[3] This was Gottfried's new world.

* * *

For Gottfried, May 8 had no significance. It was just another day in a long war. For him and many others the war was not over, and he was not safe. They were still in retreat and being pursued by the enemy, particularly the Partisans who flooded into the Austrian provinces of Styria and Carinthia. Along with the Partisans were the Soviets, and their Bulgarian allies who originally stopped at the Hungarian/Slovene border on the 7th, but then continued a westerly drive into Austria, eventually ending up near Wolfsberg and Klagenfurt on the 13th before they stopped their advance.[4]

On May 9 and 10, Gottfried and remnants of the division were trying to cross over the Koralpe in Austria, a mountain range that divides the provinces of Styria on the east and Carinthia to the west. To get to the other side of the Koralpe, they passed through the villages of Eibeswalde and Deutschlandsberg. In Eibeswalde, the Soviets cut off their group and they had to fight their way through them to avoid capture. In Deutschlandsberg, at the eastern base of the Koralpe, Partisans took half the company prisoner after a master sergeant surrendered. "The coward," Gottfried wrote. "He lets those 17-year-old Partisans intimidate him and he is the first to turn in his weapon. That example is copied and 20 men of the company do the same." Among them was his friend, Erwin Fisher. He summarized the 10th as "a lot of firing—some dangerous times." Otto Funk, another Jäger from the reconnisance unit of the 118th was not as fortunate as Gottfried. Captured by Romanian troops near Deutschlandsberg on May 10, he and other troops watched as Romanian and Partisan troops celebrated the end of the war, dancing, drinking and playing their harmonicas. A Romanian major who spoke German mocked Funk and others for allowing their leaders to return safely home, while squandering their lives. Funk's response was bold and direct to the major: it was cowardly for a German soldier to surrender. Funk and thousands of others—Chetniks, Italians, and collaborators, including women—would soon be on their way east to captivity, following the same route of the division's retreat from the Lake Balaton area.[5]

For Gottfried's group, on the 10th, at about 2pm, they were finally driving up the Koralpe under heavy fire with Soviet tanks chasing them to Glasshutten. At Glasshutten, near the top of the Koralpe, Soviet troops were successful in flanking them on both sides of a pass, cutting off about 25 of the last men in the column. Luckily for Gottfried, his vehicle reached the top. But in the deep snow and mud, their truck got stuck on the way down and they had to blow it up, along with their radios, to avoid them from falling into Soviet hands. From there, they escaped on foot down the western side of the Koralpe, making it to St. Gertraud on the 11th, the assigned meeting point for what was left of the division. Meeting up with the remnants of the division in St. Gertraud and then walking onto Wolfsberg, they then had a 60-kilometer march over the Saualpe mountain range; 40 kilometers of it was in the high mountains. "Dead tired," he wrote; they made it up to the snow line about midnight. It was here that he, Ernst, and Sepp the great scrounger, parted their ways. Being Austrians, the other two were close to home and took advantage of that. They walked home to their families and freedom. Other Austrians, including Rudy Wagner from the division, also took advantage of being home. An experienced mountaineer, Rudy told me that after the official surrender, he walked home to Innsbruck and into the arms of his girlfriend who was patiently waiting for him.[6]

On May 12 Gottfried was finally safe and the war was officially over for him—four days after the armistice was declared. The day was relatively uneventful for him. After a short four-hour break on the Saualpe, they were back on the march down the mountain, making it to Guttaring about noon, another collection point for the division. They had nothing to eat, he wrote. But, they made it to the protection of the British, despite the protestations of the Soviets who wanted them back. Lingering there for a day, on the 13th they moved onto Launsdorf. They may have been defeated, but they were still proud and showed it. He wrote that they marched on to Launsdorf under "strict military discipline," where the remains of his company set up its quarters in a school. Home was already on his mind. He wrote, "When can we go home?" Rumors were also already flying about that they would be loaded up at St. Veit, that was to the west of Launsdorf by a few kilometers, for their trip home. But for the moment they turned in their weapons to the British. "That's not too bad," he wrote about his internment. The only complaint he had was that he was hungry, and he wanted some rest. The following day he caught up on his rest. They could move about freely, but they still had nothing to eat.

* * *

Following the same route in the 21st century, the road that he took is narrow and very steep in some places. In early spring 1945, with snow and mud covering the road, it is surprising that Gottfried made it as far as he did. Moving up the crest of the Koralpe to Glasshutten and then Weinebene, at least it is then a downward slope to St. Gertraud and Wolfsburg, followed by an uphill climb again to Klippitztorl and then on down to Lolling, and then to Guttaring. Along the way, the road is lined with many small villages. Probably not seen by many of wet and dirty troops that cast the sour odor of a barnyard after a rainstorm in the springtime, they meandered their way through the villages past the many roadside monuments that commemorated the prior wars that the locals were involved in. But undoubtedly seen by retreating troops were the strewn equipment, fatigued soldiers and refugees resting on the side of road, and the fear and apprehension on the faces of those villagers who had the courage to come out their homes and cellars to watch the unending column of troops that just a few years ago were their salvation to a better life. Now they were a sin that the Soviet forces would not readily forgive. These villagers did not have to rely on radios or word of mouth to know the surrender occurred. The unending clatter from soldiers' hob-nailed boots, neighing and tired horses, and motorized vehicles that still puttered along in the slow columns composed a sad melody of annihiliation, augmented at times by the Soviet bass section of the orchestra of defeat that included distant gunfire and muffled explosions. Defeat was also written on the faces and hollow stares of the dirty and downtrodden troops who were driven by one thought—freedom from the Soviet horde.

* * *

Gottfried and his comrades were not designated as POWs by the British. When I asked his friend, Richard Wachter, about being a POW with Gottfried, he adamantly responded that he was never a prisoner of war. He was never captured or surrendered to the enemy. Instead he was classified as a "Surrendered Enemy Personnel"—an SEP. The same designation applied to Gottfried and the rest of the division that turned themselves over the British.[7]

Prior to the war ending, with the Allies anticipating their future victory, what to do with the millions of surrendering Germans became a topic of discussion. A subsequent draft instrument of unconditional surrender was written that provided that the commander in chief of Allied forces, Dwight Eisenhower, had discretion over whether the surrendering Germans would be considered prisoners of war. If they were classified as prisoners of war, then the Allies would have to follow the Geneva Convention. But, already in March 1945, Eisenhower had realized that the Allies would not be able to feed all of the prisoners to the standards set forth in the Convention, which stated that prisoners had to be fed essentially the same as what their captors ate. To skirt the Convention rules, Eisenhower sought permission from the Combined Chiefs of Staff that any troops who surrendered after May 8, 1945, could instead be designated as Disarmed Enemy Forces (DEFs). Under this designation, the Convention rules would not apply to these persons or have

Hochosterwitz Castle today. In May 1945, the fields at the base of the castle were crowded with troops from the 118th. (Author's collection)

Veterans and a military unit assemble at the division's memorial plaque at the base of Hochosterwitz Castle. The plaque reads: "On May 15th, the former 118th was disbanded on this historic soil. In gratitude for their fortunate return home and in memory of their fallen and missing comrades, the surviving members of the division erected this this memorial. Honor to the fallen and a reminder to the living. May 1965." (Author's collection)

to be followed. The British also followed suit, using the term "Surrendered Enemy Personnel" (SEP) for those they interned in their camps.[8]

Officially the division surrendered in the fields at the base of the Hochosterwitz Castle, within sight of Launsdorf, where a very large number of troops from the division were encamped. Today, the castle is a UNESCO World Heritage Site. The castle itself is imposing in nature, sitting on a large rock mound, looming about 65 meters above the farm fields that surround it. It looks out of place; there are no other hills or mountains in close proximity to it. Most likely visitors to the castle have no idea that the division surrendered here in 1945, and the whole area was swarming with troops. Only a small plaque embedded in the castle's rock base, placed there after the war by veterans of the 118th during one of their reunions, marks the official place of surrender. It is hard to find to the point that I had to ask a castle staff member where it was located. I asked around if anyone could tell me about the German surrender. My questions were met with blank stares.

Bleiburg

On May 7, the Ustaša and Croatian leadership fled Zagreb, leading to a mass evacuation of Croatian troops and civilians fleeing north to the safety of Austria. The Croatians, along with many other Axis forces, started flooding into the valleys that led into Austria. One of these was the Mežica valley that led into the village of Bleiburg, just to the south of Klagenfurt, and not too far from Gottfried. Soon after the surrender, many soldiers and civilians thought they made it to the safety of the British in Carinthia. Many more were on their way. By May 14, the commanders of the British 38th Irish Brigade received word that approximately 200,000 members of the Croatian army and another 500,000 civilians were moving toward the British lines at Bleiburg. The area was soon jammed with troops and civilians, many of whom were encamped in the fields just south of Bleiburg.[9]

On the 15th, the Croatian commander, Colonel Danijel Crljen, met with General Scott of the 38th Irish Brigade at Bleiburg Castle to negotiate their surrender to the British, while also explaining that a large number of Croatian civilians needed to escape the Yugoslav communists. It did not work. Yugoslav General Milan Basta also arrived and insisted that they surrender to the Yugoslavs. General Scott simply could not handle the large amount of people, and knowing that the Yugoslavs were planning to attack the Croats around Bleiburg, he offered the Croats three options: stay and be attacked by the Yugoslavs; keep moving into British lines where they would be attacked by the British; or, surrender to the Yugoslavs, where General Scott would try to ensure that they would be treated correctly. Basta also said that civilians would be returned to Croatia, while the soldiers would be treated as prisoners of war. They had five minutes to decide. The Croatians surrendered to the Yugoslavs.[10]

On the 16th, the Yugoslavs began moving the citizens and soldiers back across the Austrian/Slovene border. Basta lied to General Scott about the care and treatment of the prisoners and civilians. The resulting death marches were called the "Way of the Cross" by the predominately Catholic Croatians. Others had a simpler name: the Bleiburg massacre. On the long march back to Croatia, civilians and soldiers were marched in the direction of Maribor and then south to Zagreb. Many were executed on the side of the road; others were killed and dumped in mass graves, anti-tank trenches along the way, karst pits, and old mines—wherever the Partisans could hide their atrocities.[11] Many of the mass graves that dot Slovenia from the Bleiburg massacre and the expulsions from other valleys that led into Austria are still being discovered. Close to 600 mass graves have been identified that hold about 100,000 dead. It is estimated that 50,000–80,000 of them are Croatians.[12]

* * *

The area still keeps giving up the secrets of its dead. In 2010, approximately 2,000 soldiers from the Prinz Eugen division were found in one mass grave near Brežice, Slovenia.[13] With the spring sun warming their backs and their eyes to the ground, they knelt on the edge of their mass grave with their hands bound behind their backs. Thoughts about their farms, loved ones, and the gentle rolling hills of the Banat were soon destroyed by the muzzle flash and a bullet to the back of their heads as they tumbled into their common grave. They became comrades forever. Over 100,000 years of potential future life taken by the communists. For some family members, this discovery would now end the 75-year mystery of their loved ones' destinies and bring some closure. For many in the mass graves, there were no family members to grieve their death. They were also eliminated by Partisan forces and Tito's policy of mass deportations of Volksdeutsche from the new Yugoslavia.[14] And even if there were families left, identifying the dead was most likely an arduous task. Many were stripped of their clothing and identification disks prior to their execution as a futile attempt to hide who they were, if the grave was discovered. For those that still had their ID dog tag around their vertebrae, many of the names and unit numbers on the steel or zinc disks were indistinguishable because of corrosion. Even the earth did not want them to be known.

One survivor of the march was Stjepan Zivković. Sitting in his farmhouse kitchen in Croatia drinking rakija with his family, he told me his story. He and other Ustaša troops from his unit had made it to the Slovene/Austrian border after being ordered to retreat by his local Ustaša commander. After a couple of days in Bleiburg field, they were disarmed by the Partisans and marched back to Slovenia in columns of four, in the direction of Maribor. The majority of the officers and NCOs in his group were executed on the march, and others in the group were also randomly shot for having the wrong name, being too slow, or looking at their captors the wrong way. The killing was indiscriminate. Eventually, he wound up in a POW camp where conditions were very poor. Here, he was a given a choice: join the Partisans or die. He joined. While serving his patriotic duty as a Partisan for the new Yugoslavia, he was responsible for training other troops in operating and assembling the MG-42 machine gun. He said the Partisans were dumb. They had a lot of weapons left over from the war, including machine guns, but nobody knew how to clean and maintain them. After proving his allegiance to the new Yugoslav government, he was released in early 1946. Walking back to his village, still in his Ustaša uniform, he was accompanied by another Partisan from his village who had also been released from service. He talked about the irony of two persons from the same village becoming enemies during the war, and walking back together to the peace of civilian life. He returned to his life of farming. But he was never trusted by the state. Every weekend until the death of Tito, he had to turn himself in at the local police station on Friday nights, spend the weekend in jail, and then be released on Monday mornings to go home.[15]

Today, outside of Bleiburg is a monument to the massacre that was built by the Croatians. Every year, the Catholic Church and Croatians assemble there to remember the dead and missing from the forced marches. Just to the south of the Bleiburg monument are the farm fields where the troops and civilians milled

The Bleiburg memorial on Bleiburg field where thousands of troops and civilians assembled. The caption reads: "To commemorate the Croatians killed in 1945." (Author's collection)

around in May, 1945. Walking through these fields, secrets are readily given up to what happened here in 1945. A quick stroll yielded a couple handfuls of 9mm handgun and 8mm unspent rifle ammunition, left by those who reluctantly surrendered there in 1945. Headstamps on the casings showed that they were World War II-era manufacture. No longer needed by the sea of soldiers who surrendered in these fields, the flotsam of their possessions still slowly washes up to the surface to this day.

Gottfried

For Gottfried, boredom soon became the new enemy. On May 15, he wrote that already internment was getting on the nerves of some: "Some start to go crazy, the uncertainty about our fate, about the loved ones at home turns many apathetic." He, a man named Otto, and Raymund, his roommate and companion from when he was on the island of Korčula, went to a local mountain creek and bathed and sunned themselves. He wrote: "I'm lost in my thoughts, everyday, you have an undefinable feeling in your stomach area—it's not too surprising with this lack of grub… the worst times on Korčula were better than this." He also had a new friend by the name of Richard Wachter that he walked with. Little did he know at this time that Richard would become a life-long friend.

On the 16th, some of the soldiers in his circle started giving instruction in business, math, the natural sciences, and English. Now, they became teachers, instead of soldiers, to while away the time. Gottfried wrote that he attended sessions on English, business, and math in the morning "… that's the only way to train your mind and prepare it for civilian life after concentrating on death and destruction for so long." Later in the afternoon, most of the company went to the dam on the nearby Gurk river, just off the Unterbruckendorf road, to swim and bathe. Instead of going, he sorted through his old letters that he had managed to keep with him throughout the retreat, reading through the letters from Ilse that were "so dearly written… I want to be with my thoughts and think about myself. What does Goethe say? Only where you can find clarity in your life, you belong to yourself and trust yourself alone. There you enjoy beauty and good in solitude—there you make your world." His brother Georg was also on his mind. As late as May 24, troops from Croatia and from further south were still drifting into the area. Some were from 117. Jäger-Division, Regiment 737, that his brother was in. Good news was received: Georg might be in the area.

It appears that he and his unit were not greatly impacted by the SEP designation. They still had food, but he often complained that it was limited, and the quality could have been better. Throughout May, the rations consisted of dried peas and other vegetables, horsemeat, or a simple meal of rice, pea soup, or something he referred to as "army soup," and two thirds of a loaf of bread that was expected to last four days. What food they received from the British was supplemented through foraging; Gottfried would go into the mountain meadows looking for strawberries. Benevolent locals also supported him and his comrades with what they could, oftentimes giving them potatoes. One person in particular was a woman that he called "mother." She had suffered greatly in the war, losing her only son. He wrote that he was similar in appearance to her dead son. She repaired his clothes and he would stop by and have tea and apple butter with her.

Throughout May, reading books, going to movies, hiking alone or with friends, and foraging for food became his pastimes. "If only this dammed grub would improve," he wrote. "With this type of food we are slowly going to hell. If the mothers of the soldiers knew that their sons would go hungry, they would be very worried…" The division itself also provided entertainment for the troops to relieve the boredom and instill order. Usually, this consisted of movies, singing contests between companies, and dances. One thing that was clearly evident is that he now had a lot more time to write in his diary. During the war, many of the daily entries were short and factual. At times, he had no time to expand on some points or really reflect on his thoughts and feelings. Now, his entries were longer and more philosophical in nature. Obviously relieved that he had survived, his thoughts were directed more toward home and the fate of his family, while also questioning his own future.

Boredom was satiated with some responsibilities. He was still technically in the Wehrmacht, and military discipline and a chain of command existed. Already on the 16th, he was assigned as a messenger at division headquarters. Besides his messenger duties, he also had kitchen duty where he had to clean and wash potatoes. What horses the company still possessed also had to be cared for in the valley; at the end of the month, the British came and ear tagged them for inventory purposes. Unarmed guard duty of his quarters was still a requirement that he often performed at night. He also had to maintain his quarters in the school, performing general clean-up duties, while taking care of what was left of his uniform and personal equipment that he managed to carry with him on the retreat. Even military awards were still being issued. On May 19 he was awarded the War Merit Cross 2nd Class with Swords medal for his valor in a combat-related function above and beyond the normal call of duty.[16] It was received by Gottfried with some contempt:

> I don't need medals anymore that peace has come. They should have thought about us when we were under heavy bombardment. Nobody paid attention to us when we were at the front. Those gents were happy that they could stay in quiet positions. Nobody showed up at the front. Yes, that's how it was…

May soon turned into June, July, and August. In June, the weather was becoming warmer. Like the weather, rumors were also heating up, often followed by rainstorms that washed away hopes of a quick reunion with their loved ones. Already in late May, the commanders had spread the word that Austrian members of the division would be assigned to a special battalion and stay in Gösseling, and be released soon. The Germans, meanwhile, would be shipped out on June 3 to the Salzburg area to go home. The date then changed. Going home would start on June 9, when the Germans from the 118th would be sent in groups of 2,000 to Bavaria, or to Munich. Then, the rumors said that the 118th would begin loading up between the 13th and 15th, while everyone would be home by the end of August. To add hope, some of the Austrians in early June were sent to St. Veit to be processed and sent home. But, because there was no space at the transit camp, they were sent back. The hope of release made Gottfried think about where he would be released to. "Release to where—your own choice?" he wrote. One idea he had was to go to an aunt's house that was in the American zone of occupation. Concerns over his family and that they did not know about his status also pressed on his thoughts "… how worried they must be—at the moment there is nothing I can do to notify them."

Early June was filled with walks in the surrounding meadows, swimming in the local river, doing laundry, mending his clothes, picking strawberries in the high meadows, foraging for other food to supplement his rations, and attending courses, including English. On his 21st birthday on June 3, he spent the morning hiking in the high meadows and woods, buried in his thoughts. While hiking, he met a girl who picked strawberries with him. She was the first to congratulate him on his birthday, even though he wrote that he believed that his loved ones back home had done so already. Going back for lunch that consisted of horsemeat, potatoes, and gravy, he was back in the high meadows in the afternoon, reading a cheap romance novel, then making it back for dinner that consisted of beef, bread, and gravy. These walks in the meadows between courses and duties were commonplace to the point that he wrote that "I can sit there by myself by the hour—I have turned into a regular dreamer… I love to be by myself up above. There I can follow my thoughts and recall into my memory the affairs of heart because of all of the possessions of the earth, the most valuable is your own heart." Hope for reuniting with Ilse still existed, although he had not received a letter from her for some time, and had no idea where she was. Marriage was also on his mind. He wrote that "marriage after all is fulfillment and purpose of our life on earth and then I would like to have the permission and blessing of my parents—the love of my parents is deep down in my heart—profound and cherished."

His movements around the area were not very limited as an SEP, and it appeared that the British did not really care where he walked or what he did, as long as he was back for curfew, which was 10pm. Curfew even seemed to be unenforced. One night after a dance, he was out after curfew and walked by a British patrol and was not stopped or written up. But the German commanders recognized that military discipline was already starting to erode in June. They were reminded by their major that they had the strictest duty to salute their victors, while they were also ordered to restrict their contact with the civilian population. This was due in part because in early June, some of the German officers hosted an unofficial party for one of the Hungarian girls that accompanied them on the retreat. The party was not permitted or allowed by the British. Punishment for this indiscretion landed on the enlisted. Offended by their actions, Gottfried reflected on the incident and wrote that it was a sad circumstance, and their behaviors were not worthy of a German soldier. But civilian contact still went on, especially at the dances that attracted the local girls. Gottfried wrote that the girls knew the waltzes, but were not familiar with modern moves, such as the foxtrot, and tangos, suggesting their provincial naivety, or the fact that the last six years of war had robbed them of contact with the modernity of the outside world to a great degree. The girls went there for the music and the companionship of young males, which was a rare commodity during the war years. If not companionship, maybe it was hope for a glimmer of normalcy in their atypical world that ripped away years of their youth.

On June 11, he was transferred to a work battalion attached to Artillerie-Regiment 668 and was sent to St. Viet. From there, he went to the Klagenfurt area and unloaded in a large pasture where thousands of other German soldiers were just standing around. In a heavy rain with no tent or another form of shelter, with only a blanket, he endured the night in a rainstorm. The following day, he found a barn to sleep in and stumbled on an old friend, Ranier Müller, from basic training, who was from the village of Oelsnitz, about 50 kilometers to the southwest of Waldenburg. Between Ranier and himself, they managed to build a shelter from scrap wood and pine branches to protect themselves from the elements. Calling it his villa, it was something, but it was much more uncomfortable than the school he was billeted in while in Launsdorf. Ranier became a companion and someone he could pass the time with during the summer months. However, this work assignment was not good news for his release. On the 17th, many from the 118th would load up for Munich; the work units would remain for now.

He and others in the work unit were assigned to various details in the area around Klagenfurt. One of his main jobs was working in what he called the vehicle cemetery, which was a large vehicle salvage yard. Working from 8:30am to noon, and 1 to 4:30pm, with Saturdays and Sundays off, he and others were responsible for dealing with the mass of Italian and German vehicles that had made it to Austria and now littered the landscape, laying on the sides of roads, and abandoned in fields where they coughed their last breaths after breaking down, or most likely, running out of fuel. He and his partner towed abandoned vehicles to the vehicle cemetery, organized the vehicles in orderly rows, scrapped some for their parts and tires, and cobbled together others to get them working again. Working in the cemetery had its benefits. They could drive around the area and get out of the camp. And, besides being paid for his work, he traded items found in the vehicles to British troops to supplement his rations. On one day, he traded a compass for 50 cigarettes. On another day, he traded a pistol to a British soldier for 40 cigarettes and two packs of American candy.

Besides the vehicle park, he was also assigned to work in Klagenfurt, picking up the rubble and bricks from bombed-out buildings. Repairing roads, cutting firewood, and building latrines, in what would become his new camp, were other work activities.

Free time was still there. Saturdays and Sundays were spent doing laundry, and writing letters to family that he passed on to friends going home in the hopes of them being mailed and received. Going to the barber, and scrounging for books that included Schiller's poems, stories of Carinthia, opera books, *Parsifal*, *Tannhauser*, *Don Juan*, *The Flying Dutchman*, and others, also helped pass the time. In July, he also got official leave to go into Klagenfurt. Dressed as a civilian for what appears to be the first time in years, he wore a red neckerchief and a colored shirt. He caught a ride into Klagenfurt to go to the British Red Cross Office where he was able to send a message to his family in Waldenburg, using a friend's home in Obersteimer, Austria, as his permanent address. With Klagenfurt itself, he was not impressed: "I had imagined something better, I turn my back on the town," he wrote. Foraging also continued in his free time. The hunt for strawberries switched over to raspberries, now in season, which he traded with the British for crackers and dried vegetables.

In August, he was in his new camp and now had much better living conditions. The makeshift shelter was gone, and he lived in a barracks that had electricity. Hope also increased that release was coming. Now, the word was that August 17 would be the release date. It was rumored that they would be transported home by zone, beginning with the English and American zones first. Last would be the Soviet zone, which Waldenburg was in. Already on June 9, he wrote that he knew from a radio message that the Americans were pulling out of Sachsen and Waldenburg. Now, his family would be under the occupation of the Soviets, which he was anxious about. This time, release appeared to be real. Gottfried even completed a triplicate questionnaire for his release. He contemplated using his aunt's address in Swabia, just west of Munich, that was in the American zone of occupation. But he decided to use his home address in Waldenburg, even though it was in the Soviet zone of occupation. It was still home. It also appeared that the British were fattening up the SEPs for their departure. Rations included another 400–600 grams of bread daily. But these dates also passed without anyone going home.

Early September found him still working in the vehicle cemetery. On September 5, he and Pretschner, his co-worker, were taking their noonday break, laying under a vehicle to get out of the hot sun. For some reason, the vehicle fell on him, breaking his clavicle and six ribs on his left side. He was first transported to the hospital at the displaced persons camp in Tessendorf, and then to the Elizabethan Convent in Klagenfurt, that was converted into a military hospital. As he lay in bed unable to move because of the pain, Pretschner brought him his personal possessions from camp the next day. Over the days he was visited by Fritz Vandreier, Ruppert Eiffler, Thomas, Schaeidt, Neiderreiter, and other comrades, writing in his diary that he was glad that his old friends hadn't forgotten him. Pretschner also stopped by again before his release to say his goodbyes. Pretschner used an address in the American zone to get released, and then planned to cross over into the Soviet zone and to his home in Reichenbach, not too far from Zwickau and Waldenburg. Gottfried wrote a letter to his family that Pretschner took with him.

By the end of September, he was able to get out of bed and walk the streets of Klagenfurt, alone and with friends. The last week of the month was spent with more visits from friends, wandering the city, and going to movies, including *Waitress Anna*, *The White Dream*, *The Golden City*, *Summer Nights*, and *Tonelli*. Sometimes he violated the 10pm British curfew. He didn't care, writing "if we were all angels, good thing we are not." He wrote that it would be bad luck if he had to return to his work company that was now located in Annabichl, a short walk from the Klagenfurt airport.

Gottfried was getting more restless to go home. One of his doctors hinted that he might be released because of his injuries, and he was watching more of his friends leave. He had received no word from any family members. However, letters from others who had contact with family members in Germany suggested that conditions were getting better there. Writing that it was now six months since the end of the war and there was still no hope of going home, "here in Austria, the business of peace is spreading. Wine taverns, jazz music, dances and such… it would have been better if we had stayed on the front. It hurts to notice that we soldiers are considered as outcasts by Germany and now by the Austrian people, as if they had never been associated with us."

Finally, on October 10, he was released from hospital. But he was told there was no possibility of getting on a hospital train to Germany. Instead, he was sent to Feistritz in Rosental, to the southwest of Klagenfurt, where he was reunited with some of his comrades. Conditions of the camp did not agree with him. Fortunately, he was soon transferred to a company that was in Emmersdorf, to the north of Klagenfurt. Close to Tessendorf, he was able to socialize with some of his buddies from the 2nd company that were billeted there. They often received passes to Klagenfurt to go to movies and aimlessly wander around the city.

November and December were relatively uneventful. Already in October, the Karawanken Alps that loomed in the distance were growing snow. Now, in November, it was also snowing in Klagenfurt. On November 19, he was back to his work detail, cutting logs, and sometimes working in the RAF headquarters that was located at the Klagenfurt airport. On Christmas Eve, he got dressed up and he and his comrades had a celebration in their day room. There was "very little Christmas mood" he wrote: "everyone is depressed by the dark fate that is hanging over us. What kind of worries will my loved ones have because of me—unimaginable—not that I am bad off…" Following a brief speech from their commander, they sang Christmas songs and had a meal of roast pork, boiled potatoes, and vegetables. They were all given the same gift from the British that consisted of a stollen, socks, one razor blade, a handkerchief, and 25 cigarettes. His thoughts also drifted to his family in Waldenburg:

> I know that my mother lies in bed sleepless and thinks of her boys who cannot be home yet, but are locked up somewhere—and Marianne [his sister] with her two little ones… When the tree is lit, Inge and Utta will open their eyes wide, at around 5am the church bells will be ringing at home again…

The highlight of his Christmas was visiting his friend, Ernst Schaffer, and his family. Already his Austrian comrade was home in St. Donath. Like other Austrians in his unit, Ernst simply walked home at the end of the war. Ernst had sent Gottfried a letter to join him for Christmas, and the British gave him permission for leave. With his pass in hand, Gottfried left for St. Veit and boarded the train for the short trip to Huttenberg, and then walked about four kilometers to Ernst's home. Writing that he immediately connected with the family, he ate well and walked the hills with Ernst, most likely sharing their thoughts about the war, and ruminating about their futures. On the 26th, he was on his way back to his camp and to his work assignment at the RAF headquarters.

Roehler

Like Gottfried, for Roehler the end of the war did not arrive on May 8. Roehler and the rest of his machine-gun crew had made it to the Slovene/Austrian border on foot, sometimes catching rides with the other fleeing Axis troops. He and his machine-gun crew had made a pact: they would stick together at all costs. He said the woods and roads were full of troops and civilian refugees all heading north. He was not exactly sure of the date, but he thinks it was on May 9 that he made it to the border. The only date that he said he was sure of was that by his 18th birthday on May 31, he was a prisoner of war.[17]

To get into Austria from Slovenia, they had to cross through the Loiblpass tunnel, the same tunnel that he took into Slovenia in early 1945. In May 1945, the area was packed with desperate civilians and a mix of soldiers, Croatian NDH, Ustaše, Germans, and Cossacks, some with their families, all wanting to get to what they thought would be the safety of Austria, and away from the vengeance of the Partisans. They had a choice of traveling through the dark tunnel to the light of freedom on the Austrian side, or hiking over the mountain. In their condition, it was decided that the tunnel was their only option. Instead of walking, they tried to catch a ride on a hospital train that was heading into Austria. Alfred said that there were some empty wagons on the back, but before they could get on, some Partisans came down the slope, and an officer by the name of Binder, who spoke German, told them to drop their weapons and go home. The war was over. So, they dropped their weapons… "and sure enough they had us by the neck," said Roehler. The small group of them, around four to six, were ordered to strip down to their underwear and take off their shoes. Then they were marched to a larger group of

April–May 1945. Clockwise: A soldier of the once-mighty Wehrmacht sits among wreckage with his rifle on his lap, hoping to make it to Austria; a long column of Germans and their allies in Slovenia and on their way to the protection of the Allies in Austria; it was just not the Germans retreating. Here, a Chetnik (in wagon) is part of the retreat column, hoping to avoid the vengeance of the Partisans. (Author's collection)

prisoners. He was lucky though. He recalls seeing other Germans executed on the spot. Stripped of their shirts with their arms raised, the Partisans checked them for the tell-tale sign of an SS soldier, the blood group tattoo on the inside of the left arm, near the armpit. These tattoos meant instant death, said Roehler.[18]

They were marched with 15–20 other prisoners to a basement in a nearby building, and held there for the night. The next morning, they were packed into a boxcar that took them to Fiume on the Adriatic coast. They were then marched to an area where there was a rock cliff surrounding a bay that was packed with prisoners lingering on the rocky beach below, with the guards watching over them from above. There was no food or water. Most of the prisoners were in the same condition as Roehler and his comrades: hungry, tired, and without shoes and clothes. He remembers that there were a lot of Italian prisoners with the group who had joined up with the Germans after the Italian Armistice in 1943. They were there for about three days before the decision was made to escape. People, especially the older men, were already starting to die from the lack of water and food; they had to get out of there or they would die too.[19]

For the escape, they gathered up some clothes and shoes that were littered on the beach. Roehler had a mixed-up uniform including a Luftwaffe hat, just a shirt, and no tunic. Fortunately, the weather was mild along the Adriatic coast in May, so the clothing was adequate. He said his main issue was hunger. When the tide was out, the group of five snuck around the cliff, halfway submerged in the water. Their goal was to make it to Trieste to the north, and to the safety of the British. Traveling by night in the hills at most times to avoid Partisan patrols that were canvassing the roads during the day, they used the North Star to guide them on their way. About five days into their escape, a patrol found them; two of them were captured. The next day, one of the men that was captured caught up with them. His captives had gotten drunk and fell asleep, and he walked out of the hut he was detained in. They were now down to four.[20]

They never made it to Trieste. One day, they were walking down a valley and came upon a lone farmhouse with nothing else in the area:

> [W]e were looking down in the valley and there was this beautiful farmhouse with a straw roof on it, you know, the thick thatch and smoke coming out of the chimney. Man, we were almost passing out from hunger, so one of us decided he's gotta volunteer and knock on the door. A woman opened up and she took him inside, and then a few minutes later he came back out and waved at us to come on down, so we went down the hill and went in the door. Inside she had a big kettle of Polenta cooking on an open fire. And, that was so good. That was the first warm food we had in days and days and days. And we just started feeling good and the back door opens up and the old man comes into the light with a rifle. He arrested us and took us to the local police station.[21]

At the station with their hands tied behind their backs with old telephone wire, Roehler and his comrades were interrogated by the Slovenian police. After establishing that they were not Ustaše that were being hunted in the area, the police determined that they were basically harmless and sent them to another POW camp that was located in a monastery, close to the Austrian border. It was a large camp.

He estimated that at least there were 1,000 inmates. Life in the camp was tough. Inmates were triple bunked and he recalls that he was covered in lice. Food was also scare. Polenta, soup, and bread, if that, were the common meals, with the bugs in the corn serving as their protein source. Occasionally, they would catch a cat and fry it up. He said they tasted like chicken. The guards were often brutal. He said that if they were Serb, you got kicked and got the rifle butt. Some of the Serb guards would also come around at night when they were drunk and shoot inmates for fun. The Slovene guards were more humane, and in general, they did nothing to the prisoners. Big difference, he said. Eventually, the camp got a Slovene commandant who put an end to those actions, and camp life became better.[22]

In their spare time they would work in the local village and surrounding areas. By now, it was late summer and he had noticed that like the leaves, civilian attitudes were changing colors—in a positive manner toward them. In the fall, an official came to the camp and said that he needed 300 prisoners for a work detail. Alfred was selected and was separated from his buddies that he never saw again. Roehler and others were loaded up into trucks and sent to Ljubljana to work at the airport. The POWs were housed nearby in the horse stables of a disused Italian barracks. During the day they were trucked to the airport, digging, and cleaning up battle damage. Guarding the prisoners was limited. On one day, Alfred saw a British aircraft land at the airport. "I made my way over there and I said [to the crew], I'm a prisoner of war. I knew that much in English and asked, would you have an extra seat on your plane? The guy just looked at me and said 'You're nuts, get outta here.' It was worth a try! We tried!" he laughingly said.[23]

Most of the guards at the Ljubljana camp were young and naïve. He said that in most cases the guards were scared of the Schwabos, the nickname that the Yugoslavs had given to ethnic Germans that had settled in the kingdom. Alfred said:

> They were scared to death, scared to death. The poor guys. I remember one trick we used to play in the barracks. There was an older guy from Hannover, Germany. He played the hypnotist and there was a short Austrian guy that played the counterpart to it. You know, he would hypnotize him and he would jump off the upper deck of the cot and fall on the floor and then swim on the floor—all kinds of dumb stuff. He would turn and look at them [the guards] and say "now, you're next." And then the guards would be so scared, they would run out of the barracks. It was unbelievable.[24]

Others, he said, were simply stupid:

> … stupid, stupid. They were so dumb they would take a light bulb home and screw it into their walls for light. They would take a faucet off the water pipe so they would have water at home. Things like that… I mean unbelievable. We had to explain the rifle to them. They had German rifles and they wouldn't know what to do with them, so we had to show them how to take it apart![25]

While they may have been stupid, young, and naive, they were nice to the prisoners. Compared to his other experiences, he said that the guards were really nice people there. He recalled one of the Slovenian sergeants that was in charge of the kitchen would always try to get the prisoners to help in the kitchen and make cooks out of them, so they could be better fed.[26]

Freedom was still on his mind, and the Ljubljana camp was the site of another escape attempt. One night, he and two others crawled under the wire and made their way north. Their plan was to walk over the Austrian Alps, and to freedom. It almost worked until a hunting party stumbled on the three a couple days later. They were arrested and taken back to the camp. Punishment was relatively light. He and others had their heads shaved for lice, and were placed in a dark bunker for 30 days. After the 30 days, they were back in the stable and working at the airport.[27]

Things took a positive turn for Alfred in late 1945. He said that in his opinion, already in 1945 the Yugoslavs realized that they had killed off all their intelligentsia, like engineers, and professors:

> [T]he Commies realized oops, nothing's running anymore, then some smart guys said "well, we got the Germans, and they know how to do things, you know"… so sure enough they came along and said we need draftsmen, we need engineers, we need electricians, we need this, we need that. Volunteer, you know. They want to haul you into town to a factory or wherever. We were needed and were put to work and got some decent food and better uniforms. I happened to be there with the group that had to go to Electro Techna. We had some German engineers with us and they would have some old catalogs from Siemens in Germany that they had laying around down there, and they took the pictures and they would copy stuff. You know, I happened to be a draftsman, an apprentice draftsman, so they put me behind the table and said, go ahead you know, you make us a plan. And that's when life changed because they needed us.

Instead of the POW camp, he now lived at the factory, was well fed, and slept in a back room on a cot. But he was still a prisoner, and he could not go home.[28]

vonCampe

On May 8, vonCampe was in Slovenia. In the early part of 1945 he was at an officers' school in Germany. The city he was in for officer training was very close to the approaching lines, to the point that German officials were picking up soldiers who had no orders, throwing them into whatever unit and line was closest, be it the British or the Soviets. vonCampe, however, had his orders and returned by train to his unit in April, without any reservations. He also said he had no problems getting back to his unit. In the last days of the war the Soviets were still relentless, pushing them further back toward the Reich. He described the Soviets as "barbaric… There was not one soldier who didn't know what was expected when captured by the Soviets. We did not expect anything good from them…" But even in April, 1945, he said it did not occur to him that they might lose the war. It was the same conditions as usual, even though the war was reaching its end. He admitted how naïve he was. They were always talking about wonder weapons that would turn the tide of the war. And, he believed it.[29]

They knew about the surrender. They had read the orders between the Soviets and German High Command that they were to deliver their arms and tank, and then walk home. They talked about if they should turn over their tank intact. In his opinion, "we could have gotten out of the country [Slovenia], but we wouldn't most likely get over the mountains. We discussed the question, do we go, or don't we go? We were not part of a division or anything. You had tanks and people, and that was all. We were on our own… We were free even to destroy them… It was against everything I was considering… to deliver your arms to the enemy." But in the end, they decided to do it. Orders are orders, and he was a German soldier. So, they started driving in the direction of the Alps and to Austria, on what he described as a warm, sunny day. But in one town they were surrounded by Partisans, and they became prisoners of war. "That is the way the Soviet Union always operates. They promise one thing and do as they please," he said.[30]

Hilmar and the rest of his tank crew soon became part of the stream of hundreds, if not thousands, of prisoners marching south in the direction of Croatia to an unknown destination and fate. The Partisans treated them very badly. For about 10 days they were not given any food, and some soldiers were randomly executed. He had no personal equipment with him, just the clothes he was wearing. They slept in the open under the stars and never in a building. Eventually during the march, they did get some food. It usually consisted of some water with beans in it, along with some foul bread. One night, a horse was killed that they eagerly ate. He knew it was horsemeat and he didn't care. It was food. They were marched for at least a month, he said.[31]

Eventually he and about 25–30 others were placed into a work camp in a forest to cut down trees, somewhere in Croatia. They were forbidden to leave, and there was camp count every day to prevent escapes. Close by, there was a river. "And, so I went to the river every night and got mussels. So, we survived with mussels. But we survived. We survived…" Then they were transferred to a small village which had been destroyed during the war. They were supposed to build new houses. Now they slept in a barn that was much better than the crude shelters they had in the forest. To supplement what meager rations they got from the guards, at night, Hilmar and others would raid the local fields for potatoes.[32]

In the fall he concluded that he would not survive the winter, based on what he had to eat and wear. If the Partisans found out that they were stealing potatoes from the local fields, they would also be done for. Five of them decided to escape. The plan was to make it to Hungary and then cross into Austria and to freedom, instead of a more direct route through Croatia and Slovenia. Hilmar said that they believed the Hungarians were their friends; after all, they were the last of the German allies, and historically part of the old Austro-Hungarian Empire. Hopefully, they would be more sympathetic to them and supportive of their escape than the Yugoslavs who were their former enemies.[33]

Their actual escape was easy. There were no fences or other barriers. There was only one guard who had a girlfriend in the nearby village that he would visit at night.

So, the next evening, they left the barn at about 10pm. Coming into a village about midnight, they assumed that everyone was asleep, but then the shooting started. Their lead man with the map disappeared in the confusion, never to be seen again. Without a map, the rest decided that they would use the North Star to guide them northeast to Hungary.[34]

Traveling by night and hiding during the day, they worked their way toward Hungary. For food, they foraged for cabbage and bulbs in farm fields to supplement the small amount of bread that they had stockpiled for the escape. On one day during their journey, along came a man walking his dog down the road. The dog pulled his master to where they were hiding in the brush along the side of the road. He obviously was not a friend of the communists. The man looked at them, and they looked back. Nobody said a word, and he and his dog continued on. After about 10 days, they reached what they thought was the Yugoslav/Hungarian border. Hilmar recalled that it was a cold night with a full moon (which according to the lunar calendar was close to September 21). They had to cross the river. Fearing that they all would not be able to swim across, they found a small boat and made it to the other side. But it was not the border. They were still in Yugoslavia as they soon discovered by the communist slogans and graffiti that they saw scrawled on the walls of homes in a nearby village that they had snuck through that night.[35]

Two days later, they actually made it to the border. Again, they had to cross a river, this time the Drava, which is the dividing line between the two countries. Luck again was on their side. There was a boat tied to a tree on the riverbank and there were no guards on either side of the river. Crossing that night, they were finally in Hungary, and a little closer to freedom. That night, they made it to a farm, and for the first time in about a month they had something substantial to eat and a warm place to sleep, even though it was in a barn. The next evening, they continued on their march to Austria, but they realized that four people were too many for families to hide and support. So they divided into pairs.[36]

Their trip through Hungary was still dangerous. One day on their journey, Hilmar and his friend found a farm with two elderly women living there. The women gave them food and put them in the barn for the day. Suddenly, the old ladies came running and screaming into the barn, telling them that Soviet soldiers with a German shepherd dog were approaching. They grabbed their things and ran across a field and hid in some bushes at the edge of the field. Hilmar watched the Soviets approaching with their barking dog. One of the Soviets picked up the hat that had fallen off his head, but they turned around and gave up the chase, even though Hilmar's footprints could be easily seen in the plowed field. Hilmar did not know how it was possible that they did not continue tracking them, and they were not captured. After a while, they went back to the farm and asked for more food. After being fed, they went on their way.[37]

A few days later, they reached the Austrian border and stayed with another Hungarian family. The owner took Hilmar to the Austrian border, warning him to be careful of the Soviet troops in the area. He was also told that there were other Germans in the area trying to make it to Austria. Once in Austria, they now started walking by day, even though they were in the Burgenland region that was occupied by Soviet troops. He said that the locals always told them if there were Soviet troops billeted in or patrolling the area. In instances where there were troops, they always continued on, not stopping for the day or night. Eventually, his escape partner decided that he did not want to travel through villages anymore. It was too dangerous. But Hilmar wanted to get away from the Soviets as fast as possible, and he was willing to take the risk. So, they parted ways.[38]

Now on his own, he was getting closer to the demarcation line between the Soviet and British occupation zones in Austria. The only thing that now separated him was a bridge over a river. A local man told him that the bridge was guarded by the Soviets, but in the early morning, nobody had guard duty. That day, the sun was already up, it was well past dawn, but Hilmar could not wait:

> I couldn't wait another 24 hours. And I started to go up to the bridge which I did, and then I was shocked—even before I got there all of a sudden out of nowhere comes a Soviet soldier with his gun on his shoulder. And I said [to myself] no, this is not, this is not the end, after those weeks, that cannot be. I turned off the main road and knocked at the door of a local house. Nobody came. And I looked back and he was not there. He was walking back to the village where I had come from. And I crossed the bridge and I was in the free world. I realized that I had reached what I wanted. Freedom. Now comes the end of the story… I was lying on a hill and looked down into this Austrian village at British soldiers. And then I asked myself whether it was God who has taken me out of bondage, just like he had taken the Israelis out of Egypt… I have a complete lack of answer when they [the Soviets] came into the farm and didn't find us. I have a complete lack of answer for the Soviet at the bridge… He must have a purpose for me. And then I'm sitting here because He had a purpose for me. So, I prayed to God… that is my story.[39]

Even though vonCampe made it to the British zone, his story was not quite over. One of the men that he escaped with, the man with the map who they got separated from the first night of their escape, lived near Graz. Hilmar remembered his address. He went there, and the man's family took him in immediately. The following day, his partner that he separated with earlier in Austria reappeared. They were a pair again and they decided that they would go to Salzburg, which was in the American zone of occupation. But they had no money, no documents, and of course, no ticket for the train. Jumping on the train anyway, when they got to the British/American checkpoint, everyone on the train had to unload, walk over a small pass, and board the American train for Salzburg. They snuck through the checkpoint, and a former German soldier then hid them under a tarp in a boxcar that was part of the American train to Salzburg. In Salzburg, they separated. Hilmar's goal was to now make it to his grandmother's home in Westfalia that was in northern Germany. To get there, he first went to the French zone on a coal train traveling north, then crossing the border on foot back into the British zone in northern Germany, which he said was no problem. From there, he made it to his grandmother's house, discovering that his sister and mother were also there. They had fled their home in the Sudetenland from the Russians near the end of the war. His brother and father were less fortunate. His younger brother serving in the Wehrmacht disappeared on the Eastern Front, and the Soviets had arrested his father in his hometown in the Sudetenland for being a civil servant and a party member. His brother was never found. Years later he would discover that his father died in a Soviet concentration camp.[40]

Hansinger

Rudy Hansinger was perhaps the most fortunate in comparison to Gottfried, vonCampe, and Roehler. Soon after the surrender, the owner of the mountain hut where Hansinger and his comrades were holed up came to check on his black-market stash. They were discovered; it was time to leave. Hansinger and another soldier from Prinz Eugen walked down the mountain into an unknown fate. He said they found a nice little home on a hillside that had two pretty girls, who were refugees, living there with the owners. The end of the war for this family was bitter. They had lost their two sons on the Eastern Front. After the mother had fed them and gave them some of her dead sons' civilian clothes to wear, Rudy and the other comrade parted ways. Rudy soon met up with some German troops who had made it out of Greece and were camping in a nearby field. He checked in with their commander, told him that he was from the Prinz Eugen division, and spent the night in a haybarn. The next day, an American truck appeared and took Rudy and two other SS troops to Bad Aibling near Rosenheim, southeast of Munich. At Bad Aibling, he was quartered at the airport in a hangar, sleeping on straw. In the camp there was already talk that former SS would receive a 20-year prison sentence for their service to the Reich.[41]

From there, he was moved around from camp to camp, eventually ending up at the Nuremberg-Langwasser POW camp. This camp was located at the old Nazi Party Grounds in Nuremberg. Originally, it was a tent city where thousands of participants in the Nuremberg Party Rallies encamped.[42] Old films of the camp in the 1930s show *Sturmabteilung* (SA Troops) and Hitler Youth happily camping there, preparing for their perfectly choreographed marches at the Nuremberg parade ground that would be reviewed by Hitler and his leadership corps. This was not the case for the Allied POWs when it was converted to a German POW camp in 1939. Holding Yugoslavs, Russians, French, British, and later American troops, the camp's conditions were poor. Food was limited, and the inmates were required to perform forced labor activities in the area, including cleaning up the bomb damage in Nuremberg.[43]

Now, in 1945, the camp had new occupants. About 15,000 SS POWs now lived there. When Rudy first got to the camp, they lived out in the open. There weren't enough barracks for all of the SS prisoners. One of their first tasks was building more barracks to live in. He and other prisoners were trucked to the nearby city of Fürth to cut down trees and lumber the wood, haul it back to camp, and build their own barracks. Already, the camp was laid out with streets and had water lines installed, so all they had to do was build the barracks on concrete pillars. The barracks were not warm. In the winter months they were cold because they had no insulation, and there were large cracks between the wood slats, allowing the cold Bavarian winds to blow in. Rudy's clothing was limited and consisted of surplus military uniforms that were spray-painted in white "PW" (Prisoner of War) on the back and front of the tunic and pants. Food was limited to a watery soup that had potato peels in it. But he said he didn't complain much. As part of their de-Nazification process, they were shown films of the concentration camps. Seeing the starving and dead in these films, he said that one could not really complain about their food.[44]

Like the former occupants of the POW camp during the war, they too were responsible for cleaning up bomb damage in Nuremberg. Every day, he and others in the work crew were sent to the city. The city was not a city, he said. It was rubble. They would clear out an area in the middle of the street and construct a narrow gauge rail track with a cart on it, loading the cart up with bricks, and hauling it out of the area. Cleaning debris out of basements was particularly difficult. Occasionally, a body would be found. Sympathetic locals would often leave potatoes and bread scraps on the walls of the bombed-out buildings where they knew that the prisoners would be working the following day. Rudy said it was much appreciated because the rations they were receiving as POWs were very limited. One specific building that he cleaned up was the Palace of Justice.[45] Located near the center of the city, this building was the location of the Nuremberg War Crime Trials that began in November 1945, where some of his old SS bosses, including Heinrich Himmler and Ernst Kaltenbrunner, answered for, and were prosecuted in Courtroom 600 by the world for their crimes against humanity.[46]

* * *

New Year's Eve 1945 had to be a lonely time for Gottfried and his comrades. Not too different from young men in the 21st century that are bored and looking for something to do, they went searching for parties. First, they went to Tessendorf. With nothing going on, he and his buddies then went to a dance in a schoolhouse in Pörtschach am Berg, watching others dance for a while, commenting in his diary that there was a lot of terrible stomping, and lousy musicians. From there, they took off for a lonesome mountain guest house in Tanzenberg, spending a few hours sitting at a table in a contemplative circle, drinking beer. Most likely it was the Gasthaus Kollerwirt, which is the only guest house in a village of about a dozen structures. They were the only ones there:

> … so we take leave of the old year, and again my memory goes back to my loved ones back home… will we see them again in the New Year? That's our greatest desire. Each one of us is being drawn to his wife, his parents, or a girl, and where one feels at home. How will my loved ones spend the evening? Surely filled with sorrow and unrest about our fate. I want to look into the future, into the New Year, 1946.

CHAPTER 8

Captivity

In 1946, Europe was in economic and social turmoil. Most of Europe's citizens were living hand to mouth, relying upon the benevolence of the occupation forces for their survival. Mass deportations of Germans from the Soviet-occupied areas of Europe continued in earnest in 1946. The Allied Control Commission composed of representatives from the USSR, America, Britain, and France authorized that the 3.5 million Germans now living within the new boundaries of Poland, that now included East Prussia, be moved to the Soviet and British zones in Germany. The three million-plus Germans living in Czechoslovakia, Austria, and Hungary would also be moved to the American, French, and Russian zones in Germany. The deadlines for these deportations would be the end of July 1946.[1]

From late November 1945, until October 1946, the world was witnessing the Nuremberg War Crimes Trials. Some of the top Nazi leaders that could be found were charged and tried with war crimes, crimes against peace, and crimes against humanity. Other German military commanders who served in Yugoslavia and failed to escape from the country, or later fell into the hands of Tito after the war, were sitting in a Belgrade prison waiting to be tried in Tito's own version of the Nuremberg trials. Some of the other bigwigs, such as Ante Pavelić, the Poglavnik or leader of Croatia, escaped the hangman's noose. One of the versions of how he got away was that he and some of the other Ustaša leaders fled to Austria near the end of the war. Hiding initially near Salzburg with his family and then living on a farm near the village of Obertrum, about 32 kilometers from Salzburg, he stayed there until April, 1946, then moving into the British zone and hiding in Wolfnitz.[2] According to his daughter Visnja, from there he hid in a Jesuit monastery in Italy and then fled to Argentina in 1948, under the protection of the Perón regime that was sympathetic to former Nazis. After a failed assassination attempt in Buenos Aires in 1957, the family moved to Madrid and was protected by the Franco regime. Pavelić died in 1959 at the age of 70 from wounds from the previous 1957 assassination attempt.[3]

To prevent German citizens from re-sowing the seeds of national socialism, a series of proactive steps were taken by the occupying nations. When released, soldiers were sent home individually, or in small groups, by road and rail, and not allowed to march home to cheering crowds as they did in World War I. The Allied Control Commission also passed a series of directives. One in particular, Directive 30, prohibited any efforts "to preserve and keep alive the German military tradition, to revive militarism, or to commemorate the Nazi Party" under the penalty of arrest.[4] The mandates were broad and deep. Parades and other forms of military celebrations were banned. Paramilitary organizations, or the *Freikorps* that emerged after World War I to maintain order in cities, were also prohibited. Any memorial preserving the Nazi tradition was to be destroyed, and military museums were closed. The press was also controlled, while libraries were stripped of controversial and national socialistic writings. Veterans' organizations were also banned.[5]

Like Germany, Austria in 1946 was divided into American, British, French and Soviet zones of occupation, with Vienna split between the four, along with an international zone in the middle of the city that the four powers rotated through on a monthly basis. The country was in economic chaos. A provisional government was created that declared that Austria was again a Republic, but the Allies still had supreme administrative powers over the country.[6]

Yugoslavia was still a mess. Yugoslavia had laid claim to the Istrian Peninsula and the city of Trieste, arguing that the majority of its citizens were Yugoslavs. And, because they were on the winning side, they should be entitled to it. The US and Britain said it was theirs, making the city and area the southern end of the Iron Curtain between communism and the free world. An uneasy relationship existed in 1946 between the Allies and Tito's troops.[7]

* * *

January 1, 1946 found Gottfried getting back to his barracks at 4am, after a long night in Tanzenberg, drinking beer with his comrades. He was up at 9am writing "I'm pretty knocked out—but only from staying too long..." After a cold shower, his five senses returned to him. Following a three-hour nap in the afternoon, he and his buddies took another "collective beer trip" to Pörtschach and then went back to Tanzenberg.

The rest of January was work as usual, earning his 5 schillings per day, including free room and board for his labor. It was enough spending money to go to the movies, buy food to supplement his allotted rations, and keep him supplied with beer on his outings. Because of the hard work, they received special ration cards. His weekly rations now included 1400 grams of bread, 850 grams of meat and 115 grams of fat. Overall, the food was getting better in the context of quantity and quality. For most of January, he was on forest duty, felling wood. He wrote that even though it was not pleasant working in the snow and cold, "I'd rather be outside with all the fresh air in the mountains than anywhere else." His British supervisor, a soldier by the name of Lowitz, who he called "our slave driver," was actually nice to them. On one occasion, they were supposed to go fell wood, but they could not find the location. For two days all he did for work was to ride in the back of the truck as Lowitz drove around looking for the work site. Other tasks included working at RAF headquarters at the Klagenfurt airfield, sawing wood in the morning, and even working in a civilian sawmill to run the machines.

His free time was filled with chores, including laundry, and making kindling. For fun, he belonged to the camp choir that practiced during the evenings. Reading and listening to the radio were other personal pastimes. On weekends, the movies were almost a weekly event. Going to the movies at the Peterhofkino on the Ramsauerstrasse in St. Peter next to Klagenfurt, he watched *Prechtel, Loveletters, The White Dream, Luck with Women*, and the *Romantic Bridal Trip*.[8] Besides the movies, the company also filled in the free time with variety shows, that included comedy skits in the camp's day room. Dance evenings, only on the weekends, were also held in the day room of the camp. Some dances were designated ladies' choice. Going out and drinking beer was also a common weekend activity. In January, he was introduced to adult entertainment somewhere in town: "Soon I get drawn into the maelstrom—Mephisto urges me on—according to Goethe 'beautiful hours as well as beautiful talents have to be enjoyed'—I try it—just once to forget about the pressing worries at home." The following week he was back at it: "a forbidden fruit is always desirable—it will, however, always leave a bitter aftertaste," he wrote.

Politics still bubbled up to the surface at times. In late January, he wrote that General Noeldechen, their local German military commander, was arrested by the military police for his alleged involvement in the creation of a Freikorps unit in Carinthia. A rumor was spread from a person in the Austrian Democratic party that the "Korps Noeldechen" was being formed. The existence of and membership in any paramilitary units was banned by the Allied Control Council Directives.[9] Gottfried was upset about the creation of the Freikorps, suggesting his naïve youthful interests in nationalistic organizations were now gone: "Here we are being held against our will and then these gentlemen want to mess with our return home—a shame—and they call themselves officers—it is obvious that these men want to keep their position as long as possible so they won't be unemployed..." Home was still on his mind. He wrote how he dreamt about his homecoming, standing in front of his house, and finding all of his loved ones: "At the moment I reach for my mother's hand in greeting, I wake up—what a shame."

Life in February was basically the same as it was in January. His work still primarily involved felling trees in the surrounding hillsides and mountains around Klagenfurt, sometimes in the cold winter rains. On some days, he worked in the comfort of the RAF headquarters at the airport. He proudly wrote that his English had improved to the point that he would be used as an interpreter at times. Dance evenings were temporarily halted at the camp. From early to mid-February, the day room was converted into temporary quarters for about 100 German officers who were waiting to be released. He was also still looking for his brother and heard that one of the officers there was Lieutenant Weber. Unfortunately, he wrote, it was a false alarm. It was not Georg, whose fate was still unknown to him. There was still his laundry that needed to be done, which he called "women's work." Fortunately, he had found a local woman in Viktring to eliminate this activity from his list of personal chores. Later, in February, the dances started up again in the day room, as well as the variety shows, which in his opinion, were sometimes junk. Many new rumors about release were also circulating. He wrote that he lost faith in them. And, concerns about home were on his mind. In late February, it was his mother's 64th birthday: "Dear Lord, I'm worried because I don't hear from them," he wrote. Close to a year since the end of the war, he still had not received any letters from family and friends in Waldenburg.

Weekends also included going into Klagenfurt and surrounding towns. The 20-meter obelisk located at the Kardinalplatz in the center of the city, which is still there, served as an initial gathering place for Gottfried and his friends. From there, they would share the latest information on where the fun was to be found that night, and collectively try to figure out what to do, a typical activity replicated by youth throughout the world. Usually their nights involved going to dances, drinking beer, or going to the Volkskino that was located just to the south of the city's Bahnhof to watch movies, including the *Walk of Sacrifice*. Some of Gottfried's friends lived in factories or shops in the city, instead of the camp. On some free days, Gottfried would visit them. His friend Fritz Vandrier lived in the tobacco factory, while Rudi and his wife lived at the Kaiser auto repair shop. Socializing with local girls also occurred. Once in a while, he would be invited to a dance by a local girl. There was also his local friend, Mitzi, and her sister, who would visit the camp and accompany Gottfried and his friends on their outings. It appears that curfews no longer existed. If they did, they were not enforced by the British. Making it back to his barracks at 3 or 4am was a common weekend occurrence. Depending on the time and day, he would catch a ride from a passing truck, ride the bus or tram, or rely on his feet to get him to the city or back to camp.

In March, one of his social highlights was a masked ball in Pörtschach. The dance was not supposed to take place. The British ordered that all dance entertainments for SEPs were now forbidden. But the dance went on anyway. He wrote that it was his first masked ball: "An unheard of attraction for the girls. I see many beautiful costumes and masks and one wonders where the people got the material because nothing can be purchased. I don't have a mask, but I'm in good shape—I search in vain. At 22hrs all masks off. I dance every round. I entertain two girls at once—teaching one the tango step—lots of fun—ends at 0400 hours."

On March 8, 10 months after the surrender, he was finally allowed to write a weekly card home through the International Red Cross. POWs were allowed to write a maximum of 25 words on the post card. The cards were then collected, sent to Geneva, and then forwarded to their respective addresses.[10] He was also told that he could apply for another zone to be released to, but he decided to remain in the

Soviet zone. He also wrote that releases to the English and American zones would start in March. According to the radio station in Hamburg, all German prisoners of war were also to be released by the end of the year. This information was somewhat accurate. Already Britain, France, and America had agreed that all POWs would be returned by the end of 1948.[11] A new rumor also surfaced that those who were being released to the Soviets would have to go through de-Nazification and re-education: "Who knows how far we are going to be separated from our home—we may have to go for political re-education in the Urals as we heard recently. I don't believe in these rumors too much—agitation…" His tone toward Russia was slightly changing, most likely because he would now be under their yoke of oppression. He wrote, "Russia was shown during the Third Reich in an unfavorable light—everyone agrees to that." While admitting that he was perhaps influenced by the Nazi propaganda about Russia, he nevertheless still held the belief that Germany could have beaten them, writing "they could have never defeated us on their own."

In March, spring was emerging in the Karawanken Alps, and the weather was getting warmer. Hiking the mountains started up again. On Sunday, March 10, he climbed the 1022-meter Ullrichsberg, the highest mountain near Klagenfurt that overlooks the Woerthersee, with his friend Willy. Making it to the top, they toured the old Gothic church ruins of St. Ulrich that was built in the 5th century.[12] From there, they descended the mountain and hiked back to Karnburg in the rain. By 6pm, he was back to the camp. Outdoor activities were supplemented by social activities that included camp variety shows that the locals attended, dances in the town, and going to the movies. In his personal time, he would listen to jazz on the radio, read novels, and optimistically think about release and home. "I believe in a happy return and to find everyone healthy," he wrote.

On March 11, his job as a lumberjack was over. Because of spring and the sap rising in the trees, it was becoming more difficult to fell timber. Now, his job changed from cutting wood at RAF headquarters to clearing and cutting wood from bombed-out buildings in the city. Other work details were even more rigorous, including the clearing of cement rubble from destroyed buildings and hauling it by truck to the Loiblpass area, south of Klagenfurt. He also worked at the Zigguln Castle that is located in the northwest part of the city. Here, he cut firewood and carted away ash. This work, he wrote, made him as dirty as a pig.

Some clues were also emerging that release might be coming. On March 19 he had to go for a medical examination where the British checked him for any physical handicaps. Many of his comrades were also leaving camp for home; others were losing interest in camp life. The choir director had skipped the last three practices and Gottfried wrote: "The comrades show less and less interest. At every practice fewer appear—the reason is clear—upcoming release… and no accompanying instruments. I don't enjoy it any longer. We work for some time on Beethoven's "*Die Ehre Gottes aus der Natur*" ["Praise of God from Nature"]…" He also received new clothes in late March. These were not old military surplus issue, but instead were civilian clothes and good quality, resulting in him commenting about the quality black pants he was issued. Maybe it was actually time to leave.

In late March, and up to April 20, he was neglecting his diary entries. Making up for three weeks in only one page in his diary, he wrote that he wanted to:

> Retain my small memories for the future, mostly the last days as a prisoner of war in Carinthia, after weeks of storms and white glory, spring has arrived—all is wunderbar—oh beautiful nature. I greet you, my mountain with a reddish beaming peak. I greet you the sun, that gives it a lovely reflection. I also greet you, meadow full of life, whispering linden trees and the happy choir sitting on the branches. Quiet blueness that covers the greening forest, pouring without measure across the brown mountain, I have finally escaped the prison of my quarters and the narrow conversation and happily escape to you the mountain. Such wrote Schiller when he enjoyed a new spring.

Finally, in late April, he received a letter from his sister, Lena, through the International Red Cross (IRC). Shortly after getting this letter, he also received one from his aunt Liddy. Maybe the letters that he had been giving to his departing comrades reached Waldenburg. Or, maybe family had found him through the IRC that is empowered through the Geneva Convention to collect information about POWs, and share that information with families. Regardless of how the letters got to him, he was relieved. All was reasonably well back home. "I'm likely to be home soon," he wrote.

On April 20, the British required him to turn in his extra clothing. They also told him that he was only allowed to have one bag and one change of underwear when he was discharged "…so it is safe to assume I'm going home—high time—it's been a long, long, time since the last visit home. I'm full of expectation…" While he was sorting out his clothes, Mitzi and her sister stopped by to visit and planned for the next day's outing to the Ullrichsberg mountain.

Easter Sunday, April 21, would be his last climb up the mountain. He got up early that day. Despite the cold morning, he was optimistic that it would become a beautiful day. With his friend, Paul Boeber, he had a quick breakfast of milk soup prior to leaving camp. Before 7am, they were on their way to their rendezvous point where Mitzi, her sister, and a Viennese refugee girl, waited, and set off for the Ullrichsberg peak. He wrote that they did not sweat on the ascent because it was still cool, and the trail was crowded with slow walking people who were also moving up the dark, silent path, to the top. At about 11am, they made it to the top and had breakfast that consisted of farmer's bread, Tiroler homemade sausage, eggs, and smoked meat. "I lay back and laze—close my eyes, and dream. Mitzi reads from a book without interruption for almost 3 hours… After a final look from the Kaerntener Alpen to the Karawanken, the Gerlitzen and Saualpen and the rest in the round—full of happiness—I take in once again this wonderful view from above and recall full of mourning that this land blessed by the Lord will soon be in the past…" That night, he was back in the camp and performed his obligatory guard duty.

The prior day's activities must have been strenuous. On Easter Monday he wrote: "Weber, Weber, you are becoming a bum, you were supposed to be on guard, but slept the whole time, really solid…" His excuse was that his relief, Willy, did not wake him, because Willy had also slept through his guard duty. He was on another sightseeing trip on the Worthersee that day, planning to meet up with his friend Rudi, to take a boat tour. The lake itself is one of the major sightseeing attractions in the Klagenfurt area. About 16 kilometers long and two kilometers wide, tourists then and now can view the shoreline from a tour boat, stopping at various locations on the north and south shores along the way.

Catching a ride into Klagenfurt, he then took the tram to the lake. He never found Rudi. The dock was filled with people waiting to board the tour boat:

> I was one of the fortunate ones to illegally battle for a seat in the true sense of the word—I jumped in over the side of the boat. Thank goodness I'm in. At the dock, one half the crowd is left behind and cannot get on. The boat is rocking in the waves. Off we go at exactly 9am. The sun beams down from an azure blue sky—it's still cool on the water. I stand in front on the bow and look down on how the blue water is being sliced by the keel. And then again, my eyes are drawn across to the south of the Karawanken chain. It's very unique here where everything comes together—the snow covered peaks, blooming meadows, trees, ice, and water. The nicest part of the lake is probably Maria Woerth—very impressive small peninsula with an old church…

At 10am, he was at Pörtschach looking for Rudi at the Kaiser auto repair where he was quartered. They never met up. Walking home along the edge of the lake about 14 kilometers to the tram station, he then went to St. Georgen and met up with Mitzi at her home. Mitzi's mother immediately served him up a good and ample meal of eggs, ham, Tyrolean sausage, and horseradish. Later that day, he walked back to his barracks in the rain, getting soaked. Reflecting on one of his last days in Klagenfurt he wrote: "It was nice, wonderful. And now I want to come to the end of my diary notations. I'm out of pages and what is more important, I am going home."

The next day on Tuesday, April 24, his time in Klagenfurt was over. He was going home. He was first sent by truck to the English release camp at Feistritz, just south of Klagenfurt on the Drau river, and processed out of being under the custody of the British. From there, he went to the American exchange camp in Karlsruhe. For a few days, he sat and sat and sat, waiting to be processed out of the American zone. On May 5, he made it to the Soviet zone of occupation and was sent to the quarantine camp at Elsterhorst by Hoyerswerda, near Dresden.

Camp Elsterhorst originally served as a Soviet POW camp during the war. Then, the Soviets used it as collection camp for German prisoners right after the war ended, where Colonel Hans von Luck, a relatively famous panzer commander on the Eastern Front, was appointed the camp commandant.[13] In 1946, it was now serving as a Displaced Persons camp and a quarantine camp for German POWs waiting to be released into the Soviet occupation zone. The camp was large. In August 1946, the civilian side of the camp held about 15,000 displaced persons living on meager rations of bread and soup. In the other side of the camp there were about 20,000 German prisoners in quarantine. Gottfried spent 14 days at the camp on the quarantine side, getting medically cleared for his release, and most likely being questioned by Soviet state security personnel about his time in the Wehrmacht and in Yugoslavia to determine if he committed crimes against the Motherland and if he was a threat to the Soviet occupiers. He wrote that it was a "test of his nerves and it was a starvation diet… the last fat disappears. I'm going home, so it's completely immaterial."

Waldenburg

"I greet you my homeland—on May 22 in Waldenburg…" He was home. His arrival was probably nothing like his departure in 1943. Neither his mother nor any other family members were at the train station to greet him. Skinny and malnourished from his quarantine period with the Soviets, his reception committee was most likely Soviet troops who suspiciously reviewed his documents, considering him an enemy of the state. He also had to immediately register with the local police and military officials to document where he was living in Waldenburg, and so he could obtain his ration cards. His family probably had no idea he was coming home.

On the short walk up the Bahnhofstrasse from the train station to home, not much had physically changed. The town itself was lucky in the sense that it was spared from the large air raids, only experiencing damage from some small air attacks, and the short fighting that occurred there in spring, 1945.[14] Those citizens on the streets or looking out of their windows at him walking up the street at a distance would have been filled with hope that maybe it was one of their loved ones who made it home. Getting closer, some probably looked at him with envy that the neighbors' kid made it home in one piece. Their loved ones were dead, still missing, or had not yet returned from captivity. Over the last three years, Gottfried had probably physically changed to the point where neighbors may have had difficulty recognizing who he was. But at least it was one more Waldenburger who made it home.

It was not the town he had left in 1942 for his RAD service. On July 1, 1945, the Soviets took over occupation duties from the Americans. In advance of the Soviet troops, the Soviet propaganda machine was already in full swing and had flags placed on the city hall and police station. Even though any types of meetings were restricted by the Americans, the communists and social democrats had nevertheless met and created an action committee to remove any Nazis from city positions, and to create a committee to oversee municipal operations and remove any of the capitalistic rich social class who remained. In comparison to the Americans, the Soviets had far fewer tanks and were using captured German vehicles and motorcycles. They were also described as being more sloven in appearance than the American occupiers.[15]

The first official act of the Soviets was firing the acting mayor. This was followed by removing some of the town's residents from their homes to quarter Soviet troops. Unlike the Americans who had their own food, the Soviets also required that the locals feed their troops, without any form of compensation. The Soviet command staff also moved into the left wing of the Waldenburg Castle. Over the months, the rest of the castle occupants were removed and the owner, Günther Fürst von Schönburg-Waldenburg was arrested, but soon escaped captivity, making it to the West. Through the Soviet land reforms, the castle later became state property. One of the castle's buildings was also converted into a jail with cells to hold some locals for denazification purposes. Probably some of the pro-Nazi locals had most likely developed amnesia about their actions or denied their membership with the Nazi Party. But the Soviets would remember, thanks to the detailed record keeping that the Nazi Party had maintained. Other parts of the castle were also redecorated for the Soviet command. They even had a sauna installed. Perhaps the highlight of the renovations was the banner at the entrance that stated: "We are right, we have won, we have liberated Europe," along with a large red Soviet star that was attached to the wall. Later in 1946, part of the castle was also converted into a hospital for Soviet troops that were still convalescing.[16]

Young men in Waldenburg had to be relatively scarce. Many of the units in Sachsen had been deployed to the east, and simply decimated. Others were yet to be released from captivity. Those that were home were the crippled and infirm who made it home in pieces before the end of the war. Their status as veterans could easily be seen at times because of the lack of limbs. The convalescent hospitals also served as reminders that the war was over, but the wounds of the war were still healing. For many, it would take a lifetime. Personally, for Gottfried, homecoming had to be bittersweet. Some of his friends from his youth that he chummed around with had to be dead.

His old hangouts, such as the Gewerbehaus and Grünfelder park, were still there. But the atmosphere was different. Photos of the Führer were gone, replaced by images of the new dictator, Stalin, that adorned shop windows and public buildings. There were no longer any eager Hitler Jugend wandering the streets either. Instead, young rosy-cheeked Soviet replacement troops who had not fought in the war patrolled the streets. And in the bars, the new occupants spoke a different language—Russian. This new language, and its Cyrillic alphabet, would now be taught in the schools as the primary language, followed by German. There was no longer a patriotic buzz in the town. That was replaced by the quiet solemn gaze of a defeated nation. But red flags still flew throughout the town. In the center of these flags, the swastika representing national socialism was replaced with the communist hammer and sickle. This was Gottfried's new normal that he and the other millions fought for. Like the town itself, it was time to pick through the ruins of his youth and rebuild.

Lives Beyond War

Yugoslavia was still in turmoil in 1946 and beyond. The civil war was still brewing to some degree in certain areas of the former kingdom. Croatian fascists now calling themselves Crusaders were defending their Christian culture and beliefs: Serb Chetniks loyal to the monarchy, Muslims in Bosnia, and Albanians called Ballists who were defending Kosovo, were also resisting Tito's new communist government.[1] Tito was also still seeking vengeance on the civilians of Yugoslavia. Volksdeutsche who could not prove their allegiance to the Partisans or Yugoslavia during the war were executed or placed in camps throughout the Vojvodina to starve, or later be deported. Those that survived were stripped of their civil rights and lost all of their property. Names of villages throughout the Banat were renamed to remove any clue of a Volksdeutsche presence, while anything "German" was eliminated from the landscape. Even German war graves and Volksdeutsche cemeteries were stripped of their gravestones and erased from existence. No longer would there be a presence of the Volksdeutsche communities that thrived in the Banat, and no German culture would exist in the new state of Yugoslavia. To this day, German field cemeteries are being discovered in farm fields and construction projects throughout the former kingdom. It didn't stop with the Germans. In one of Tito's first postwar operations, the graves of Italian soldiers, and domestic enemies including Ustaše, Chetniks, and collaborators were also obliterated.[2]

Tito was also still extracting his vengeance on the former occupiers. In 1946, Draza Mihailović, the leader of the Chetniks, was captured, tried, and then executed for high treason against the state. In the later Belgrade Process trials in 1947, General Alexander Löhr, commander in chief of Army Group E, and who was the person responsible for planning the bombing of Belgrade in 1941; General Johann Fortner, the commander of the 718. Infanterie-Division from 1941 to March 1943; and General Josef Kübler, who commanded the 118th until July 1944, were found guilty of "mass executions of non-combatants, especially of women and children, destruction and razing of homes, kidnapping of Yugoslav civilians to concentration camps, and torture and murder of POWs." Along with some others, they were executed by hanging outside of Belgrade on February 26, 1947.[3]

Artur Phleps, the original commander of Prinz Eugen, had died in battle in 1944. His successor, Otto Kumm, never fell into the clutches of Tito or other war crimes tribunals. After the war, he became a businessman and never gave up on his SS comrades. He was the founding chairperson of HIAG: *Hilfsgemeinschaft auf Gegenseitigkeit,* or the Mutual Aid Association for Waffen-SS members, after the Allies allowed for the creation of and re-emergence of veteran organizations in 1951. This right-wing organization lasted until 1992.[4] Kumm wrote a division history about Prinz Eugen, using Phleps' personal notes as the foundation for the book. He wrote about the pride he had in his troops, concluding the book with the comment: "… we did our duty and leave everything else in the hands of fate, and hope that our sacrifice will be remembered."[5] Kumm died at the age of 95 in 2004 of natural causes. Post-war photos show him proudly wearing his Knight's Cross with Oak Leaves and Swords, the highest military award that one could have earned in the Third Reich.[6] He was described by one author as "the ever un-reformed Nazi enthusiast."[7]

* * *

The story of many of Gottfried's comrades from Yugoslavia did not stop in 1946. Between 175,000 and 200,000 German soldiers were prisoners in Yugoslavia after the war.[8] Many would not be released until 1948.[9] Compared to other countries, such as the Soviet Union, the Yugoslavs were actually more benevolent and faster in releasing German POWS; the new nation simply did not have the resources to care for them. In 1946, the Yugoslavs were already repatriating those POWs that had been reformed, and were displaying anti-fascist attitudes. The remaining POWs were educated on the faults of fascism and the benefits of communism in their POW camps to prepare them for their release in post-fascist Europe.[10]

One POW was Ludwig Glanz who was captured on May 9 and living as a prisoner in Belgrade in October 1945. He lived in a large camp of about 3,500 prisoners. His family was back home in the American zone in Erbach im Odenwald, to the south of Frankfurt, and was not doing well. His wife wrote that there were food shortages and his young son had to run his meat delivery business. His wife also had to have surgery in late 1946, and was still recuperating in early 1947, which made him worry. Her father had also recently died. Now, as a prisoner, he was her support, writing,

> Any person in your shoes would have lost their faith. I am very proud of you my beloved Anni because you mastered all the obstacles that crossed your path bravely and loyally, and you lived your life for our children and me. So, my darling, remain strong in your heart, because one day fate will be for our benefit.[11]

Conditions back home were getting worse in 1948. Because the business was failing and Anni's health had not improved, Ludwig advised her to move in with his mother, and the kids could go to school in nearby Reichsheim.[12]

Ludwig was moved from camp to camp. Until 1947, he was in Belgrade. In March, 1947, he was moved to Maglaj in northern Bosnia. Later in 1948, he found himself in Sarajevo where he was assigned to work crews, lumbering in the nearby forests. Even though conditions were not good back home, Anni and other family members still sent him packages. Cigarettes, writing paper, razor blades, and clothes were often sent through the civilian mail system to his prison camp. Based on comments in his letters, the packages arrived in a timely manner. But he would be home soon—hopefully. In his letter to his wife on February 23, 1947, he wrote that only the ill were currently being sent home. In a July 15, 1948, letter to his wife, he wrote that he was told that the last prisoners were to be sent home by December 31, 1948.[13]

Another POW was Willy Ellerstein. Willy's family lived in Hanover, which was in the British zone of occupation. His unit was in Greece in 1944 and he was part of the retreat of Army Group E through Yugoslavia, but he never made it to the Fatherland. Like other POWs, Willy was allowed to write three letters a month home—no more than 30 lines per letter. He could also receive packages from loved ones from back home, who sent him writing paper, tobacco, tooth powder, sausages, and clothing, especially a jacket for the winter months that he was very thankful for. These packages could not be over 5kg in weight. In one of his letters he wrote, "when your packets get here, I am better equipped than any refugee, but smoking is a rare thing in here," writing that a lot of his comrades had given up the habit.[14]

One of the first Yugoslav POW camps that Willy lived in in 1946 was in the area of Bitsra and Borovnica, in southern Slovenia. In the early months of 1947, he was moved to Zavidovići in central Bosnia, north of Sarajevo. Later in 1947, he was transferred to Šamac on the Sava river. He described camp life in Šamac in a letter to his children:

> At 5am is when we get up, except for Sundays. We work from 6am to 12pm. Our lunch break is from 12pm till 2pm. Then we go back to work and put the final touches to the day from 2pm till 4pm. So, it is basically an 8-hour job except for overtime when urgent work needs to be done, but that is paid just like a civilian worker. This, however, is an arrangement made by the minister in Belgrade, and each POW camp interprets it as they wish. You can then use the money to buy fruits and vegetables, even cigarettes, when available. Sometimes when you're lucky, you can buy a can of beans. There's not a lot of things you can buy here, but we're happy and it helps us forget. Our camp chaplain has been visiting us lately and bringing us some music as well. Then we have some political education and so time goes by…[15]

His work duties varied in the camps. In Zavidovići, he was working as a carpenter, where his skills were questionable to the point that he wrote that he felt like a

Holzkopf, or idiot. He also worked in other camps as an electrician. In the spring and summer of 1947 when he was near Šamac, he was a crane operator on a barge, repairing and building bridges. He wrote that the weather was hot, and they would cool off by jumping in the river. They completed a railroad bridge over the Sava river on July 14, 1947, writing that it was a big celebration for them. For their hard work, they had the 15th and 16th off, and were given some extra food, and cigarettes.[16]

It appears that the prisoners had some freedom from the camps. Around Christmas 1947, Willy was near Sokolac in Bosnia. The company that he worked for gave them some money for their work in November, and some of the men from his camp were driven into Sarajevo, where they bought meat, sweets, alcohol, and tobacco. These items made his Christmas much better, he wrote. There were even summer and fall sports championships between the camps. In 1947, they were driven to other camps with a guard to compete against one another in handball and soccer matches. Later in May 1948, they took a one-hour train trip to Sarajevo, spending the night there. The next day, they participated in inter-camp handball and soccer tournaments, then taking the train back to their camp the following day. In the winter, activities included table tennis and chess.[17]

In September 1948, Willy was still in a small work camp in the municipality of Sokolac, living in a log cabin with 30 other POWs. He described his work in a letter home:

> … I was first a telephone man [operator] and then became a writer which means I leave early in the morning with a group of civilians to go to the log loading area. There, I have to measure and write down the logs that are being loaded to the trucks. Usually it would have been the job of a civilian, but a lot of Germans are employed here as writers and receive full confidence and trust from the company, because as Germans we do our job well and on time. You really can't complain about the provisions either. It's enough for now and we also have cornbread.

His letters contained statements of reassurance to his loved ones about conditions as a POW. "Being in prison is not a vacation," but he was doing fine under the circumstances. In another letter he wrote: "So far, I have had good working comrades and at the moment, our camp is working together. When you're working together with old comrades, everything seems bearable. Well, everything else orally later," suggesting that he may have been sugarcoating his conditions and was concerned that there would be repercussions from censors reading the letter. But in some letters, he was despondent about being a POW. He felt abandoned: "As a prisoner of war in a strange land behind barbed wires, I can't save my country the accusation that they seem to have forgotten us…"[18]

In some of his letters back home to his wife and children Willy was also optimistic about release. Letters were filled with reassurance to his 24-year-old wife in 1947: "Willy is the same as back then… When I come home, we can make up for all the things… The best times of our lives are ahead of us." He was also reassuring her that he would be released soon: "Just be patient my love, and keep your head up and everything will be OK," he wrote on April 2, 1947. In October 1947, he wrote that his Austrian comrades had been discharged, raising his optimism that release for the Germans would be soon. A year later, in October 1948, he wrote that the Volksdeutsche were being released from camp, and he would be home in Germany on December 16.[19]

For others held captive in Yugoslavia, freedom would finally come in the 1950s. These individuals were most likely re-classified as criminals, had their puppet trials, and were imprisoned. This was reserved for some of the troops from Prinz Eugen. As late as 1957, some of the troops of Prinz Eugen, who did not escape the Partisans, finally made it home. On September 6, 1957, Frederich Heinemann from Prinz Eugen was released from a Yugoslav POW camp. As part of his release, he completed Red Cross questionnaires that sought information about his missing comrades. In the case of *Sturmmann* (senior private) Hermann Baur of the *Sturmgeschütz Batterie 7*, Heinemann wrote that he was killed defending the Sava river in the direction of Belgrade on October 20, 1944. Because of the retreat, Heinemann wrote that no missing person's report could be sent to family members. For Rudi Braunrath, another Sturmmann with Sturmgeschütz Batterie 7, Heinemann was also able to confirm that he was killed on October 16, 1944, near Batajnica, a suburb of Belgrade. He was buried in a field grave. At least two families now had some closure.[20]

Alfred Roehler

Out of all of the persons in this book, Roehler was the last man remaining a POW after 1946. Freedom for him would finally come in 1950. Still working at the Electro Techna factory in Ljubljana, and living in the back room, it got to the point that he had his own drafting table. There were no guards. He said that occasionally, a political commissar would stop by and check on them. In the evenings, he and other prisoners would go out, socializing with women in the parks, and at dances. The last couple years of captivity he said were not too bad: "There was a lot of Slovenian girls that had the eyes on us… yeah, that was a good time for the last year or two…" He was never without food. He was fed at the factory, and co-workers would bring him food. Even girls would bring him food, and the side money that he made from his co-workers to do their jobs also permitted him to buy civilian clothes, and other foodstuffs.[21]

He said that he finally just got fed up being a POW. From the money that he had saved up, he purchased a forged Slovenian passport on the black market, and had another document made that stated that he was a Slovenian engineer who was traveling to Germany to buy equipment. He took the train to Austria, traveling through the same tunnel where he was captured in 1945, and then stopped in Klagenfurt:

> And there's the British, you know… control. I said I'm a POW and I am escaping, and he didn't believe me and he said I'm gonna send you back… No no no you're not sending me back. I had… I was lucky enough to have a copy of my birth certificate. I had no other papers you know, that was all lost and I shoved that birth certificate under his nose, and he said OK, go

on. So, then I went back to the train and to Salzburg and then there was the German border and they wouldn't let... the Americans wouldn't let me go through there. Some big guy said where are you going? I want to go home, I said. He said, well go over there, and there was the German police, the border police, and there again was somebody from my hometown sitting there. That was my lucky thing, and he said go home. Well, it's how simple it was.

Well, I went home, walked up the stairs to my parents' house, and knocked on the door. My mother fell over—passed out. We were all... how do I say this... German families were toughened up because of the war. My dad got all beat up at the end of the war. He was in World War I and II. He was anti-aircraft. He ended up in Africa and Sicily and God knows where else. My older brother was in Russia, mostly on the front. The [unit] made it into Austria and the Americans turned them over to the Russians. His whole division got sent back. The Russians got him and they took him to Siberia. Nine years later he came home.

So, I tried to find my old place back where I was working as a draftsman, you know. I was an apprentice, but it was too late after the war. Everything was filled up and there was no way. So, you start thinking what to do, and I got to know people again. We had the American army occupying an airport close to the town. 7th Artillery as a matter of fact... a lot of American soldiers running around, and it was taxi cabs that hauled Americans, you know. So, I finagled enough money together to make a down payment on a taxi and the license and started hauling GIs around. That's where I learned speaking English. That went on for quite a while and I met a fella from California. He came home to us and lived at my house. He felt at home and he was lonesome—a young fella, German background you know... and he said I'll sponsor you anytime you want to come, and you can do a lot better in the states. In the meantime, I got married and had two boys. I said OK, and it took two years to get the visa and the papers together and enough money to fly. And bang, here I am.[22]

He immigrated to California and worked three jobs to save up to buy a house and a car before his family came over a few months later. He started driving dump trucks and operating heavy machinery, becoming a mechanic for Caterpillars and trucks for five years, until he got his citizenship. He ended up buying some property in a rural area and started farming, raising birds for a living. The bird business snowballed. Southern California's climate, he said, was perfect for the bird business. He said that he was raising hundreds of birds at a time—canaries, parakeets, finches, doves, and macaws. He had a good friend who was an importer, so he always got good breeding stock directly from the jungle. Eventually, he sold his business and moved to a retirement community near Palm Springs. His wife had passed on, and his sons did not have an interest in the bird business. Both sons joined the US military; one was in the army and served in Vietnam. The other went through the Air Force Academy and became a career officer.[23]

Rudy Hansinger

On July 4, 1946, Hansinger was discharged as a POW from Langwasser camp in Nuremberg. He knew that his parents and family were in Munich, and requested that he be sent there to live, and find a job. In 1944, with the fall of Belgrade, his family had already evacuated to Germany and became displaced persons. After reporting to and registering with the police in Munich, he was assigned quarters in a former camp that was built for foreign workers to live in during the war. Living conditions were simple, he said. He slept on a bunk bed in a communal room, and picked up odd jobs when he could. Every day for food, he would visit his family at the DP camp and eat with them. His father was talking about moving back to Yugoslavia, which Rudy said was simply not possible due to their family's German background, and the repressive actions of the Tito regime. Reflecting on his own and his family's living conditions, he said that the local authorities and Red Cross could not have done any better; the amount of displaced people that needed help was immense.[24]

Rudy married a German woman that served in the equivalent of the female Hitler Youth during World War II. He and members of his family made it to the US in the 1950s. Already, he had two uncles that had emigrated to the US and Canada after World War I. His cousin from Florida, who fought in Europe during World War II on the American side, sponsored them. He chose to live in the Milwaukee area, building a home on a small lake outside the city. He told me that he chose the area because it was peaceful and quiet. He said this is what he wanted: peace in his life. When I interviewed him, I could tell that he made a good life for himself. He was content and was cared for in his final years, surrounded by loving and caring family members who were also interested in hearing his story. Remnants of his youth in the Banat and his Volksdeutsche heritage still remained. The family still spoke German.[25]

After he retired from his career in the automotive industry, he spent his free time researching his family tree, his life in the Banat, and the Prinz Eugen division. The Banat that he never got to see again and his time in Prinz Eugen became his passion. He had a small room in his house that served as a library where he kept his books related to Prinz Eugen, even writing his own story about his time in the division that he wanted preserved for the family, before the clouds of time obscured them from his memory. In the margins of books published about Prinz Eugen, he provided his own comments, adding to the story. I asked him if he had any good memories during the war. He said there were none. "No good memories, I do not smile today. It was a sad, sad part of my life. I am sometimes more bitter with the Germans than the Partisans," he said, telling me about how he and the other Volksdeutsche felt used by, and then abandoned by the Germans later in the war, left at the mercy of the Partisans and communists. In late 2011, I received an e-mail from his grandson that he was not doing well. Later, in November, he passed away, surrounded by his loving family.[26]

Others from Prinz Eugen in this book were less fortunate. Erwin Ellmer was never to be seen again. Like Hansinger, he was at the SS-Artillerie-Schule II in Beneschau by Prague until April, 1945. After this, his whereabouts are unknown. Hans Preuss, the volunteer from Berlin, was also never seen again. A search for both him and Ellmer on the Volksbund Deutsche Kriegsgräberfürsorge, or German War

Graves Commission site, showed that they were never registered as dead. They may have been killed and buried in a field grave, wound up in a Soviet gulag, or even made it home. Or, they met their fate in Slovenia, or later in Serbia, left to rot in a roadside ditch or mass grave. In my conversations with vonCampe he described the men of Prinz Eugen division who he fought with as "very good and very humane. None of them were volunteers… basically German families that were ordered into the SS uniform." vonCampe had a hunch of what happened to them: "Wearing an SS uniform meant death," he said.[27]

The Others

Others in this book that served in the Wehrmacht started rebuilding their lives in 1946. Rudy Wagner can be best described as a man that lived for adventure. Immediately after the war he became a smuggler. Probably using some of the same mountain trails that he used to get home to Innsbruck, he now hauled cigarettes, alcohol, and other black-market goods in his rucksack, even writing a book on his post-war smuggling adventures. He married his sweetheart, and he became a writer and world traveler. His son Rudy, calling himself "little Rudy," told me that his father died in Punta Arenas, Chile, in 2010 on his last journey, after a great life.[28] Richard Wachter, meanwhile, returned to Munich and worked as a civil servant for the city of Munich.[29]

vonCampe had a different life journey. After the war, he moved to Mexico and started up an automotive parts company. He proudly told me how he had built the company from the ground up, and had a deep respect for his employees. This respect was reciprocated to him in the form of loyal employees who were dedicated to the company. He became rich. Later, he moved to the United States, and pursued his primary passion of service to God. He never forgot the day that he made it out of the Soviet occupation zone in Austria and realized that God had a purpose for him. He tirelessly educated people and wrote books on the dangers of totalitarianism, living and preaching the word of God until his death in 2012.[30]

The Allies

Of the Allies that fought in the war, most came home to intact homes and cities, parades, and nations grateful to them for defeating fascism. They were appreciated, and to this day, there is deep respect for their service. This was much different from their former enemies. For the Germans, the atrocities of the camps added to their collective guilt, where most likely, many veterans themselves kept their service quiet and not detailed, probably only explaining that they served "*im Osten, Westen, Nord, or Sudlich*" (in the East, West, North, or South). Their visible wounds and the psychological trauma revealed in their faces was enough to validate that they served. Perhaps some had survivor's guilt, wondering why they were spared while so many millions met their fate in battle. With military decorations initially banned, it would not be until 1957 that veterans in West Germany could wear their de-Nazified awards from the war.[31] In the East, meanwhile, they were not worn until after 1990, when the Berlin Wall fell. The Allies, though, wore their uniforms with their ribbon bars. Proud mothers pranced them to social events and church, and their uniforms probably served as chick magnets at the local bars and dances. In all cases, they were glad to be home and they continued on with their civilian lives.

Bob Bishop from No.2 Commandos first went back home to England and soon moved to Canada and then Florida, then moving back to Canada, and settling in the Toronto area. He worked as an engineer. On November 13, 2009, I received an e-mail from his wife Janet. Bob had died. He had a heart attack while flying home from his commando reunion at the old commando training center at Achnacarry, Scotland. The aircraft made an emergency landing in Montreal to get him to a hospital, but it was too late. She also wrote that he had a wonderful holiday where he met up with another commando from the war. They were the only No. 2 Commandos present from World War II. She wrote it was over very quickly for Bob. He did not suffer. Like other families, they had never recorded their loved ones' memories. Janet asked for copies of the recordings of our conversations. This would soon become a recurring request as more of the veterans interviewed for this book started passing away.

Frank Lashinsky moved back to New York and eventually settled in Pennsylvania. After the war, he took advantage of the GI Bill and finished college, becoming a chemical engineer and working for Pfizer for 31 years. He was very active in his unit's reunion organization and the Air Force Escape and Evasion Society, an organization for downed US aircrews. After retiring, he went back to Hungary with officials from the Pentagon to find one of his crew members that never made it back. They found him buried in a local cemetery, and had his remains repatriated to the United States. They also found the debris field of his B-24. He took home a piece of the aluminum skin from a wing section of the aircraft as a memento. Frank died in 2016.[32]

Andrew Mousalimas, along with others from his Greek-American OSS unit, completed his service in Greece, and was caught up in the Greek civil war that was brewing at the end of World War II. After his service, he returned home to Oakland, California, married a nice Greek-American girl, and raised a family. He was in the restaurant business throughout his working career, and his claim to fame is that he was the originator of fantasy football. After retiring from the restaurant business, he spent his free time writing about his unit.[33] He died in 2020.

Milorad Kristović became a displaced person after the war. He had no home to go to. He was now considered a war criminal by Tito. After being ordered by Mihailović to leave the kingdom, he and his unit, along with many civilian refugees, had made the long trek north to Fiume and then Trieste and the safety of Italy.

From there, in 1947, he was sent to a displaced persons camp in Germany, where he met his wife. Immigrating to the United States in the 1950s, he attended college, studying mechanical engineering at Talladega College in Alabama, and settled in South Carolina where he had his own engineering business. He was loyal to King Alexander, King Peter, and the Kingdom of Yugoslavia throughout his entire life. He even named his two sons Alex and Peter. He considered Mihailović a martyr for the Yugoslav monarchy, and his puppet trial and execution by the Tito regime in 1946 as an international travesty of justice. On one of my visits to Mike in South Carolina, I asked him what the secret to longevity was. He was 94 at the time. I assumed that he would tell me that walking his German shepherd every day and eating healthy was his secret. Instead, he started to cry, telling me that he was afraid to die because God would never forgive him for what he did in the war.[34] Mike died in 2018. He was 99.

118. Jäger-Division

The division itself did not disappear after the war. It now became a reunion association. Beginning with its first reunion on September 29, 1952, in Klagenfurt, the division had biennial reunions in Germany and Austria that included Munich, Innsbruck, Salzburg, Klagenfurt, Graz, Bregenz, and Bad Reichenhall, where the original companies and regiments of 718. Infanterie-Division and later 118. Jäger-Division were located prior to and during the war.[35] During some reunions, symbolic treks back to Hochosterwitz Castle occured, followed by a solemn ceremony to remember the dead and missing. The association even published a couple books; one was based on the division's movements during the war, while the other included stories from members of the division in their travels throughout the war.[36]

For some veterans their service in the 118th would remain a significant part of their life. A couple photo albums that I obtained from someone that served in the 118th shows that he and his wife attended many of the reunions. The early reunion photos are black and white and then transition to color in the later years, showing the progression of aging gray-haired chubby vets laughing and reminiscing with their comrades with their wives at their sides. For some veterans, it appears that the war and service with 118. Jäger-Division was the defining moment of their lives. One such person was Heinrich Hermann. Born in Munich in 1899, Heinrich was a career soldier, earning the Iron Cross Second Class in World War I while serving in the field artillery regiment *Prinz Leopold*. After World War I he remained in the Reserve Army in Munich and joined the Nazi Party in January 1933. In August 1939, he was on active duty status and attached to the *Jäger-Ersatz Regiment 136* in Innsbruck, and then transferred to 718. Infanterie-Division division command staff in April 1941, serving as the division's intendant or administrative officer. Leaving

Memorabilia from 118th reunions held over the years. (Author's collection)

Veterans from the 118th at one of the division's reunions that were held in Austria and Germany. Top to bottom: One of the vets with his wife holds a 118. Jäger-Division pennant; vets gather at a reception table, one of them wearing a fez, during their reunion in Graz, Austria; vets celebrating a 60th birthday with the 118th veteran flag in the background. (Author's collection)

his posh quarters located in the Hotel Niedersachsischer Hof in Goslar, he then became the division's chief of staff for the quartermasters in Sarajevo in 1942, and later moved with the division through Montenegro and to the Dalmatian coastline in 1943 and beyond, ending up at the division's main headquarters in Prague in 1944. Heinrich's photo albums provide a glimpse into the life of an officer in the 118th in Sarajevo—riding horses, going to parades and funerals, conducting inspections, and accompanying troops in the field.

Other materials from his estate show that he attended many of the reunions after the war and collected information related to his missing comrades. One of his documents from his estate includes a 1953 Red Cross list of all the missing from the 118th. With some of the names underlined with colored pencil, maybe persons that he knew from the various regiments and companies, it appears that he never gave up trying to locate some of his missing comrades. Of the 1,000-plus missing, 18 were from his own headquarters unit. Most of them disappeared in 1944 and were NCOs and lower officer-grade ranks which suggests they were on the front lines and not in the relative safety in the rear when they went missing.[37]

Rudy Wagner also made it to some of the reunions. But towards the end of the first decade of this century, Rudy stopped going to them. The reunions were getting smaller, Rudy said. The later reunions simply consisted of "widows sipping tea."[38] Time had taken its toll on the surviving members. While conducting research for this book, I actually found a person that was involved with the 118th Reunion Association in Klagenfurt. He told me that the reunions were over, and the association's materials were locked away in a storage garage somewhere in the Klagenfurt area.

Gottfried

Compared to other German and even American families, Gottfried's family was fortunate. Nobody was killed. It was probably a rare occurrence that in a war that led to the combat deaths of over four million Germans, there was not a photo of a young teen hanging in one's home with a black ribbon draped across it. His older brother Georg, who fought in Greece and Yugoslavia, also made it home. Georg settled in Darmstadt, West Germany, opting not to return to a life under communist rule. He died in 1999. While writing this book, Gottfried's daughter told me that Georg's wife was still alive but had no interest in reliving that part of her life with me.

Gottfried lived his life in Waldenburg. After his short stint in construction and demolition work, he became a bookkeeper for the stocking manufacturer Haase. Gottfried never reunited with Ilse, his love during the war. One night at a dance in Waldenburg, he met Hildegard née Giselhar, most likely charming her over with his moves on the dance floor, and probably teaching her how to tango. He was never one to let his feet rest at a dance. Hildegard would become the love of his life. They married in 1950 and had two children. Their son was born in 1954, and later in 1964, their daughter Claudia was born.

Claudia told me that they had a happy childhood and that her parents were very caring and loving. They always wanted the best for her and her brother. Both kids went to college. From a man who quoted famous philosophers in his diary, it is no surprise that he wanted a college education for his children—something he had been deprived of due to the war. Claudia earned her degree in food science, and his son became a physician. The family never talked about the war and politics. Claudia said in the post-war German Democratic Republic critics of the regime had to expect reprisals. Therefore, the political opinions of her parents were very reserved and discreet. Her father and mother were what she said the Germans called a *Mitläufer*—a fellow traveler—not convinced of communism, but nevertheless accepting it and not raising any issues. She said that she and her brother had very good relationships with their parents.[39]

World War II and 118. Jäger-Division remained part of Gottfried's life. He did not completely avoid the memories of the war, but occasionally relived his time in the Wehrmacht with his old comrades. After the wall fell, he managed to make it to a few of the division's reunions that were held in Austria. His old comrades were the people that understood the war and what they did in Yugoslavia. They were therapists. They helped him make sense, were not judgmental, and did not make him fully confront the truth of the war, but instead provided a sanitized version of the war, based on their comradeship. Gottfried also stayed in touch with Richard Wachter who he met when he was a SEP. Wachter even visited Gottfried in 1978, and later in August 1984, when he was in hospital in Waldenburg. The leg injury he received during the invasion of Korčula in 1943 had flared up and needed to be operated on. Richard also sent the Weber family parcels from the West that contained items that were difficult or impossible to obtain in the GDR. Wachter summarized Gottfried in this way: "Gottfried was a good, friendly, and a helpful person. I really appreciated him."[40]

While writing this book, I was often asked: What do you think Gottfried was like? In my opinion, he was a kid caught up in the victories of the German nation, filled full of patriotism, and influenced by the propaganda machine that basically controlled all of Germany in the 1930s, until the end in 1945. Based on his diary entries, he was educated, and detail oriented. He was also religious. He would always write in his diary what major religious holidays and festivals were occurring for that particular day. It appeared that he was not shy and was considerate of others. If he grew up in modern society, he might be considered by some to be a model child. He was also full of insight and was excited about life. Unfortunately, he, and millions more, were sucked into the Nazi philosophy, collectively engaging in actions where human values, morality, and natural law no longer applied, contributing to the conflagration that would subsequently change their lives and the world. To a degree, he willingly placed himself in a very bad situation, and most likely had regrets later in his life for serving and supporting the Third Reich. He had dirty hands that helped keep the machine alive.

But this book was not just a story of one German soldier. It is the story of the many conscripts who were called into service to fight the Bolsheviks, and later fight for the survival of Germany itself. Their duty to serve was engrained in them; it was genetic—a reflex. Just like their fathers who fought in World War I, and their ancestors who helped create the German Empire in 1871, true German patriots served the Fatherland. God was even on their side. Stamped on their Wehrmacht belt buckles was the motto *Gott Mit Uns*, or "God is With Us," which further reinforced their duty to serve. So, they went, fought, came home, and made lives for themselves. In most cases, their patriotism and motives were most likely not too different from the soldiers on the Allied side who were interviewed for this book. This is also a contemporary story that has been repeated many times since the end of World War II. There are many Gottfrieds in the world today. Believers in a cause, good or bad, and willing to fight for it. Nations still need, want, and groom Gottfrieds. More are being bred and born every day.

Every story has a conclusion, and Gottfried's came in the first decade of the 21st century. In 2004, Gottfried's wife Hildegard was diagnosed with severe Alzheimer's disease and was placed in a nursing home. Gottfried was devastated. He died three months later in 2005. They were married for 55 years.[41]

Thanks for the adventure.

Endnotes

Introduction

1   G. Hennes (personal communciation, January 29, 2009).

Chapter 1

1   Lukacs, John (2001). *The Last European War: September 1939–December 1941*. Yale University Press.

2   Gardner, W. J. R. (2014). *The Evacuation from Dunkirk: "Operation Dynamo", 26 May–June 1940*. Routledge.

3   Hough, R., Hough, R. A., & Richards, D. (2005). *The Battle of Britain: The Greatest Air Battle of World War II*. WW Norton & Company.

4   Hartmann, C. (2013). *Operation Barbarossa: Nazi Germany's War in the East, 1941–1945*. Oxford: Oxford University Press.

5   Williamson, G. (2012). *Afrikakorps 1941–43*. Bloomsbury Publishing.

6   Hall, R. C. (2002). *The Balkan Wars 1912–1913: Prelude to the First World War*. Abingdon, UK: Routledge.

7   Hooton, E. R. (2017). *Prelude to the First World War: The Balkan Wars 1912–1913*. Fonthill Media.

8   Williamson, S. R. (1990). *Austria-Hungary and the Origins of the First World War*. New York: Macmillan International Higher Education.

9   Becherelli, A. (1914). "Remembering Gavrilo Princip." *The First World War: Analysis and Interpretation*, *1*, 17–33.

10 Jagodić, M., & Radonjić, O. (2015). "Pyrrhic Victory: The Great War and its Immediate Consequences for Serbia's Economy." In I. Vujacic & M. Arandarenko (eds.), *The Economic Causes and Consequences of the First World War*. Belgrade: Faculty of Economics, University of Belgrade, pp. 219–235.

11 Crampton, R. (1997). *Eastern Europe in the Twentieth Century—And After*. Abingdon, UK: Routledge.

12 Lampe, J. R. (2020). "Overview: armies and occupations, peace settlements and forced migrations." In Lampe, J. R. & Brunnbar, U. (eds.), *The Routledge Handbook of Balkan and Southeast European History*. Abingdon, UK: Routledge, pp. 147–154.

13 Hoptner, J. B. (1962). "The Roots of Crisis." In *Yugoslavia in Crisis 1934–1941*. New York: Columbia University Press; Bartlett, W. (2003). *Croatia: Between Europe and the Balkans*. London: Routledge.

14 Ramet, S. P. (2006). *The Three Yugoslavias: State-building and Legitimation, 1918–2005.* Bloomington, IN: Indiana University Press.

15 Rendic-Miocevic, I. (2002). "Retracing the past to the cradle of Croatian history." *East European Quarterly, 36*(1), 1–25.

16 Fine, J. V. A. (1991). *The Early Medieval Balkans: A Critical Survey from the Sixth to the Late Twelfth Century.* Ann Arbor, MI: University of Michigan Press.

17 Goldstein, I. (1999). *Croatia: A History.* McGill-Queen's University Press.

18 Biondich, M. (2020). "The Croat Peasant Party: From Stjepan Radić to Vladko Maček." In Lampe, J. R. & Brunnbar, U. (eds.), *The Routledge Handbook of Balkan and Southeast European History.* London: Routledge, pp. 263–271; Gordon-Smith, G. (1925). "The Croatian capitulation." *Advocate of Peace through Justice, 87*(7), 421–424; Kršljanin, N. (2020). "The Parliament of the Kingdom of Serbs, Croats and Slovenes: Projects, the Constitution, and Reality (1918–29)." *Parliaments, Estates and Representation, 40*(2), 245–259.

19 Biondich, M. (2016). *Stjepan Radić, the Croat Peasant Party, and the Politics of Mass Mobilization, 1904–1928.* University of Toronto Press; Kosnica, I. (2021). "State Authority and Competing Arrangements in the Kingdom of Serbs, Croats and Slovenes/Yugoslavia (1918–1941)." *Administory, 5*(1), 152–166.

20 For more information on the HSS in pre-war Yugoslavia see: Gaži, S. (1973). "Stjepan Radić: His Life and Political Activities (1871–1928)." *Journal of Croatian Studies, 14,* 13–73.

21 Pavle Radić and Đuro Basariček were the two persons that were killed.

22 Radan, P. (2018). "The Serbs and Their History in the Twentieth Century." In Radan, P. & Pavkovic (eds.), *The Serbs and Their Leaders in the Twentieth Century.* London: Routledge, pp. 1–29.

23 Miljan, G. (2018). *Croatia and the Rise of Fascism: The Youth Movement and the Ustaša During WWII.* Bloomsbury Publishing.

24 Gligorijević, B. (2018). "King Aleksandar I Karađorđević." In Radan, P. & Pavkovic (eds.), *The Serbs and Their Leaders in the Twentieth Century.* London: Routledge, pp. 140–157.

25 Radan, P. (2018). "The Serbs and Their History in the Twentieth Century." In Radan, P. & Pavkovic (eds.), *The Serbs and Their Leaders in the Twentieth Century.* London: Routledge, pp. 1–29.

26 McCormick, R. B. (2014). *Croatia Under Ante Pavelic: America, the Ustaše and Croatian Genocide in World War II.* London: Bloomsbury Publishing.

27 Goldstein, I. (2006). "Ante Pavelić, Charisma and National Mission in Wartime Croatia." *Totalitarian Movements and Political Religions, 7*(2), 225–234.

28 McCormick, R. B. (2014). *Croatia Under Ante Pavelić: America, the Ustaše and Croatian Genocide in World War II.* Bloomsbury Publishing.

29 Sadkovich, J. J. (1988). "Terrorism in Croatia, 1929–1934." *East European Quarterly, 22*(1), 55–79.

30 Adriano, P., & Cingolani, G. (2018). *Nationalism and Terror: Ante Pavelić and Ustaša Terrorism from Fascism to the Cold War.* Budapest: Central European University Press.

31 McCormick, R. B. (2014). *Croatia Under Ante Pavelić: America, the Ustaše and Croatian Genocide in World War II.* London: Bloomsbury Publishing.

32 Miljan, G. (2018). *Croatia and the Rise of Fascism: The Youth Movement and the Ustaša During WWII.* London: Bloomsbury Publishing.

33 Ibid.

34 Ramet, S. P. (2007). "Vladko Maček and the Croatian Peasant Defence in the Kingdom of Yugoslavia." *Contemporary European History, 16*(2), 215–231.

35 Ibid.

36 Adriano, P., & Cingolani, G. (2018). *Nationalism and Terror: Ante Pavelić and Ustaša Terrorism from Fascism to the Cold War.* Budapest: Central European University Press.

37   Miljan, G. (2019). *Croatia and the Rise of Fascism: The Youth Movement and the Ustaša During WWII*. London: Bloomsbury Publishing.

38   Ibid.

39   Adriano, P., & Cingolani, G. (2018). *Nationalism and Terror: Ante Pavelić and Ustaša Terrorism from Fascism to the Cold War*. Budapest: Central European University Press.

40   Deroc, M. (1990). "Demise of the Yugoslav Army." *East European Quarterly, 24*(1), 57–64.

41   Miljan, G. (2019). *Croatia and the Rise of Fascism: The Youth Movement and the Ustaša During WWII*. London: Bloomsbury Publishing.

42   Ibid.

43   Ibid.

44   Dizdar, Z. (2005). "Italian Policies Toward Croatians in Occupied Territories During the Second World War." *Review of Croatian History, 1*(1), 179–210.

45   Biondich, M. (2020). "The Croat Peasant Party: From Stjepan Radić to Vladko Maček." In Lmoe, J. R. & Brunnbauer, U (eds.), *The Routledge Handbook of Balkan and Southeast European History*. London: Routledge, pp. 263–271.

46   Pavlowitch, S. (2008). *Hitler's New Disorder: the Second World War in Yugoslavia*. London: Hurst & Company Limited.

47   Onslow, S. (2005). "Britain and the Belgrade Coup of 27 March 1941 Revisited." *Electronic Journal of International History, 8*, 1–57.

48   Svolopoulos, C. (1987). "Greece and its Neighbours on the Eve of the German Invasion of the Balkans, 1941." *Balkan Studies, 28*(2), 355–371.

49   Milazzo, M. J. (2019). *The Chetnik Movement and the Yugoslav Resistance*. Baltimore, MD: Johns Hopkins University Press; Hoptner, J. B. (1963). *Yugoslavia in Crisis*. London: Columbia University Press.

50   Onslow, S. (2005). "Britain and the Belgrade Coup of 27 March 1941 Revisited." *Electronic Journal of International History, 8*, 1–57.

51   Mezger, C. (2020). *Forging Germans: Youth, Nation, and the National Socialist Mobilization of Ethnic Germans in Yugoslavia, 1918–1944*. Oxford: Oxford University Press.

52   E. Sakasitz (personal communication, February 16, 2009).

53   Ibid.

54   Killen, J. (2013). *The Luftwaffe: A History*. Barnsley, UK: Pen & Sword Aviation.

55   Prusin, A. (2017). *Serbia Under the Swastika: A World War II Occupation*. Chicago: University of Illinois Press.

56   From: https://www.wikiwand.com/en/Bridges_of_Belgrade; https://en.wikipedia.org/wiki/King_Alexander_Bridge; https://en.wikipedia.org/wiki/Pan%C4%8Devo_Bridge.

57   Z. Kellerman (personal communication, May 12, 2009).

58   Heaton, C. D. (1998). "Taking Belgrade by Bluff." *World War II, 12*(5), 30–35.

59   Alexander, P. (2017). *Serbia Under the Swastika: A World War II Occupation*. Chicago: University of Illinois Press.

60   Tanner, M. (2010). *Croatia: A Nation Forged in War*. New Haven, CT: Yale University Press; Goldstein, I. (2006). "Ante Pavelić, Charisma and National Mission in Wartime Croatia." *Politics, Religion & Ideology, 7*(2), 225–234.

61   Yeomans, R. (2012). *Visions of Annihilation: The Ustaša Regime and the Cultural Politics of Fascism, 1941–1945*. Pittsburgh: University of Pittsburgh Press.

62   Tomasevich, J. (1969). *Yugoslavia During the Second World War*. Berkeley, CA: University of California Press, pp. 59–118.

63 Ristović, M. (2001). "Yugoslav Jews Fleeing the Holocaust, 1941–1945." In *Remembering for the Future*. London: Palgrave Macmillan, pp. 512–526.

64 Bieber, F. (2020). "Building Yugoslavia in the Sand? Dalmatian Refugees in Egypt, 1944–1946." *Slavic Review, 79*(2), 298–322.

65 Prusin, A. (2017). *Serbia Under the Swastika: A World War II Occupation*. Chicago: University of Illinois Press.

66 Bartlett, W. (2004). *Croatia: Between Europe and the Balkans*. London: Routledge.

67 Hehn, P. N. (1971). "Serbia, Croatia and Germany 1941–1945: Civil War and Revolution in the Balkans." *Canadian Slavonic Papers, 13*(4), 344–373.

68 Goldstein, I. (2006). "Ante Pavelić, Charisma and National Mission in Wartime Croatia." *Politics, Religion & Ideology, 7*(2), 225–234.

69 Redzic, E., & Donia, R. (2004). *Bosnia and Herzegovina in the Second World War*. London: Routledge, p. 202.

70 Calic, M. J. (2019). *A History of Yugoslavia*. Perdue University Press; Prusin, A. (2017). *Serbia Under the Swastika: A World War II Occupation*. Chicago: University of Illinois Press.

71 Dizdar, Z. (2005). "Italian Policies Toward Croatians in Occupied Territories During the Second World War." *Review of Croatian History, 1*(1), 179–210; Pavlowitch, S. (2008). *Hitler's New Disorder: The Second World War in Yugoslavia*. London: Hurst & Company Limited.

72 Dizdar, Z. (2005). "Italian Policies Toward Croatians in Occupied Territories During the Second World War." *Review of Croatian History, 1*(1), 179–210.

73 Pirjevec, J. (2018). *Tito and his Comrades*. Madison, WI: University of Wisconsin Press.

74 Redzic, E., & Donia, R. (2004). *Bosnia and Herzegovina in the Second World War*. London: Routledge, p. 202.

75 McConville, M. (2007). *A Small War in the Balkans: British Military Involvement in Wartime Yugoslavia 1941–1945*. Uckfied, UK: Naval & Military Press, Ltd., pp. 25–26.

76 Dizdar, Z. (2005). "Italian Policies Toward Croatians in Occupied Territories During the Second World War." *Review of Croatian History, 1*(1), 179–210.

77 Redzic, E., & Donia, R. (2004). *Bosnia and Herzegovina in the Second World War*. London: Routledge, p. 202.

78 Pirjevec, J. (2018). *Tito and his Comrades*. Madison: University of Wisconsin Press.

79 Redzic, E., & Donia, R. (2004). *Bosnia and Herzegovina in the Second World War*. London: Routledge, pp. 202, 204.

80 M. Kristović (personal communications, 2008–2009).

81 McConville, M. (2007). *A Small War in the Balkans: British Military Involvement in Wartime Yugoslavia 1941–1945*. Uckfield, UK: Naval & Military Press, Ltd., p. 23.

82 Trew, S. (1998). *Britain, Mihailovic and the Chetniks, 1941–42*. New York: Springer.

83 Bax, M. (2000). "The Celebration of a Violent Past: About Some Local Sources of the Recent War in Bosnia-Herzegovina." *Narodna umjetnost: hrvatski časopis za etnologiju i folkloristiku, 37*(1), 115–131.

84 Veljan, N., & Ćehajić-Čampara, M. (2020). "A Dangerous Nexus? History, Ideology and the Structure of the Contemporary Chetnik Movement." *Democracy & Security in Southeastern Europe, 7*(1), 22–40.

85 Cohen, P. J. (1997). "The Ideology and Historical Continuity of Serbia's Anti-Islamic Policy." *Islamic Studies, 36*(2/3), 361–382.

86 Tasić, D. (2021). "The Emergence of New Paramilitary Organizations in Bulgaria and Yugoslavia after the First World War." *Nationalities Papers, 49*(6), 1–13.

87 Tasić, D. (2019). "The Institutionalization of Paramilitarism in Yugoslav Macedonia: The Case of the Organization Against the Bulgarian Bandits, 1923–1931." *Journal of Slavic Military Studies, 32*(3), 388–413.

88 Tasić, D. (2021). "The Emergence of New Paramilitary Organizations in Bulgaria and Yugoslavia after the First World War." *Nationalities Papers*, *49*(6), 1–13.

89 Ramet, S. P. (2007). "Vladko Maček and Croatian History: An Introduction." *Contemporary European History*, *16*(2), 199–202.

90 Tasić, D. (2020). *Paramilitarism in the Balkans: Yugoslavia, Bulgaria, and Albania, 1917–1924*. London: Oxford University Press.

91 McConville, M. (2007). *A Small War in the Balkans: British Military Involvement in Wartime Yugoslavia 1941–1945*. Uckfield, UK: Naval & Military Press, Ltd., p. 24.

92 Bartlett, W. (2003). *Croatia: Between Europe and the Balkans*. London: Routledge.

93 McConville, M. (2007). *A Small War in the Balkans: British Military Involvement in Wartime Yugoslavia 1941–1945*. Uckfield, UK: Naval & Military Press, Ltd.

94 M. Kristović (personal communications, 2008–2009).

95 Ibid.

96 Glantz, D. M. (2011). *Operation Barbarossa: Hitler's Invasion of Russia 1941*. Stroud, UK: The History Press; Prusin, A. (2017). *Serbia Under the Swastika: A World War II Occupation*. University of Illinois Press.

Chapter 2

1   Piehler, G. K., & Grant, J. (eds.), (2023). *The Oxford Handbook of World War II*. New York: Oxford University Press.

2   Budig, U. (2000). *Erinnerungen and den Frühling 1945*. Neiderfrohna, Germany: Mironde-Verlag.

3   Lepage, J. D. G. (2009). *Hitler Youth, 1922–1945: An Illustrated History*. London: McFarland.

4   Ibid.

5   See "Law on the Hitler Youth." Alpha History. From: https://alphahistory.com/nazigermany/law-on-the-hitler-youth/ and HJ Research. From: https://www.hj-research.com/forum/f85/hj-streifendienst-questions-772/.

6   "Law on the Hitler Youth." Alpha History. From: https://alphahistory.com/nazigermany/law-on-the-hitler-youth/.

7   "The Hitler Jugend (The Hitler Youth Organisation)." From: https://www.ibiblio.org/hyperwar/NHC/NewPDFs/GERMANY/GER%20Hitler%20Jugend.pdf.

8   Stokes, L. D. (1978). "The Social Composition of the Nazi Party in Eutin, 1925–32." *International Review of Social History*, *23*(1), 1–32.

9   Ambrose, S. E. (1990). *Handbook on German Military Forces*. Baton Rouge, LA: LSU Press.

10 Military Intelligence Division (1944, April). The German Replacement Army. Washington D.C.: War Department.

11 Patel, K. K. (2005). *Soldiers of Labor: Labor Service in Nazi Germany and New Deal America, 1933–1945*. Cambridge University Press.

12 Fritz, S. (1997). *Frontsoldaten: The German Soldier in World War II*. Lexington, KY: University Press of Kentucky.

13 van Pelt, R. J., Krause, U., & Wienert, A. (2019). *Reflections on Camps – Space, Agency, Materiality*. Vienna: Vandenhoeck & Ruprecht.

14 Patel, K. K. (2005). *Soldiers of Labor: Labor Service in Nazi Germany and New Deal America, 1933–1945*. London: Cambridge University Press.

15 Gönner, R. V., Seipp, P., & Scheibe, W. (1937). *Spaten und Ähre: das Handbuch der deutschen Jugend im Reichsarbeitsdienst*. Heidelberg: Kurt Vowindel Verlag, p. 213.

16 Ibid.

17 van Pelt, R. J., Krause, U., & Wienert, A. (2019). *Reflections on Camps – Space, Agency, Materiality.* Vienna: Vandenhoeck & Ruprecht.

18 E. Sakasitz (personal communication, February 16, 2009).

19 "Infanterie-Regiment Plauen Infanterie-Regiment 31." Lexikon der Wehrmacht. From: https://www.lexikon-der-wehrmacht.de/Gliederungen/Infanterieregimenter/IR31.htm.

20 Scapini, A. & Gorzanelli, A. (2013). *The Wehrpass and Soldbuch of the Wehrmacht.* Richmond, MI: B&D Publishing.

21 Bollow, M. E. (1999). *The Recruit: A Primer, Tutorial and Refresher Course for Young Soldiers.* Chicago: Infoblitz Publications.

Chapter 3

1 Gilbert, M. (2014). *The Second World War: A Complete History.* New York: Rosetta Books.

2 G. Hennes (personal communication, April 10, 2009).

3 For more information on 24. Infanterie-Division, see: https://en.wikipedia.org/wiki/24th_Infanry_Division_(Wehrmacht).

4 For a review of 718. Infanterie-Division go to: https://d6kvd4uory7vz160tdyh5zuwuq-jj2cvlaia-66be-lexikon-der-wehrmacht.translate.goog/Gliederungen/Infanteriedivisionen/718ID.htm.

5 Shepherd, B. (2012). *Terror in the Balkans.* Boston: Harvard University Press.

6 Ibid.

7 For more information on Jäger-Divisions go to: https://www.flamesofwar.com/Default.aspx-?tabid=112&art_id=1883&kb_cat_id=34;TM-E-451, or the *Handbook on German Military Forces* that can be found at: https://www.scribd.com/document/35474263/Handbook-on-German-Military-Forces-Text, and, "List of German Divisions in World War II." Wikipedia. at: https://en.wikipedia.org/wiki/List_of_German_divisions_in_World_War_II.

8 Shepherd, B. (2009). "With the Devil in Titoland: A Wehrmacht Anti-Partisan Division in Bosnia-Herzegovina, 1943." *War in History, 16*(1), 77–97.

9 Dr. Erhard Morgenstern. *In Weisst Du noch Kamerad! Geschichte der 118. Jäger-Division.*

10 R. Wagner (personal communication, October 17, 2007).

11 Ibid.

12 Ibid.

13 Wagner, R. *Our Small War. Under the Edelweiss and Oak Leaves. The 118. Hunter Division at the Balkans.* Author's collection.

14 Donia, R. J. (2006). *Sarajevo: A Biography.* Ann Arbor, MI: University of Michigan Press.

15 Hein, P. (1971, Winter). "Serbia, Croatia and Germany 1941–1945: Civil War and Revolution in the Balkans." *Canadian Slavonic Papers/Revue Canadienne des Slavistes, 13*(4), 344–373.

16 MacIsaac, J. J. (nd). "Op 31–Sarajevo West Marshalling Yards." The WWII History of James MacIsaac and RAF No. 37 Squadron. From: http://natureonline.com/37/42-op31.html; "Combat Missions." 450th Bomb Group Memorial Association. From: http://www.450thbg.com/real/html/missions.shtml.

17 deZeng, H. (nd). *Luftwaffe Airfields 1935–45: Yugoslavia.* From: http://www.ww2.dk/Airfields%20-%20Yugoslavia.pdf.

18 Greble, E. (2011). *Sarajevo, 1941–1945.* Ithaca, NY: Cornell University Press.

19 For more information on Sarajevo, go to: http://hmh.ba/wp-content/uploads/2017/04/KAMPUS-competition.pdf.

20 R. Wagner (personal comunication, October 17, 2007).

21 E. surname omitted to maintain confidentiality (June, 2007). Egor's grandparents lived through the occupation in Sarajevo.

22 Greble, E. (2011). *Sarajevo, 1941–1945.* Ithaca, NY: Cornell University Press.

23 Ibid.

24 Miller, P. B. (2016). "The First Shots of the First World War: The Sarajevo Assassination in History and Memory." *Central Europe, 14*(2), 141–156.

25 "What's that for? Memorial Plaque for Gavrilo Princip." Deutsches Historishes Museum (June 28, 2023). From: https://www.dhm.de/blog/2023/06/28/whats-that-for-memorial-plaque-for-gavrilo-princip/.

26 "Organization German Jäger Divisions 16 May 1941–15 October 1942." Ike Skelton Combined Arms Research Library. From: https://cgsc.contentdm.oclc.org/digital/collection/p15040c0116/id/1360/.

27 *Handbook on German Military Forces, 1943.* Baton Rouge, LA: Louisiana State University Press.

28 R. Wachter (personal communication, June, 2007).

29 "Wireless Communications of the German Army in World War II." Wikipedia. From: https://en.wikipedia.org/wiki/Wireless_Communications_of_the_German_Army_in_World_War_II#Torn.Fu_Series.

30 *Technical Manual: Handbook on German Military Forces (1943).* Washington, D.C.: War Department.

31 Ibid at 22.

32 Lepage, J. D. G. (2007). *German Military Vehicles of World War II: An Illustrated Guide to Cars, Trucks, Half-Tracks, Motorcycles, Amphibious Vehicles and Others.* London: McFarland.

33 Ibid at 22.

34 Kumm, O. (1995). *Prinz Eugen: The History of the 7. SS Mountain Division "Prinz Eugen."* Winnipeg, Manitoba: Fedorowicz Publications.

35 Shepherd, B. (2012). *Terror in the Balkans.* Boston: Harvard University Press.

36 M. Kristović (personal communications, 2008–2009).

37 Hoare, M. A. (2013). *The Bosnian Muslims in the Second World War: A History.* New York: Oxford University Press, Inc.

38 Ibid.

39 M. Kristović (personal communications, 2008–2009).

40 Ibid at 32.

41 Kennedy, R. M. (1989). *German Antiguerrilla Operations in the Balkans, 1941–1944* (Vol. 104, No. 18). Center of Military History, US Army.

42 "Case White." Military History Fandom. From: https://military.wikia.org/wiki/Case_White.

43 "Case Black." Military History Fandom. From: https://military.wikia.org/wiki/Case_Black.

44 For a comprehensive review of the Italian-Chetnik relationship, see: Redzic, E. (2005). *Bosnia and Herzegovina in the Second World War.* New York: Frank Cass.

45 Balkan War History. From: http://www.balkanwarhistory.com/search/label/battle.

46 "Case Black." Wikipedia. From: https://en.wikipedia.org/wiki/Case_Black#Axis_preparations; http://wikipedia.us.nina.az/wiki/Operation_Schwarz#Phase_V:_Partisan_breakthrough_toward_eastern_Bosnia_(10_June_%E2%80%93_15_June).

47 Mit III./750 in Jugoslawien. (nd). *Erinnerungen an die 118. Jäger-Division (frühere 718. Infanterie-Division).* Kameradschaft d. ehem. 118. Jäg.Division, p. 126.

48 "Civil War in the Balkans: Interview with Two Former Yugoslav Nationals Who Recall the Conflict." Historynet. From: https://www.historynet.com/civil-war-in-the-balkans-interview-with-two-former-yugoslav-nationals-who-recall-the-conflict-of-world-war-ii/.

49 Kennedy, R. M. (1989). *German Antiguerrilla Operations in the Balkans, 1941–1944* (Vol. 104, No. 18). Center of Military History, US Army.

50 Lenormand, P. (2022). "A History of Yugoslavia, Marie-Janine Calic." *Revue Historique des Armees, 304*(1), 131–132.

51 Rill, H. & Stojcic, H. (1972). *On the Trail of the Danube Swabians in Vojvodina.* Centre for Nonviolent Action. From: https://nenasilje.org/publikacije/pdf/On_the_Trail_of_the_Danube_Swabians_in_Vojvodina.pdf.

52 Ibid.
53 "History of Vojvodina." Wikipedia. From: https://en.wikipedia.org/wiki/History_of_Vojvodina.
54 Zakic, M. (2014). "The Price of Belonging: Volksdeutsche, Land Redistribution and Aryanization in the Serbian Banat, 1941–4." *Journal of Contemporary History. 49*(2), 320–340.
55 Zakic, M. (2017). *Ethnic Germans and National Socialism in Yugoslavia in World War II.* Cambridge University Press.
56 Rill, H. & Stojcic, H. (1972). *On the Trail of the Danube Swabians in Vojvodina.* Centre for Nonviolent Action. From: https://nenasilje.org/publikacije/pdf/On_the_Trail_of_the_Danube_Swabians_in_Vojvodina.pdf.
57 Kumm, O. (1995). *Prinz Eugen: The History of the 7. SS Mountain Division "Prinz Eugen."* Winnipeg, Manitoba: Fedorowicz Publications.
58 Information from the *Familienbuch der katholischen Pfarrgemeinde der Stadt Gross Betschkerek im Banat sowie ihrer Filialen 1753–1945. Arbeitsgemeinschaft fur Veroffentlichung Banater Familienbucher* shows that his stepmother's name was Elisabeth Amalia Freidman. Her father's name was Sigmund Friedmann and his grandmother was Sidonia Goldmann. Both were listed as Jewish in the book.
59 SS Wehrpass and documents of Erwin Ellmer. Author's collection.
60 Soldbuch, documents, and photos of Michael Fingerhut. Author's collection.
61 "Interview with Adalbert Lallier April 24, 2008 RG-50.030*0525." United States Holocaust Memorial Museum. From: https://collections.ushmm.org/search/catalog/irn36914.
62 R. Hansinger (personal communication, October 8, 2011).
63 Ibid at 55.
64 SS Wehrstammbuch and documents of Hans Preuss. Author's collection.
65 Savich, C. K. (2001). "Prinz Eugen SS Division, 1941–1945." Project Rastko - Banja Luka: Electronic Library of Culture and Tradition of Bosnian Krajina. From: https://www.rastko.rs/rastko-bl/istorija/kcsavic/csavich-eugen_e.html.
66 Hart, S. (2017). "Partisans: War in the Balkans, 1941–1945." BBC History. From: https://www.bbc.co.uk/history/worldwars/wwtwo/partisan_fighters_01.shtml#:~:text=Murder%2C%20rape%20and%20mass%20executions,brutality%20in%20war%2Dtime%20Yugoslavia; Tomasevich, J. (1975). *War and Revolution in Yugoslavia, 1941–1945: The Chetniks.* Stanford: Stanford University Press; Shepherd, B. (2012). *Terror in the Balkans.* Boston: Harvard University Press.
67 Yves, T. (2010). "Massacres in Dismembered Yugoslavia, 1941–1945." SciencesPo. From: https://www.sciencespo.fr/mass-violence-war-massacre-resistance/en/document/massacres-dis-membered-yugoslavia-1941-1945.html; Dizdar, Z. (2005). "Italian Policies Toward Croatians in Occupied Territories During the Second World War." *Review of Croatian History, 1*(1), 179–210.
68 "Operation *Foča*." Codenames: Operations of World War II. From: https://codenames.info/operation/foca/; "Anti-Partisan Operations at the Beginning of 1942." Balkan War History. From: http://www.balkanwarhistory.com/2017/12/anti-partisan-operations-at-beginning.html; "Operation *Trio*." Wikipedia. From: https://en.wikipedia.org/wiki/Operation_Trio.
69 Bassett, R. (2005). *Hitler's Spy Chief: The Wilhelm Canaris Mystery.* London: Cassell; "Armistice of Cassibile." Wikipedia. From: https://en.wikipedia.org/wiki/Armistice_of_Cassibile.
70 "Armistice with Italy: September 3, 1943." Yale Law School. The Avalon Project: Documents in Law, History and Diplomacy. From: https://avalon.law.yale.edu/wwii/italy01.asp.
71 "The Italian Declaration of War on Germany, October 13, 1943." Original Sources. From: https://www.originalsources.com/Document.aspx?DocID=EY4Y5ZC4S7Q32LE.
72 D. Cupcovic (personal communication, May 8, 2008).
73 "Nikšić." Spomenik Database. From: https://www.spomenikdatabase.org/niksic; Afiero, M. (2016); *An Illustrated History: The 7th Waffen-SS.* Atglen, PA: Schiffer.
74 R. Wagner (personal communicaton, December 12, 2007).

75 Ibid.

76 Dr. Erhard Morgenstern. *In Weisst du noch Kamerad! Geschicte der 118. Jäger-Division.*

77 *Erinnerungen an die 118. Jäger-Division (frühere 718. Infanterie-Division).* Kameradschaft d. ehem. 118. Jäg.Division, p. 152.

78 Document NOKW-1354, "Prosecution Exhibit 447: Extracts of Daily Reports from Commander in Chief Southeast, 9/19-28/1943, to Operations Section, OKH: Extract of 9/28/1943", in Trials of War Criminals Before the Nurernberg Military Tribunals Under Control Council Law No. 10. Vol. 11: *United States of America v. Wilhelm List,* et al. (Case 7: "Hostage Case"). US Government Printing Office, District of Columbia: 1950. 1085–1086.

79 Kumm, O. (1983). *7. SS-Gebirgs-Division Prinz Eugen im Bild.* Djurhamn, Sweden: Hugin & Munin.

80 Ibid.

81 "The German Operation Autumn Storm." (2017). Balkan War History. From: http://www.balkanwarhistory.com/2017/02/the-german-operation-autumn-storm.html.

82 Maclean, F. (2015). *Eastern Approaches.* London: Penguin, p. 288.

83 Kennedy, R. M. (1989). *German Antiguerrilla Operations in the Balkans, 1941–1944* (Vol. 104, No. 18). Center of Military History, US Army.

84 R. Wagner, (personal communication, September 17, 2007).

85 Wagner, R. (nd). *Bruckenschlag und Ruckschlage. Quer durch den Balkan auf den Spuren Zweier Bergstiefel.*

86 *Handbook on German Military Forces, 1943.* Baton Rouge, LA: Louisiana State University Press.

87 Wagner, R. "Unter Edelweiß und Eichenlaub Die 118. Jägerdivision am Balkan." From: http://rudolf-nautilus-wagner.info/5.htm.

88 William, C. (2015). *Third Reich Collectibles: Identification and Price Guide.* London: Penguin.

89 K. Gadson (personal communication, October 8, 2008.)

90 Werner, F. (nd). *Erinnerungen an die 118. Jäger-Division (frühere 718. Infanterie-Division). Kameradschaft d. ehem. 118. Jäg.Division.*

91 "Operation *Herbstgewitter.*" Vojska.net. From: http://www.vojska.net/eng/world-war-2/operation/herbstgewitter-1943/.

92 "War Diary: German Naval Staff Operations." Internet Archive. From: https://archive.org/stream/wardiarygermann521943germ/wardiarygermann521943germ_djvu.txt.

93 "The German Operation *Autumn Storm.*" Balkan War History. From: http://www.balkanwarhistory.com/2017/02/the-german-operation-autumn-storm.html.

94 "Operation *Herbstgewitter.*" Vojska.net. From: http://www.vojska.net/eng/world-war-2/operation/herbstgewitter-1943/.

95 Mandel, L. (2018). *Sterling Hayden's Wars.* Oxford, MS: University Press of Mississippi.

96 Rutz, P. X. (2017). "Troubled Waters." Historynet. From: https://www.historynet.com/troubled-waters.htm.

97 Mandel, L. (2018). *Sterling Hayden's Wars.* Oxford, MS: University Press of Mississippi.

98 Botica, J. (nd). "A Proud Australian." From: https://www.wa.gov.au/system/files/2020-01/Botica_Jakov%20%28Jim%29.pdf.

99 Ibid.

100 "Stranica nije pronađena." Sword Dances: Project by the Institute of Ethnology and Folklore Research. From: https://macevni-plesovi.org/en/mjesta/korcula/.

101 "History of Korčula". Korculainfo.net. From: https://www.korculainfo.com/history/.

102 "Hotel Korčula Photos." Korculainfo.com. From: https://www.korculainfo.com/photos/hotel-korcula/.

103 "Korčula Town." Split Croatia Travel Guide. From: https://split.gg/korcula-town/.

Chapter 4

1   Gilbert, M. (2014). *The Second World War: A Complete History.* New York: Rosetta Books.

2   McConville, M. (2007). *A Small War in the Balkans: British Military Involvement in Wartime Yugoslavia 1941–1945.* Uckfield, UK: Naval & Military Press, Ltd.

3   King-Clark, R. (1997). *Jack Churchill "Unlimited Boldness."* Knutsford, UK: Fleur de Lys Publishing.

4   For more information regarding Mad Jack, go to: https://www.historynet.com/the-daring-exploits-of-mad-jack-churchill.htm.

5   For more information on No. 2 Commandos, see: https://www.commandoveterans.org/2CommandoContent.

6   B. Bishop (personal communication, June 4, 2008).

7   Ibid.

8   See Perdue, R. E. (2010). *Behind the Lines in Greece: The Story of OSS Operational Group II.* AuthorHouse. A more detailed account of the 122nd was written by Andrew Mousalimas and can be found at: http://www.pahh.com/oss/pt1/p3.html.

9   Ibid.

10 Ibid.

11 A. Mousalimas (personal communication, May 3, 2008).

12 Several internet websites provide additional insight on the gg400 generator and its use in WWII. For more specifications on the gg400 generator, go to: https://tigertank181.com/51_GG400.htm or http://lucafusari.altervista.org/page1/page10/GG400.html.

13 Leibovitz, L. & Miller, M. (2009). *Lili Marlene: The Soldier's Song of World War II.* New York: W. W. Norton & Co., p. 201.

14 Raberstein was killed on July 2, 1944 near Caen, France. He earned the EK 1 & 2 and Fighter Operational Clasp. He is credited with shooting down a total of five Allied aircraft. From: http://www.aircrewremembered.com/KrackerDatabase/?s=900&q=Schneider,%20Walter%20Jap&qand=&exc1=&exc2=&search_type=&search_only=.

15 See Macksey, K. (2015). *Invasion: The Alternative History of the German Invasion of England, July 1940.* Barnsley, UK: Pen and Sword; Kieser, E. (1997). *Hitler on the Doorstep: Operation Sea Lion: The German Plan to Invade Britain, 1940.* Annapolis, MD: US Naval Institute Press.

16 B. Bishop (personal communication, June 4, 2008).

17 A. Mousalimas (personal communication, May 3, 2008).

18 Ibid.

19 Ibid.

20 B. Bishop (personal communication, June 4, 2008).

21 Ibid.

22 Ibid.

23 Reynolds, L. C. (2009). *Dog Boats at War: Royal Navy D Class MTBs and MGBs 1939–1945.* Cheltenham, UK: The History Press.

24 The remains of 61 German soldiers were exhumed on Korčula. From: https://zdravlje-slobod-nadalmacija-hr.translate.goog/dalmacija/na-korculi-ekshumirani-ostatci-61-njemackog-vojni-ka-294703?_x_tr_sl=hr&_x_tr_tl=en&_x_tr_hl=en&_x_tr_pto=sc.

25 Information from the German War Graves Commission states the following: "Herbert Volland has not yet been transferred to a military cemetery set up by the Volksbund. According to the information available to us, his grave is currently still in the following location: Korčula–Croatia. The Volksbund is trying to find the graves of the German soldiers on the basis of war grave agreements and to give them permanent resting places. We hope to find Herbert Volland's grave in the not too distant future and to be able to transfer the remains to a military cemetery." From: https://www.volksbund.de/en/erinnern-gedenken/gravesearch-online.

26 Dear, I. (2010). *Sabotage and Subversion: The SOE and OSS at War*. Cheltenham, UK: The History Press; Smith, B. F. (1983). *The Shadow Warriors: OSS and the Origins of the CIA*. New York: Basic Books.

27 Dear, I. (2010). *Sabotage and Subversion: The SOE and OSS at War*. Cheltenham, UK: The History Press; Smith, B. F. (1983). *The Shadow Warriors: OSS and the Origins of the CIA*. New York: Basic Books. The OSS records state that the raid was July 12–19.

28 Barčot, T. (2011). "The Administration of the Independent State of Croatia on the Island of Korčula." *Radovi Zavoda za povijesne znanosti HAZU u Zadru, 53*, 313–358.

29 "Operation *Shoot.*" Codenames: Operations of World War II. From: https://codenames.info/operation/shoot/.

30 Ladd, J. D. (1998). *By Sea, by Land: The Royal Marines, 1919–1997: An Authorised History*. New York: Collins.

31 "Landing on Korčula." Wikipedia. From: https://translate.google.com/translate?hl=en&sl=s-r&u=https://sh.wikipedia.org/wiki/Desant_na_Kor%C4%258Dulu&prev=search&pto=aue; Mirko Novović, Stevan Petković: PRVA DALMATINSKA PROLETERSKA BRIGADA, Vojnoizdavački zavod, Beograd 1965, str. 283–284.

32 Barčot, T. (2011). "The Administration of the Independent State of Croatia on the Island of Korčula." *Radovi Zavoda za povijesne znanosti HAZU u Zadru, 53*, 313–358.

33 Reynolds, L. C. (2009). *Dog Boats at War: Royal Navy D Class MTBs and MGBs 1939–1945*. Cheltenham, UK: The History Press, p. 208.

34 Novović, S. & Petković, S. (1965). The First Dalmatian Proletariat Brigade. Belgrade: War Publications Institute.

35 Freivogel, Z. & Rastelli, A. (2015). *Adriatic Naval War, 1940–1945*. Zagreb, Croatia: Despot Infinitus.

36 Ibid.

37 Novović, S. & Petković, S. (1965). *The First Dalmatian Proletariat Brigade*. Belgrade: War Publications Institute.

38 Churchill, T. B. L. (1987). *Commando Crusade*. London: Kimber.

39 Barčot, T. (2011). "The Administration of the Independent State of Croatia on the Island of Korčula." *Radovi Zavoda za povijesne znanosti HAZU u Zadru, 53*, 313–358.

40 R. Wagner (personal communications, October & November 2007).

41 B. Bishop (personal communication, June 4, 2008).

42 "Operation *Farrier* - Yugoslavia." Royal Marines History.com. From: https://www.royalmarineshistory.com/post/operation-farrier-yugoslavia.

43 From: http://oss-og.org/balkans/yugo_island.html.

44 A. Mousalimas (personal communication, May 3, 2008).

45 Ibid.

46 "41-28685 *Leading Lady.*" American Air Museum in Britain. From: http://www.americanairmuseum.com/aircraft/21391.

47 *Summary of the Squadron History for the Month of August, 1944*. From: https://461st.org/History/765th%20History/PDFs/765%20August%201944.pdf.

48 Ibid.

49 Ibid.

50 "Stalag Luft 4." 392nd Bomb Group. From: https://www.b24.net/powStalag4.htm.

51 Meyer, H. F. (2002). Von Wien nach Kalavryta: Die blutige Spur der 117. Jäger-Division durch Serbien und Griechenland (Vol. 12). Bibliopolis.

52 See Trifković, G. (2017). "'The German Anabasis': The Breakthrough of Army Group E from Eastern Yugoslavia 1944." *The Journal of Slavic Military Studies, 30*(4), 602–629; Clive, N. (1985). *A Greek Experience, 1943–1948*. Norfolk, UK: Michael Russell Publishing.

53   Mazower, M. (1992). "Military Violence and National Socialist Values: The Wehrmacht in Greece 1941–1944." *Past & Present*, *134*(1), 129–158.

54   Central Registry of War Criminals and Security Suspects (CROWCASS). *Consolidated Wanted Lists* (1947). 2005, Uckfield, UK: Naval & Military Press, Ltd. Information can also be found at: https://search.archives.un.org/unwcc-publications-war-crimes-submitted-by-governments-yu-goslavia-summary-of-first-six-reports-of-the-state-commission-for-the-investigation-of-the-crimes-of-the-invaders-and-their-assistants-2.

55   For more information on Partisan activities on Korčula, go to: https://inavukic.com/2016/02/03/victims-of-communism-on-island-of-korcula-croatia/.

56   As an example, see Jim Botica's written memories at: https://www.wa.gov.au/system/files/2020-01/Botica_Jakov%20%28Jim%29.pdf.

57   Barčot, T. (2011). "The Administration of the Independent State of Croatia on the Island of Korčula." *Radovi Zavoda za povijesne znanosti HAZU u Zadru, 53*, 313–358.

58   *The Allied Presence on Vis 1943–45*. From: https://www.451st.org/Stories/Pdfs/Allied%20Presence%20on%20Vis,%201943-45.pdf.

59   King-Clark, R. (1997). *Jack Churchill "Unlimited Boldness"*. Knutsford, UK: Fleur de Lys Publishing. Also see: http://www.deddingtonhistory.uk/__data/assets/pdf_file/0004/13657/UnlimitedBoldnessApril2015.pdf.

60   Saunders, L. H. S. G. (2016). *The Green Beret: The Story of the Commandos, 1940–1945*. Protomac, MD: Pickle Partners Publishing.

61   Thompson, S. L. (2011). *Gulaschkanone: The German Field Kitchen in World War II*. Altgen, PA: Schiffer Publishing.

62   "The Origin of the Goldfish Club." The Goldfish Club. From: https://www.thegoldfishclub.co.uk/history-of-the-goldfishclub.

63   "Flight Lieutenant 'Blondie' Walker". The Telegraph. (10 December 2008). From: https://www.telegraph.co.uk/news/obituaries/3703352/Flight-Lieutenant-Blondie-Walker.html.

64   Saunders, L. H. S. G. (2016). *The Green Beret: The Story of the Commandos, 1940–1945*. Protomac, MD: Pickle Partners Publishing; For a comprehensive review of the origin and activities of commandos, see: http://www.raidingsupportregiment.com/operations/.

65   *The Allied Presence on Vis 1943–45*. From: https://www.451st.org/Stories/Pdfs/Allied%20Presence%20on%20Vis,%201943-45.pdf; "Grandfather I" report, RSR War Diary, WO 170/1364.

66   Ibid.

Chapter 5

1   Deletant, D. (2006). *Hitler's Forgotten Ally: Ion Antonescu and His Regime, 1940–1944*. New York: Springer.

2   Miller, M. (1975). *Bulgaria During the Second World War*. Stanford, CT: Stanford University Press; Adams, S. (2008). *The Eastern Front*. New York: The Rosen Group.

3   "Operation *Seydlitz (vii)*." Codenames: Operations of World War II. From: https://codenames.info/operation/seydlitz-vii/; See also: http://www.vojska.net/eng/world-war-2/operation/seydlitz-1944/.

4   "Operation *Eisbär*." Vojska.net. From: http://www.vojska.net/eng/world-war-2/operation/eisbar-1944/.

5   "Operation *Kranich*." Vojska.net. From: http://www.vojska.net/eng/world-war-2/operation/kranich-1944/.

6   "Operation *Zirkus*." Codenames: Operations of World War II. From: https://codenames.info/operation/zirkus/.

7   R. Wagner (personal communication, December 12, 2007).

8   "Battle of Vukov Klanac." Axis History Forum. From: https://forum.axishistory.com/viewtopic.php?t=67294&start=15.

9   Redzic, E. (2005). *Bosnia and Herzegovina in the Second World War*. New York: Taylor and Francis. 109.

10 R. Hansinger (personal communication, October 8, 2011).

11 Ibid.

12 Ibid.

13 Ibid.

14 Afiero, M. (2016). *The 7th Waffen SS*. Altglen: Schiffer.

15 R. Hansinger (personal communication, October 8, 2011).

16 Ibid.

17 For more information on Ustasha Brigades, go to: https://axishistory.com/ustasha/.

18 Šejtanić, S. (2016). "Mostar between 1941 and 1952 with Special Reference to the Period of Reconstruction and Development from 1945 to 1952." *European Journal of Social Sciences Studies*, *1*(2), 118–147.

19 "Battle of Vukov Klanac." Axis History Forum. From: https://forum.axishistory.com/viewtopic.php?t=67294&start=15.

20 Dulić, T. (2005). *Utopias of Nation: Local Mass Killing in Bosnia and Herzegovina, 1941–42*. Doctoral dissertation, Uppsala University, p. 162.

21 Hoare, M. A. (2013). *The Bosnian Muslims in the Second World War: A History*. New York: Oxford University Press, Inc.

22 "Chetniks Terrible Crimes Against Bosnia's and Croats." World War II Graves. From: https://ww2gravestone.com/69681-2/.

23 "Petar Baćović." Wikipedia. From: https://en.wikipedia.org/wiki/Petar_Ba%C4%87ovi%C4%87.

24 Hoare, M. A. (2013).*The Bosnian Muslims in the Second World War: A History*. New York: Oxford University Press, Inc.

25 Marjanović, D., et al. (2015). "Identification of Human Remains from the Second World War Mass Graves Uncovered in Bosnia and Herzegovina." *Croatian Medical Journal*, *56*(3), 257–262.

26 Ibid at 15.

27 Redzic, E. (2005) *Bosnia and Herzegovina in the Second World War*. New York: Taylor and Francis, p. 109.

28 Kurapovna, M. (2009). *Shadows on the Mountain: The Allies, the Resistance, and the Rivalries that Doomed WWII Yugoslavia*. Nashville, TN: Turner Publishing.

29 Borić, I., Ljubković, J., & Sutlović, D. (2011). "Discovering the 60 Years Old Secret: Identification of the World War II Mass Grave Victims from the Island of Daksa near Dubrovnik, Croatia." *Croatian Medical Journal*, *52*(3), 327–335.

30 Trifković, G. (2020). *Parleying with the Devil: Prisoner Exchange in Yugoslavia, 1941–1945*. Lexington, KY: University Press of Kentucky, p. 325.

31 F. Lashinsky (personal communications, October 8 & 11, 2008).

32 Ibid.

33 Ibid.

34 Ibid.

35 Ibid.

36 Ibid.

37 Bork, B. (2021). *StuG III Brigade 191, The Buffalo Brigade in Action in the Balkans, Greece and from Moscow to Kursk and Sevastopol*. London: Greenhill Books.

38 H. vonCampe (personal communication, June 17, 2009).

39   Bork, B. (2021). *StuG III Brigade 191, 1940–1945. The Buffalo Brigade in the Balkans, Greece, and from Moscow to Kursk and Sevastopol*. London: Greenhill Books.

40   Ibid.

41   R. Hansinger (personal communication, October 8, 2011).

42   "The Yugoslavian Theatre of War As the Cornerstone of the Southeren Section of the Eastern Front (October 1944 to May 1945)." Ebrary.net. From: https://ebrary.net/116934/political_science/yugoslavian_theatre_cornerstone_southern_eastern_front_october_1944_1945.

43   "Interview with Adalbert Lallier April 24, 2008 RG-50.030*0525." United States Holocaust Memorial Museum. From: https://collections.ushmm.org/search/catalog/irn36914.

44   Trifković, G. (2017). "'The German Anabasis': The Breakthrough of Army Group E from Eastern Yugoslavia 1944." *The Journal of Slavic Military Studies*, *30*(4), 602–629.

45   Trifković, G. (2016). "Carnage in the Land of Three Rivers: The Syrmian Front 1944–1945." *Militärgeschichtliche Zeitschrift*, *75*(1), 94–122.

46   R. Hansinger (personal communication, October 8, 2011).

47   Trifković, G. (2016). "'Damned Good Amateurs': Yugoslav Partisans in the Belgrade Operation 1944." *The Journal of Slavic Military Studies*, *29*(2), 253–278.

48   Trifković, G. (2016). "Carnage in the Land of Three Rivers: The Syrmian Front 1944–1945." *Militärgeschichtliche Zeitschrift*, *75*(1), 94–122.

49   Ibid.

50   Ibid.

51   Fellgiebel, W. P. (2004). *Die Träger des Ritterkreuzes des Eisernen Kreuzes 1939–1945: Die Inhaber der höchsten Auszeichnung des Zweiten Weltkrieges (mit Ergänzung)*. Eggolsheim, Germany: Podzun-Pallas Verlag GmbH.

52   R. Wagner (personal communication, December 12, 2007).

53   For more information on the Iron Cross see: Maerz, D. & Alt, M. (2020). *The Iron Cross 2. Class*. Richmond, MI: B&D Publishing.

54   Hoare, M. A. (2013). *The Bosnian Muslims in the Second World War: A History*. New York: Oxford University Press, Inc.

55   Catherwood, C. (2017). *Churchill and Tito: SOE, Bletchley Park and Supporting the Yugoslav Communists in World War II*. London: Grub Street Publishers.

56   Nikolić, K. (2011). *The Serbian Political Emigration in Western Europe, 1945–1946*. Belgrade: Institut za savremenu istoriju, p. 168.

57   M. Kristović (personal communications, 2008–2009).

58   Ibid.

59   A. Roehler (personal communication, March 18, 2009).

60   Ibid.

61   Ibid.

62   Ibid.

Chapter 6

1   Stone, D. R. (2023). "'The Eastern Front', 1943–1945." In Pieher, G. K. & Grant, J. (eds.), *The Oxford Handbook of World War II*. New York: Oxford University Press; Liedtke, G. (2008). "Furor Teutonicus: German Offensives and Counter-Attacks on the Eastern Front, August 1943 to March 1945." *Journal of Slavic Military Studies*, *21*(3), 563–587.

2   Hitler's January 1, 1945 Speech to the Wehrmacht. From: http://der-fuehrer.org/reden/english/45-01-01.htm.

3   Nash, D. E. (2021). *From the Realm of a Dying Sun: Volume III: IV. SS-Panzerkorps from Budapest to Vienna, February–May 1945*. Casemate; Liedtke, G. (2008). "Furor Teutonicus: German

Offensives and Counter-Attacks on the Eastern Front, August 1943 to March 1945." *Journal of Slavic Military Studies, 21*(3), 563–587; Nevenkin, K. (2012). *Take Budapest!: The Struggle for Hungary, Autumn 1944*. Stroud, UK: The History Press; George, E. E. (2006). "The Siege of Budapest: One Hundred Days in World War II." *East European Quarterly, 40*(2), 245–254.

4   Mustafa, S. A. (2008). *The Long Ride of Major Von Schill: A Journey Through German History and Memory*. Lanham, MD: Rowman & Littlefield Publishers.

5   Isaev, A., & Kolomiets, M. (2014). *Tomb of the Panzerwaffe: The Defeat of the Sixth SS Panzer Army in Hungary 1945*. Warwick, UK: Helion; Trifković, G. (2023). "'Liberated Territory' vs. 'Battle of Annihilation': Partisan and German Strategies in Yugoslavia 1941–1945." In Newman, J. P., Škodrić, L. & Ristanović, R. (eds.), *Anti-Axis Resistance in Southeastern Europe, 1939–1945*. Paderborn: Brill Schöningh, pp. 143–163; Nevenkin, K. (2012). *Take Budapest!: The Struggle for Hungary, Autumn 1944*. Stroud, UK: The History Press.

6   "Operation *Spring Awakening*." Wikipedia. From: https://en.wikipedia.org/wiki/Operation_Spring_Awakening.

7   *Volksbund Deutsche Kriegsgräberfürsorge Gräbersuche-Online*. From: https://www.volksbund.de/erinnern-gedenken/graebersuche-online.

8   Ibid.

9   Craven, W. F. & Cate, J. L. (1983). *The Army Air Forces in World War II. III Europe: Argument to V-E Day, January 1944 to May 1945*. From: https://apps.dtic.mil/sti/pdfs/ADA440398.pdf.

10 F. Lashinsky (personal communication, March 21, 2011).

11 Ibid.

12 Ibid.

13 Ibid.

14 Ibid.

15 Ibid.

16 Ibid.

17 A. Roehler (personal communication, March 18, 2009).

18 Ibid.

19 Ibid.

20 Ibid.

21 Ibid.

22 Ibid.

23 Ibid.

24 Ibid.

25 Budig, U. (2000). *Erinnerungen and den Frühling 1945*. Neiderfrohna, Germany: Mironde-Verlag.

26 Bedessem, E. N. (1996). *Central Europe: The U.S. Army Campaigns of World War II*. Washington, D.C.: US Army, Center of Military History (CMH). An electronic version can be found at: https://history.army.mil/brochures/centeur/centeur.htm.

27 Budig, U. (2000). *Erinnerungen and den Frühling 1945*. Neiderfrohna, Germany: Mironde-Verlag.

28 Ibid.

29 Ibid.

30 "HASAG: Hugo Schneider Aktiengesellschaft Metalwarenfabrik." Holocaust Education & Archive Research Team. (2013). From: http://www.holocaustresearchproject.org/nazioccupation/hasag.html.

31 The owner and his wife are reported to have committed suicide near the end of the war; no HASAG personnel were ever tried as war criminals. From: http://www.holocaustresearchproject.org/nazioccupation/hasag.html.

32 "HASAG: Hugo Schneider Aktiengesellschaft Metalwarenfabrik." Holocaust Education & Archive Research Team. From: http://www.holocaustresearchproject.org/nazioccupation/hasag.html.

33   Ibid.

34   Budig, U. (2000). *Erinnerungen and den Frühling 1945.* Neiderfrohna, Germany: Mironde-Verlag.

35   Ibid.

36   Ibid at 10.

37   *Combat History of the 4th Armored Division.* Page: April 49-9. From: https://mcoecbam-coepwprd01.blob.core.usgovcloudapi.net/library/ABOLC_BA_2018/Research_Modules_C/Singling/804_AD_414.pdf.

38   Ibid.

39   Budig, U. (2000). *Erinnerungen and den Frühling 1945.* Neiderfrohna, Germany: Mironde-Verlag.

40   Ibid.

41   Ibid.

42   A. Roehler (personal communication, March 18, 2009).

43   Ibid.

44   Ibid.

45   R. Hansinger (personal communication, October 8, 2011).

46   Ibid.

47   Ibid.

48   M. Kristović (personal communications, 2008–2009).

49   Nikolić, K. (2011). *The Serbian Political Emigration in Western Europe, 1945–1946.* Belgrade: Institut za savremenu istoriju, p. 55.

50   M. Kristović (personal communications, 2008–2009).

51   Petrov, B. (2010). "Revolutionary Justice in Serbia, 1944–1946: The Problem of Collaboration." *Études Balkaniques,* (1–2), 60–88.

52   Nikolić, K. (2011). *The Serbian Political Emigration in Western Europe, 1945–1946.* Belgrade: Institut za savremenu istoriju, p. 67.

53   M. Kristović (personal communications, 2008–2009).

54   Ibid.

55   Nikolić, K. (2011). *The Serbian Political Emigration in Western Europe, 1945–1946.* Belgrade: Institut za savremenu istoriju, p. 67.

56   M. Kristović (personal communications, 2008–2009).

57   Ibid.

58   Barne, A. & Barne, C. (2019). *Churchill's Colonel: The War Diaries of Lieutenant Colonel Anthony Barne.* Barnsley, UK: Pen & Sword Military, p. 300.

59   M. Kristović (personal communications, 2008–2009).

60   R. Wagner (personal communication, December 12, 2007).

61   In the late hours of May 8th and the early morning hours of the 9th, another surrender document, with some modifications to the original May 7th surrender document, was demanded by the Russians. This May 9th surrender document that was signed by General Keitel in Berlin, ordered all German troops to cease all military actions against Allied armies, disarm and disband, and be taken into captivity. While they had already surrendered in the West, now, they had until the end of the 9th to surrender to the Russians. If the Germans refused to surrender, then they would be punished. See Zigo, P. E. (2019). *Unconditional Surrender: Witnessing History–May 1945: Nazi Germany's Surrender to the Allies Ending World War II in Europe.* Bloomington, IN: Archway Publishing.

62   Brown, M. (2005). *Day Peace Broke Out: The VE-Day Experience.* Cheltenham, UK: The History Press.

63   F. Lashinsky (personal communications, October 8 & 11, 2008).

64   R. Hansinger (personal communication, October 8, 2011).

65   A. Roehler (personal communication, March 18, 2009).

66   R. Wagner (personal communication, December 12, 2007).

Chapter 7

1   Mitcham, S. W. (2007). *German Order of Battle: Panzer, Panzer Grenadier, and Waffen SS Divisions in World War II* (Vol. 3). Mechanicsburg, PA: Stackpole Books.

2   *February 11, 1945 Yalta Conference Agreement, Declaration of Liberated Europe.* From: https://digitalarchive.wilsoncenter.org/document/116176.pdf?v=66b99cbbf4a1b8de10c56b38cf4fc50d. Later at the Postdam Conference in July–August 1945, the US and Great Britain tried to control Stalin's mass deportation activities of ethnic Germans. Under Potsdam, there would now be an "orderly transfer of ethnic Germans—all 12 million of them." It was also agreed that the Nazi leadership would also be brought to justice.

3   *February 11, 1945 Yalta Conference Agreement, Declaration of Liberated Europe.* From: https://digitalarchive.wilsoncenter.org/document/116176.pdf?v=66b99cbbf4a1b8de10c56b38cf4fc50d.

4   "Nagykanizsa-Kormend Offensive." Wikipedia. From: https://en.wikipedia.org/wiki/Nagykanizsa%E2%80%93K%C3%B6rmend_offensive.

5   Funk never made it to the Soviet POW camp. He and another prisoner escaped from a moving train and eventually made it back to Britsh lines. From: Funk, O. (1986). *Der Sprung in die Freiheit.* Schifferstadt, Germany: Geier-Druck.

6   R. Wagner (personal communication, December 12, 2007).

7   R. Wachter (personal communication, June 2007).

8   "Disarmed Enemy Forces." Wikipedia. From: https://en.wikipedia.org/wiki/Disarmed_Enemy_Forces.

9   Matkovich, B. (2017). *Croatia and Slovenia at the End and After the Second World War* (*1944–1945*). Boca Raton, FL: Brown Walker Press.

10   Ibid.

11   Rulitz, F. T. (2016). *The Tragedy of Blieburg and Vitring, 1945.* DeKalb, IL: Northern Illinois University Press.

12   Matkovich, B. (2017). *Croatia and Slovenia at the End and After the Second World War* (*1944–1945*). Boca Raton, FL: Brown Walker Press.

13   Schwarz, K-P. (2010, November 11). "Massengrab in Slowenien entdeckt: Eine eineinhalb Meter starke Schicht von Skeletten." *Frankfurter Allgemeine.* From: https://www.faz.net/aktuell/politik/ausland/massengrab-in-slowenien-entdeckt-eine-eineinhalb-meter-starke-schicht-von-skeletten-11070164.html.

14   For more information on the Volksdeutsche in the Banat after WWII, see: Black, M. (2013). "Expellees Tell Tales: Partisan Blood Drinkers and the Cultural History of Violence after World War II." *History & Memory,* 25(1), 77–110; Merten, U. (2017). *Forgotten Voices: The Expulsion of the Germans from Eastern Europe After World War II.* Abingdon, UK: Routledge; Owen, L. L. (2002). *Casualty of War: A Childhood Remembered* (Vol. 18). Texas A&M University Press.

15   S. Zivković (personal communication, October 2009).

16   Maerz, D. & Stimson G. (2017). *The War Merit Cross and Higher Grades.* Richmond, MI: B&D Publishing.

17   A. Roehler (personal communication, March 18, 2009).

18   Ibid.

19   Ibid.

20   Ibid.

21   Ibid.

22 Ibid.
23 Ibid.
24 Ibid.
25 Ibid.
26 Ibid.
27 Ibid.
28 Ibid.
29 H. vonCampe (personal communication, June 17, 2009).
30 Ibid.
31 Ibid.
32 Ibid.
33 Ibid.
34 Ibid.
35 Ibid.
36 Ibid.
37 Ibid.
38 Ibid.
39 Ibid.
40 Ibid.
41 R. Hansinger (personal communication, October 8, 2011).
42 Wilson, J. (2012). *The Nazis' Nuremberg Rallies*. Havertown, PA: Casemate.
43 "The Nazi Party Grounds in Nuremberg: A Site of Nazi Forced Labor." The Research Project "POWs in Nuremburg." From: https://museums.nuernberg.de/documentation-center/further-research/pows-in-nuremberg; "The Nuremberg POW Camps 1939–1945." Rijo Reasearch 2.0. From: http://www.rijo.homepage.t-online.de/pdf/EN_NU_WK2_stalag.pdf; "Stalag XIII-D." Wikipedia. (2021). From: https://en.wikipedia.org/wiki/Stalag_XIII-D.
44 R. Hansinger (personal communication, October 8, 2011).
45 Ibid.
46 Pathak, B. (2019). "Generations of Transitonal Justice in the World." *Advances in Social Science Research*, 6(7), 18–83.

Chapter 8

1 *Enactments and Approved Papers of the Control Council and Coordinating Committee, Allied Control Authority Germany, 1945, Volume 1*. Legal Division Office of Military Government for Germany (US). From: https://tile.loc.gov/storage-services/service/ll/llmlp/61035888_Volume-I/61035888_Volume-I.pdf.
2 Delić, A. (2011). "On the Concealment of Ante Pavelić in Austria in 1945–1946." *Review of Croatian History*, 7(1), 293–313.
3 DeLlano, P. (2020, April 3). "Visnja Pavelic: The Daughter of a Croatian Dictator who Lived as a Recluse in Madrid." *El Pais Semanal*. From: https://english.elpais.com/eps/2020-04-03/visnja-pavelic-the-daughter-of-a-croatian-dictator-who-spent-50-years-as-a-recluse-in-madrid.html.
4 *Control Council Directive No. 30 Liquidation of German Military and Nazi Memorials and Museums. Allied Control Authority, Germany, Volume 3*. March–June 1946. From: https://www.loc.gov/rr/frd/Military_Law/Enactments/Volume-III.pdf.
5 Biddiscombe, P. (1999). "The End of the Freebooter Tradition: The Forgotten Freikorps Movement of 1944/45." *Central European History*, 32(1), 53–90.

6   Britannica Online. "Restoration of sovereignty." From: https://www.britannica.com/place/Austria/
      Restoration-of-sovereignty.

7   Sluga, G. (2001). *The Problem of Trieste and the Italo-Yugoslav Border: Difference, Identity, and
      Sovereignty in Twentieth-Century Europe.* Albany, NY: SUNY Press.

8   The theater opened in 1930 and could hold about 300 people. It was torn down in 2005. From:
      https://www.kinogeschichte.at/peterhof.htm.

9   Lieutenant General Ferdinand Noeldechen commanded the 438th Replacement Division. Its
      headquarters was located in Klagenfurt, Wehrkreis XVIII. The division was created on November
      1, 1943. This unit took over "Schützengebites Karnyten" in Carinthia. The division was respon-
      sible for guarding the Austrian-Yugoslav frontier in the XVII military district that made up the
      southeastern part of Austria. From Mitcham, S. W. (2007). *German Order of Battle: 291st–999th
      Infantry Divisions.* Mechanicsburg, PA: Stackpole Books. He died in 1951 at the age of 56.

10   Bossy, S. (1952). "The International Red Cross." *International Journal, 7*(3), 204–212.

11   "Prisoners of War of the Second World War–Kriegsgefangene des Zweiten Weltkrieges." From:
      https://second.wiki/wiki/kriegsgefangene_des_zweiten_weltkrieges#cite_note-6.

12   Stillwell, R. & MacDonald, W. L. (2007). "Ulrichsberg Carinthia, Austria." The Princeton
      Encyclopedia of Classical Sites. From: http://www.perseus.tufts.edu/hopper/text?doc=Perseus%3A-
      text%3A1999.04.0006%3Aalphabetic+letter%3DU%3Aentry+group%3D1%3Aentry%3Dul-
      richsberg.

13   Von Luck, H. (1989). *Panzer Commander: The Memoirs of Colonel Hans Von Luck* (World War II
      Library). New York: Dell Publishing.

14   Budig, U. (2000). *Erinnerungen and den Frühling 1945.* Neiderfrohna, Germany: Mironde-Verlag.

15   Ibid.

16   Ibid.

Epilogue

1   Greble, E. (2021, September 21). "Conflict in Post-War Yugoslavia: The Search for a Narrative."
      The National WWII Museum, New Orleans. From: https://www.nationalww2museum.org/war/
      articles/conflict-post-war-yugoslavia.

2   Rill, H. & Stojcic, H. (1972). *On the Trail of the Danube Swabians in Vojvodina.* Centre for
      Nonviolent Action. From: https://nenasilje.org/publikacije/pdf/On_the_Trail_of_the_Danube_
      Swabians_in_Vojvodina.pdf; Korb, A., & Pohl, D. (2022). "Mass Violence and its Immediate
      Aftermath in Central and Eastern Europe during the Second World War, 1939–47." In Böhler, J.,
      Borodziej, W. & von Puttkamer, J. (eds.), *The Routledge History Handbook of Central and Eastern
      Europe in the Twentieth Century, Volume 4: Violence.* Abingdon, UK: Routledge, pp. 122–193.

3   Meyer, H. F. (2009). *Blutiges Edelweiß: Die 1. Gebirgs-division im zweiten Weltkrieg.* Berlin: Ch.
      Links-Verlag.

4   Wilke, K. (2008). "Geistige Regeneration der Schützstaffel in der frühen Bundesrepublik?: Die
      Hilfsgemeinschaft auf Gegenseitigkeit der Angehörigen der ehemaligen Waffen-SS (HIAG)." In
      Schulte, J. E. (ed.), *Die SS, Himmler und die Wewelsburg.* Paderborn: Ferdinand Schöningh, pp.
      433–448.

5   Kumm, O. (195). *Prinz Eugen: The History of the 7 SS Mountain Division "Prinz Eugen."* Winnipeg:
      Fedorowicz Publishing, p. 281.

6   "Bandenkampf in Jugoslawien, 1945–1945." From: http://bandenkampf.blogspot.com/2015/08/
      bk0030.html.

7   Parker, D. S. (2014). *Hitler's Warrior: The Life and Wars of SS Colonel Jochen Peiper.* Cambridge,
      MA: Da Capo Press.

8   Böhme, K. W. (1962). "The German Prisoners of War in Yugoslavia." In Böhme, K. W. & Maschke, E. (eds.), *On the History of the German Prisoners of War of the Second World War*. Bielefeld: Verlag Ernst und Werner Gieseking, pp. 42–136, 254. See also: https://second.wiki/wiki/kriegsgefangene_des_zweiten_weltkrieges.

9   Verheyen, D., & Soe, C. (2019). *The Germans and Their Neighbors*. London: Routledge.

10 Niebuhr, R. (2016). "Between Victors and Vanquished: Wehrmacht Prisoners of War in Yugoslavia." *Journal of Slavic Military Studies, 29*(1), 139–159.

11 Personal letters from Ludwig Glanz. Author's collection.

12 Ibid.

13 Ibid.

14 Personal letters from Willy Ellerstein. Author's collection.

15 Ibid.

16 Ibid.

17 Ibid.

18 Ibid.

19 Ibid.

20 Deutsche Rotes Kreuz Suchdienst of Hermann Baur and Rudi Braunrath. Author's collection.

21 A. Roehler (personal communication, March 18, 2009).

22 Ibid.

23 Ibid.

24 R. Hansinger (personal communication, October 8, 2011).

25 Ibid.

26 Ibid.

27 H. vonCampe (personal communication, June 17, 2009).

28 R. Wagner (Jr) (personal communication, July 9, 2021).

29 R. Wachter (personal communications, June 2007).

30 H. vonCampe (personal communication, June 17, 2009). vonCampe published books on his experience, one of which is *Defeating the Totalitarian Lie* (Anomalos Pub Llc).

31 Brazier, K. (2021). *The Complete Knight's Cross: The Years of Victory 1939–1941* (Volume 1). Fonthill Media.

32 F. Lashinsky (personal communications, October 8 & 11, 2008).

33 A. Mousalimas (personal communication, May 3, 2008).

34 M. Kristović (personal communications, 2008–2009).

35 A reunion letter from 118. Jäger-Division. *Kameradschaftsbund* stated that their first reunion was on September 27, 1952 in Klagenfurt. Author's collection.

36 These books include: *Erinnerungen an die 118. Jäger Divsion (frühere 718. Infanteriedivision)* that was published by the Kameradschaft d. ehem. 118. Jäg.Division (the veteran's group) and sold at 118th veteran reunions. Richard Wachter kindly sent the author a photocopy of the book. The second book is titled: *In Weisst Du noch Kamerad! Geschichte der 118. Jäger Division* by Dr. Erhard Morgenstern.

37 Information obtained from materials from the estate of Dr. Heinrich Hermann. Author's collection.

38 R. Wagner (personal communication, December 12, 2007).

39 C. surname omitted to maintain condifentiality (personal communication, August 6, 2007).

40 R. Wachter (personal communications, June 2007).

41 C. surname omitted to maintain condifentiality (personal communication, August 6, 2007).

Index